Has Corinne Been a Good Girl?

Has Corinne Been a Good Girl?

by Corinne Calvet

St. Martin's Press/New York

Design by Manuela Paul

Library of Congress Cataloging in Publication Data

Calvet, Corinne.
    Has Corinne been a good girl?

    1. Calvet, Corinne. 2. Actors—France—Biography.
3. Moving-picture actors and actresses—United States—Biography. I. Title.
PN2638.C23A32 1983   791.43'028'0924 [B] 83-2911
ISBN 0-312-36405-9

First Edition
10 9 8 7 6 5 4 3 2 1

Contents

Sections of photographs follow pages 85, 199, and 295.

I had bought this bikini in Paris. Little did I know that it would be considered daring in Hollywood in 1948.

Acknowledgments

I am indebted to my two sons, Robin Stone and Michael Calvet, for having never failed to believe in me and this book. I want to thank my literary agent, Mike Hamilburg, who never doubted the value of the manuscript. My grateful appreciation to my editor, Toni Lopopolo, for not changing the meaning of my life, and to my publisher, Tom McCormack. I would also like to thank David Lyon, who took all of my one thousand handwritten pages, corrected my English, and researched facts. I extend my gratitude to Robert Orth for his support of this project.

My appreciation goes to Andy Carpenter for the design of the jacket, and to Karen Johnsen and Carol E. W. Edwards for keeping things organized.

Credit should go to two talented photographers, the great Whitney Shaefer, who took the front jacket photo in 1949, and Richard H. Hodge, who photographed me for the back jacket in 1983. Most of the other photographs come from Marvin Page's great *Motion Picture and Television Research Review* in Hollywood.

I am grateful to all the people who have appreciated and supported me and whose names may not appear in this book. My heart goes out to all of you.

C. C.

My first American romance: Rory Calhoun had me under his spell. This photo was taken during the filming of *Powder River*. *Movie Star News*

I felt very elegant in my Edith Head design for the film *My Friend Irma Goes West*.

Preface
Outcast in Hollywood

It was the autumn of 1947. As I awoke, in the late morning, the sun was filtering through the open windows. It was going to be one of those beautiful California days. My suite at the Bel Air hotel was situated directly under Joan Crawford's love nest. The hotel, a favorite of the movie colony, was nestled among the imposing foliage of Bel Air, Beverly Hills' exclusive park section. I had been awakened during the night by the intermittent moans and groans coming from Joan Crawford and her lover, who, at that time, according to Harrison Carroll's movie gossip column, was a young man-about-town attorney.

Their love-making aggravated my acute loneliness. It had already been six months since I had left Paris. I longed for a simple family dinner with familiar faces. I yearned for the closeness of my French love, Jean-Pierre. After whirlwind experiences with Cary Grant, Clark Gable, and Errol Flynn, I needed someone to love—I felt that I had no real friends. Most men approached me with only sex in mind. Their conversation was always punctuated with *"Ooh, la la . . . Voulez-vouz couchez avec moi?"* And the women I had met had been distant, rejecting my gestures of friendship.

A last look in the mirror made me smile. My French bikini, light green with white polka dots, showed off my slender body. Covering myself, I walked amidst the luscious flowers, saying good morning to the white swans that gracefully adorned the water lily pond.

After a light lunch I dropped my robe and walked over to a lounging chair. I heard air escaping from the lungs of the group of men who were playing gin rummy. A few whistles punctuated their admiration.

I pretended not to hear, closed my lids, and concentrated on letting the sun make love to my bare skin. Before long I felt impelled to open my eyes. They fluttered as I caught sight of a young man walking toward me, his coat slung casually over one shoulder. He was dressed in impeccable gray slacks and a light green polo shirt that blended with the concentrated coolness of the pool. When he passed by to join the gin rummy group my whole body wanted to rise and move toward him. My eyes remained fixed on the back of his head. He turned and caught my glance. I lowered my face. Seconds went by. I was aware of my heart beating impetuously. Then I felt a towering shadow blocking the sun's rays. I looked up at Rory Calhoun as he introduced himself. I tumbled into the dazzling whirlpool of his eyes. It was as refreshing as the light green spring meadows when the leaves are still new. There was a fire in the depth of his glance that consumed all my resistance. It was too strong, too intoxicating. I looked down, wanting to break the spell, but his hand was on my elbow, directing me toward two chairs away from the crowd. His touch had ignited me. Desire flowed through my body. My mouth was unexpectedly dry.

Our romance was spontaneous and electric. It was soon exploited by the Selznick studio, which was grooming Rory for a place in its pantheon of stars. He was tall and slender, with thick black hair. Rory wanted me to leave the Bel Air hotel and move into an apartment where we could enjoy greater privacy. He had me in his power. My longing for a home, marriage, and family was rekindled. So I took a two-bedroom apartment in Westwood.

Rory's mentor was Henry Willson, the brilliant talent scout who recruited material for Selznick's school for young film hopefuls. Henry had a slender, immaculate charm which he combined with a penchant for crème de menthe. In the beginning, Rory and I went out a lot with Willson and his fiancée, Diana Lynn. When they broke their engagement our foursome slid easily into a threesome. I was swept away by the bliss of Rory's attention.

Despite this new and exciting diversion. I did not forget my quest for fame. Images blur as I recall a candlelight dinner for two, a burned coq au vin that didn't seem to matter, and then the anticipatory reaction I had at the newspaper headline: "Rita Hayworth Gives up Hollywood to Marry Aly Khan." It was the perfect romantic destiny for a Hollywood queen like Rita.

I knew her only through Orson Welles, whose undying love

for her had granted her a position upon the highest pedestal in my impressionable mind. I had met Welles while I was playing little sister to Errol Flynn and his crowd of cronies soon after I arrived in America. Welles had invited me to join him for dinner. We went to a little restaurant on Beverly Glen that featured inimitable early canyon cuisine. Welles made a tremendous impact on me. Under his masterful gaze I was totally pliant and malleable, willing to be molded by the master, a rare sensation I found excruciatingly pleasant. Welles had a distant longing in his eyes, and every time I attempted to speak he frowned and requested that I be silent. He said that when he was with me he lived in the illusion that I was Rita, and that he was still with her. He would break out of his trance and touch my chin deftly, modifying the angle of my face ever so slightly to improve the resemblance to his former wife. I was being touched by the hand of a genius. I was impressed by his brilliant mind although I could not grasp some of the meanings in his orations.

I remembered feeling the same awe when I had been in the presence of other great men back in France. I was filled with an elation comparable to desire, although Welles was not physically the type of man I was usually attracted to.

One evening after a romantic dinner by candlelight at Marion Davies' former beach house, by then a very private club with rooms upstairs for private encounters, Orson was quiet for a moment. He was looking at me, seeing right through my elegant black dinner dress.

"Let's go some place where we can be alone!" he whispered, lowering his eyes.

I always felt the same hesitation when faced with a sexual proposition. If I turned him down, would he be insulted and then never want to be with me again? But he's not with me. He thinks he's with Rita! The thoughts were flashing through my mind.

"I want to make love to you." His voice was a husky whisper.

I blushed. "You want to make love to me or to Rita?" I blurted out, not daring to look at him.

The silence that ensued was unbearable. I had said the wrong thing. I could feel it. Suddenly the yearning to be in his arms was overwhelming.

"Let's go," I said, touching his hand.

A somber look was on his face. His eyes had grown sad.

"I'll take you home." He reached for my wrap.

Not a word was spoken. I did not see him again until years later when we met in Venice, Italy.

I may have not wanted to be a surrogate Rita in the bedroom but I certainly would have liked to play Rita's parts on the screen. I read avidly about her life in the two columns beneath the headlines, her beginning in films, her marriages and triumphs. The center page was full of photographs. Looking at them was like looking at one of my own kind. Her widow's peak, unlike mine, had needed electrolysis, and was a little too regular, but it still framed her Latin eyes effectively. Hers were brown, mine blue green. Her mouth was bigger, her smile fuller. And there it was, that same three-quarter view that Welles had tried to recreate at the Beverly Glen restaurant. From that point of view we were almost indistinguishable. But she was taller than I, and my bones were smaller.

As I read the text of the article I could not help feeling the imprint of some impending event of great importance. The sub-headline stuck in my mind: "Columbia Looking for Rita Look-Alike." The words, of course, were planted by the studio, wisely chosen to hide their anger. They prepared for the future without Rita, threw a smoke screen over past mistakes, and yet allowed for the possible return of the prodigal daughter. This well-conceived ploy from the public relations department was contradicted, however, by Columbia studio head Harry Cohn. His anger at Rita's defection was stated without equivocation, his revenge already in the making. It would be redundant to dwell on Mr. Cohn's legendary personality. He was one of the fiercest studio dragons any young actress had to face.

I put the paper down with a certain apprehension about my future, and a strong yearning for what I knew Cohn could make happen: a world of power and international fame.

Rory was living on the valley side of Laurel Canyon, where he shared a house with his mother. She was a species of bland Americana who looked as if she had just stepped out of a Norman Rockwell painting. The place had early American decor, with wood paneling on the walls. Deliberately keeping herself in ignorance of Rory's doings, which were already seasoned with pungent rumors, she was cordial, but uninvolved. I had always been attracted to men who were close to their mothers. It gave me a false feeling of security. Through them, was I looking for the mother I yearned for? Or did I feel safer thinking they had to be more affectionate, gentle, and capable of sharing and experiencing emotions? I thought that a man influenced by his mother was less likely to feel superior to women. I was searching for equality in union, but vive la difference in participation.

No phone had yet been installed in my Westwood apartment. When I finished reading about Rita I called Rory's house from a pay phone, and was informed that he had left for the studio early that morning. A second call established that neither Rory nor Henry Willson was there. Continuing to sense that something important was about to happen, I was full of anticipation when the doorbell rang. It was a telegram instructing me to call Walter Kane immediately. My premonitions had been well founded. Walter Kane was a close associate of Harry Cohn. Kane knew Cohn and all of his secrets intimately. He was like a Bengal cat observing his master, an alter ego, inseparable, yet retaining a distant, untouchable identity of his own.

I called Kane at once, and was informed that the studio had four pictures ready to roll that had been tailor-made for Rita Hayworth. Cohn was interested in talking with me about signing with Columbia. It was happening. The applause was already beginning to echo in my mind.

"We're leaving this afternoon on Mr. Cohn's yacht for a weekend in Catalina. Can you be ready? I'll pick you up in an hour," Kane informed me.

I hesitated. I would be gone for the weekend. I had been unable to reach Rory, who would wonder what had happened to me. Kane took my silence as acceptance of Cohn's invitation.

"It's the opportunity of a lifetime," Kane went on. "Be ready."

I heard the click of the phone putting a period on the summons from Harry Cohn. I had to let Rory know where I was going. I tried once again to call his mother. The line was busy. I had no time to wait, and left Rory a note. Hurriedly I gathered a few pieces of clothing before Kane arrived. We drove to Long Beach where he escorted me onto a boat that was more like an old-fashioned wooden luxury liner than a yacht. Cohn was sitting like a pasha in the elegant salon. He was even more formidable than I had imagined, and did not get up when I entered.

"Sit down," he said.

Kane covered my anxiousness with fluent small talk. He made a woman feel confident, as if his friendship was not dependent upon her beauty alone. Cohn's snakelike eyes were piercing my clothes, examining each part of my body. Then he met my glance, squinting as if he did not want me to read his thoughts, and ordered Walter to take me up on deck.

A few minutes later when I leaned against the rail, the coast was already fading into the distance. The rolling sea sprinkled the deck with salty spray. I was licking the taste from my lips when I returned to the salon and naïvely inquired about the presence of Mrs. Cohn. Cohn knit his heavy eyebrows into a straight line that nearly bisected his pudgy face. Kane covered the awkward moment skillfully.

"Mrs. Cohn does not enjoy the crossing. Particularly when the seas are a little rough like they are today."

I suddenly had the sensation of being alone with two complete strangers and a crew who reminded me of the haughty Gestapo operatives I had observed in Paris during the war.

"She'll be joining us in Catalina," Kane went on smoothly. "She'll take a plane later."

Since the beginning of time, potentates have had someone at their side to cover for them. So it was with the omnipotent studio moguls. Kane was good at it, very good. I began to relax. The butler brought drinks. The evening began to take on a certain charm. Gulls followed our boat into idyllic Avalon bay as we put in and dropped anchor. Our position in the tiny harbor felt safe and protected. Dinner was served. More wine warmed my tongue, bringing on an attack of the giggles. I was happy and at ease when the captain brought a message he had ostensibly received on the ship's radio.

"Mrs. Cohn does not feel well, and wants to be excused for not making the trip. She hopes that Mr. Cohn will have a relaxing and pleasant weekend."

Once more I felt a creeping panic. The fresh air had made me sleepy. I suppressed several yawns, my eyes watering with the effort. Kane got up.

"Well, I'll say goodnight."

"I will too," I said decisively.

We went out on deck where Kane fetched his suitcase. A deckhand called a small boat to take him to shore.

"Where are you going, Walter?" I asked with alarm.

"To shore."

"Why?"

"I can't sleep on a rocking boat. It makes me sick. It's terra firma for me. I'm going to the clubhouse. See you in the morning."

The small boat arrived. I told myself there was nothing to worry about. They had behaved like perfect gentlemen.

When Kane departed I said goodnight to Mr. Cohn as sweetly as I could.

"Goodnight," Cohn replied. He pulled me toward his gross body and tried to kiss me.

"Please, don't."

He let me go, and I ran into the cabin where I was to sleep. I closed the door, and looked for a lock. There wasn't any.

Coming to Long Beach with Kane I had felt like a person suddenly caught up in a cyclone, filled with a kind of exhilarating fear. I knew how rare it was to make it big, and I thought I was about to reach my goal. I had constantly visualized myself as a big star. I had dubbed Rita Hayworth's pictures in France. I was familiar with the parts I would be playing. I was not just a young starlet hoping to be put under contract. The more I conversed with the two men who had my destiny in their hands, the more certain I became. I was the actrice they needed. I felt serene. I had no doubt that I would reach the top where I belonged. I was going to be the one who would take Rita's place.

But all that had vanished when Cohn tried to kiss me. There was a price to pay. I was desperately alone in an unlocked cabin.

What am I going to do, I thought? I just don't want to have sex without love, and on top of it he's so ugly. I was lying on the berth fully dressed. The door opened. Cohn stood there in his pajama bottoms, his hairy chest bare, his eyes narrowed with lust. I felt like the heroine in a silent movie facing the villain. I tried to curl back into the wall as far as I could. I demanded that he leave. He moved toward me, laughing. I tried to push him back, but he pulled me up and pinned me against the wall. I jabbed my knee under his overstuffed belly. He let out a loud yell.

"Help," I screamed. "Help."

One of the deckhands came to the door.

"Call the shore boat and get this French bitch off my yacht," Cohn said with vicious finality. His words had the impact of a guillotine. I felt that it was not personal defeat that energized Cohn's stride as he stomped away from me, but hatred for all women, particularly actresses. Driven by Rita's decision to desert him, the venom was projected onto me.

The bright lights of the harbor shocked me back into reality. Carrying my suitcase, I felt people pressing against me. I took a pedicab to the airfield and hitched a ride in a plane that took me quickly back to the Santa Monica airport. From there I took a taxi to Westwood. It was just about midnight when I arrived.

I was not prepared for what I found. The apartment was a shambles. Furniture had been overturned. Shards of broken mirrors were everywhere. I knew at once that it was Rory. Judging from his behavior, he must have concluded that I had given in to Cohn.

A livid Rory came out of the bedroom. I told him what had happened. All of his anger toward me was suddenly redirected. Without a word he picked me up and carried me down the stairs, planted me in the seat of his car, and started to drive. I was too frightened to ask where we were going, but I soon recognized the same route I had traveled earlier with Walter Kane. We were on our way to Long Beach. When we arrived at the pier Rory rented a boat and we set out immediately for Catalina. The rough weather had worsened. The boat was like a cork on the monumental swelling of the angry sea. I was very frightened. I felt we were going to drown. Rory's valiant effort to control the boat seemed futile, and he was unable to keep his stomach under control. He abandoned the wheel and hung over the railing while his insides gushed out into the dark water. With the strength of a woman who sees her loved one sick and in danger, I took the wheel, found superhuman energy, and managed to keep our heading for the island.

Suddenly the wind died down and the sea became calm. When we arrived at Avalon, Rory tipped the attendant generously and was permitted to anchor in the section reserved for large yachts. We would be gone in a few hours, he said. The boat beside us looked disturbingly familiar. It was Cohn's.

"Rory, why here?" I protested. "That's Harry Cohn's boat."
"I know," he answered.

Inside the cabin Rory undressed me with loving care. I could not resist. Our love-making was always filled with the sense of conqueror and victim. When he wanted me his eyes would envelop me, removing every trace of my own desire and personality. I was content to lie close to him like a docile antelope taking a place beside a magnificent lion. I was Rory's prey.

"You're my goddess," he said, as he knelt lovingly at my feet, resting his cheek against my navel. "You belong to me."

Rory's kisses and the cold air sweeping through the cabin door had my breasts strung tight as a bow. The image of Rory as a lion persisted in my mind. He was indolent and beautiful, yawning with the satisfaction that comes after a feast.

"Let's go out on deck," he suggested. "I want to make love to you in the moonlight."

"Yes," I said passionately, in anticipation of the novel experience I was about to enjoy. Indeed, the novelty quickly exceeded my expectations. No sooner were our bodies joined than Rory began pinching me. At first I laughed.

"Stop it," I said.

He would not stop. I tried to suppress my screams. He pulled my hair and twisted my arms. Still my screams were not loud enough to meet the demands of his well-conceived plan.

"Scream," he ordered. "Louder."

The lights on Cohn's yacht came on. The crew stood leaning over the railing in search of the source of the disturbance. Rory had me pinned down on my knees, my head flat on the deck. He was watching the activity along the railing of the yacht. Suddenly Cohn appeared, still clad in his pajamas. As Cohn reached the edge of the rail Rory grabbed me by the waist and lifted my nude body into the revealing beam of a searchlight. I hid my face in my hands.

"Take a good look, Mr. Cohn," Rory's voice boomed. "This is the closest you'll ever get."

I was immobile as Rory lowered me to the deck of our small boat. I was completely overcome by the shame of my position, and the immensity of the insult that had been leveled against Harry Cohn. In a few seconds we had both incurred his eternal hatred and a prime place on his blacklist, the roster of those who would never under any circumstances work in a Columbia film.

Rory pushed me back into the cabin, where I became nauseated. He took up anchor and cruised slowly around the coast of the island to Isthmus cove. Rory was laughing softly. I remained in a corner, feeling sick and mortified.

The next day, Saturday, like children in the garden of Eden, we were playing, running, swimming, laughing.

"Well, I guess you're the one," Rory said, holding me at arm's length. "Any woman who can make me lose my temper that way deserves to be my wife."

On Sunday, Rory gave me orders.

"Tomorrow, go and buy a new dress. Have your hair done. I want you to look special. I'll pick you up at six in the evening, we'll go out to dinner, and announce our engagement to the press. I'll make all the arrangements with the studio."

I was filled with happiness the next day as I cleaned the mess in the apartment. Then I attended efficiently to all of Rory's commands. Six o'clock came. Six-thirty. Seven. I went to the nearby gas station and called his mother.

"I don't know, Corinne," his mother said somewhat warily. "He left about an hour ago. I heard him make a dinner date with Henry."

"Did he tell you anything about our plans?"

"No, what plans?"

I hung up and raced back to the apartment, frantic with a building sense of betrayal. Then a young actor I knew only slightly rang the doorbell, looking for Rory. Standing on the front porch I took him into my confidence. As we talked, I heard the cuckoo clock inside ring nine. It had miraculously survived Rory's fit of destruction. I had to find Rory. I had to have an explanation. A cold rage began to stiffen my spine.

"Let's do every restaurant in town until we find them," I said. "I know they're together."

His hesitation was obvious, yet he was reluctant to pass up the chance to be mentioned in the gossip columns with me.

"The columnists will think we are a new romance." That was the deciding factor. We started on what would soon become one of the most bizarre evenings in my life.

Fueled by building anger, my anxiety continued to rise. We

doggedly moved from restaurant to restaurant. Two hours and three stops later, long past any reasonable dinner hour, the in crowd would now be dancing at Ciro's, putting on a calculated display under the argus eyes of the reporters. Rage and fatigue had slowly left me, but the Gallic indomitability of my ancestors had hardened my will. I stalked into Ciro's, confident that the search was over. Almost as if guided by a power beyond myself, I did not even bother to examine the crowd of faces in search of Rory's visage. Guided by the maître d', who knew me as a European star, I walked majestically to an excellent table. My meek escort followed like a somewhat bedraggled member of the queen's court.

"They're here, they're here," he whispered anxiously, as if he suddenly realized he was consorting with the enemy.

"Where?" I said, as I looked down into my purse for my cigarettes.

"In the corner, on our right."

"Good," I said with satisfaction.

"Can I go now?"

"No. You made a bargain with me. You stay until I tell you. Champagne," I ordered. "Dom Pérignon."

Rory and Henry sat next to each other in interesting proximity. A bottle of iced champagne rested between them. The smile on Henry's face gripped my heart with fingers as cold as the bed of ice surrounding the bottle. I was overcome with a feeling of love mixed with a sense of death. It was as if I found myself suddenly in a great cathedral of such height that the eye could see only the majestic shadows of the Gothic arches overhead. I became one with the candles inside, about to burn out. My body seemed stiff and erect. I felt detached, as if my life energy were slipping through my feet like sand.

"Are you all right?" the young actor asked.

"Let's go," I answered, putting some bills on the table. As I was preparing to leave the actor nudged my arm.

"Wait for the change."

Just as I turned to go I was handed a note from Henry, an invitation to join them at their table. Undoubtedly he wanted to know more about what was going on between Rory and me than he had been able to find out from my wild Irish lover, particularly about our spectacular Catalina weekend. As I crossed the room the waiter pushed a table up against theirs and brought my champagne. We became an uneasy foursome, small talk flowing with forced spontaneity. Cat and mouse was the name of the game. But who was the cat and who was the mouse? We were still feeling each other out. Rory remained silent, his jaw set, his eyes narrowed to a hostile glare.

Nothing was said about why he hadn't kept our engagement dinner date. The orchestra leader became aware of our presence, and started to play "Golden Earrings," which Rory and I considered our song.

"Dance with me, Rory. Please."

"No." He was adamant.

"Oh come on, Rory, dance with her," Henry ordered sweetly.

Rory got up reluctantly. I tried to abandon myself against the taut body of a cold stranger, grasping for the tattered remains of a dream I had held for twenty-four hours. We danced in mechanical silence. At last I was unable to maintain the facade.

"Why, Rory? What happened? Why weren't you there?"

"I couldn't."

"Why? I have a right to an explanation." I could see Henry intently watching us from a short distance away, the Svengali forever in control.

"The studio doesn't want me to get married."

"You mean Henry doesn't want you to get married. Why?"

"Why? I'll ask you why. Why did you follow us here? You're a pest, a nuisance."

"We had a date, Rory." I was nearly pleading with him. "This was supposed to be our engagement night."

He said nothing.

"I'll leave," I went on hopefully. "Walk me to my car and kiss me goodnight. Then I'll know everything is all right."

"I wouldn't kiss you if my life depended on it," he snarled. The words cut me like a knife. He stopped dancing, and directed me back to our table. My brain no longer functioned. A kind of temporary insanity took possession of my mind. I became obsessed with his refusal to meet my demand for a kiss.

"Tell me about your weekend, Corinne," Henry said, with casual cynicism. "Did you have fun?"

Rory's look had lost its power over me. I was not melting any longer.

"It started out badly, but Saturday turned out to be perfect. Rory and I got engaged. I'm going to be his wife."

"Don't listen to her, Henry," Rory said between clenched teeth. "Nothing could make me marry her."

I got up in total calm, gathered my mink wrap and purse, deliberately picked up the champagne bottle by its sweaty neck, and slowly poured the contents over Rory's head. He sat frozen in disbelief. I walked away.

Driving home after sending my escort away in a cab, I thought it over. How could Rory have changed so drastically in a few short hours? I had to know what he was really feeling. The way he was behaving now was a nightmare. If only he would kiss me everything would be the way it was before. I wanted that goodnight kiss. It would either banish a bad dream or tell me truly that our relationship was fini. I made a quick U-turn, and parked on a hill facing the exit door of Ciro's. I left the motor running, but turned off the headlights. The wait seemed endless. I was about to give up when I saw them coming out.

I watched as an attendant brought Rory's Packard. I crept down the hill in my car, ready to follow. They seemed to be arguing. I followed them up Stone Canyon where Henry lived. I turned off my lights, and stopped a short distance from where Rory parked his car in Henry's driveway. They went inside. I rang the doorbell. My love was dead, but I still wanted to seal the tomb with a kiss.

Henry came to the door.

"I want to see Rory. I want to kiss him goodnight."

"It's late." Rory, looking angry, appeared at the door.

"Where are the keys to my car, Henry? I want to get out of here," he grumbled.

"On the table where you left them."

Rory was going to leave without speaking to me. I ran outside and drove my car across the driveway, blocking his.

"Move your car!" Rory ordered. He was standing in the doorway, framed in the light from behind.

A part of me was detached, as if watching my own performance. I was the heroine in a film. I dangled the car keys in front of him impishly, and then dropped them into the cleft between my breasts.

"I'll go. Just kiss me goodnight. Please Rory, just one kiss."

I knew how irritating my stubbornness was becoming, but I didn't care. Rory went back into the house. Thinking I had won round one, I went to my car and sat behind the wheel, waiting. Before I could plan my next move Rory reappeared, now followed by a hysterical Henry Willson. Rory's hand clasped a small automatic pistol. He pointed it directly at me as he stood by the hood of my convertible. The whole scene was completely incongruous in this quiet canyon road.

"Move, or I'll shoot."

"No, Rory! No!" Henry screamed.

"You don't believe me?" Rory challenged in a white rage. He shot a bullet across the hood of my car and into dark trees at the side of the driveway.

"Stop, I beg you. Stop." Henry was down on his knees, hanging onto Rory's leg, pleading.

I was paralyzed with terror. Rory was at the door of the car, the gun at my temple.

"Move your car," he said with determination. Suddenly I didn't care whether I lived or died.

"You'll never get away with it, Rory," I said. "They'll put you away forever. Just kiss me and I'll leave."

There was a deadly moment of hesitation. Then Rory opened the door and pulled me out of the car. He handed the gun to Henry, who ran back into the house and slammed the door.

Rory's kiss was fierce. It was deep and total. Our sobs came simultaneously. We were interrupted by sirens. The shot had been heard by the neighbors.

"Go up half a mile, turn off your lights, and then duck under the steering wheel until the police leave," Rory instructed.

I did as he directed. A police searchlight skimmed my parked vehicle. I waited a little longer, then drove back down the canyon road to Sunset. Rory's car was still parked in Willson's driveway. The entire house was dark.

I drove home and parked my car a block from the Westwood apartment, ran inside, and double-locked the door. I was desperately afraid of Rory's reaction to what I had done. Shaking uncontrollably, I crawled into a corner. Finally I fell asleep.

The next morning I walked about in a daze, exhausted. I felt beaten by Hollywood. I had refused to use my body to advance my career, and I had already ruined my chances with three major studios. Then Rory had betrayed me. I felt forsaken, desperate, and defeated. I wanted the solace of my own country. I decided to go back to France.

PART ONE

Search for Identity

Chapter 1

It was the late 1920s. Paris was beginning to vibrate to strains of social change. Metaphysics, jazz, drugs, and sexual freedom invaded the Parisian atmosphere, already exhibiting the wild release of energy and libido that followed recovery from World War I. Josephine Baker had shocked and won Paris with her exuberant and daring Negro dances, art and music flourished, and the French cinema, in its childhood, was beginning to produce the early masterpieces of René Clair and Jean Renoir. Picasso, the Russian Ballet, Cocteau, Stravinsky, the list of geniuses who had gathered in Paris to pursue revolutionary creative work seemed endless. Politically, amid this cultural ferment, there were talks of disarmament, treaties and agreements, a frantic search for a sense of community in Europe. Almost everyone had a mistress, almost everyone a lover, but the family unit remained sacred. Discretion was the motto, even if everyone knew what went on behind closed doors.

Our house in Passy was in the most exclusive quarter of the city. It was a tall four-storied building next to the sumptuous Bois de Boulogne. Its beautiful facade was decorated with a relief of sandstone plates in the shape of keystones, and the curved balconies on all the windows were surrounded by intricate ironwork railings of light green filigree which stood out against the sandstone in fragile elegance. Our staff included a chauffeur, a cook, two maids, a butler, and an English governess, Isabelle, who had been with the family for many years.

I was born into this environment late one night in April, 1925. My father, Pierre Dibos, was a tall, handsome, soft-spoken, brown-haired man sporting a dashing moustache. He was a chemical engineer, an inventor, and a comte. He wasn't one to brandish his title except once when he met my mother, Juliette

Munier, the daughter of a wealthy industrialist family from the Lorraine region in the eastern part of France.

The marriage was arranged. The groom was said to be penniless but was regarded as a genius by his classmates. So on the day of their wedding, my mother, a ravishing, elegant, spoiled young woman barely nineteen, her green eyes shining with excitement, married her prince charming and became Madame la Comtesse, soon to be the toast of the 1900s, "tout Paris."

By the time I arrived, there were already three girls, Christiane, Colette, and Chantal, and a boy, Hughes, all spaced four years apart. At the age of ten, when I became aware of this precise spacing, I asked Isabelle if my parents only made love every four years. "I don't know what you're talkng about," Isabelle replied curtly. Nor did I ever get an explanation of why all the girls' names started with C. I added my presence to the household at Two Avenue Montmorency exactly four years after Chantal had arrived. I was a beautiful baby, pink and dimpled.

As a child I found my home, despite all the people in it, empty of affection. My father was fascinated with his work and spent many long hours in the laboratory, hours that were to yield the secret of manufacturing a kind of glass that would be impervious to heat, glass he called Sibor, better known to the world today as Pyrex. Nor was his absence made up for by my mother. She too was often away. Only a few minutes in her busy daily routine were allotted to her children. So I found pleasure in other ways, by sharpening my powers of observation, and by creating a whole imaginary world in which I could converse with invisible people, such as the personages whose pictures decorated my parents' study.

This room was a masterpiece of comfort and elegance. The Louis XIV desk had been in the family since its creation by the king's cabinetmaker for our ancestor whose ornate gold-framed oil portrait dominated one of the reception rooms. There was a brown velvet Napoleonic lounging sofa, protected from the night chill by a heavy, jade green embroidered curtain. The thick beige wool carpet was complemented by the cream-colored peau de soie lining the walls. The green marble fireplace had been imported from Italy. Above it, the mirror gave back a view of an impeccable Rodin white marble nude. In the corner where the sofa stood, was a photograph of the divine Sarah Bernhardt framed in gold filament. Next to it was an autographed picture of Colette, the famous novelist, which read "Juliette, my love for you is sweet like the violets you love so much." There were also pictures of Bernard Shaw, with his majestic long beard, of Clemenceau in full military uniform, Tristan Bernard, the novelist and playwright, his chin resting on a gloved fist, Sacha Guitry, the actor, writer and producer, with his famous profile, and the mystic Gurdjieff with his hynotic eyes. I would sneak into this room whenever I could and admire the photos of my mother's friends.

Each evening, after our baths, the younger children were dressed in clean clothes and taken down to this room by Isabelle for inspection. Christiane and Colette, were old enough to dine with the grown-ups. My mother, her softly curled sandy hair disarranged, would recline, exhausted from an afternoon of shopping, surrounded by boxes and baubles. Our visit was never long enough to satisfy my need to fathom her mysteries.

"Did you have a good day, Chantal?"

"Yes Maman."

"And you, Hughes?"

"Yes Maman."

"Has Corinne been a good girl?"

"Yes Maman."

Often Isabelle would tell about me not finishing my spinach, climbing trees, and being disobedient.

Maman would try to look severe, but sometimes I thought there was a glint of complicity in her eyes.

"Well?" she would manage to utter beneath Isabelle's stern expression.

During the brief silence which followed I wondered what might be in all the beautiful new packages sticking halfway out of their ephemeral wrappings.

"Well then. Good night."

"Good night, Maman."

One by one, like well-behaved little soldiers on parade, we were allowed to walk close by and curtsy. When Isabelle had no misconduct to report, Maman, extending a bejeweled arm, would pull me close for a light kiss on the forehead. There would follow a few moments of delicious bliss, the closeness to my mother's skin the aphrodisiac quality of her perfume, pushed me to the edge of dizziness. Love for me became something infinitely beautiful, and mostly out of reach. Lying in bed at night, unable to sleep, I would strain to hear the words which inevitably preceded the laughter of my parents and their guests.

Often I could not resist the lure of the voices from downstairs, and embarked on a dangerous adventure, traveling out of my room under the cover of darkness, maintaining furtive silence down the stairs and into the salon where my mother's bohemian soiree was in full swing, with music, laughter, and elevated talk of mysterious subjects. There was only one open space to traverse, a few moments of extreme hazard, from the door of the stairway across the entrance hall to a long sofa.

The trip was soon over, for safety and concealment were close at hand in the form of heavy drapes drawn across the curved bay. Behind was a long narrow veranda. Feeling secure, I could peek into the entire room through three convenient separations in the drapes. Sometimes I fell asleep, for I couldn't bring myself to leave. I didn't want to miss anything. The trip back was made when I awoke, after the guests had left. It was then that I decided that to be with and loved by my mother I would have to become famous like all of the brilliant people in her salon.

As I grew older, I searched for my own identity in the past of famous people, looking for qualities I wanted to develop in myself. In the fourth grade I learned of Joan of Arc, the French heroine. Studying her portrait, looking deeply into her eyes, I sometimes waited for fifteen or twenty minutes before the facial expression began to move slightly. That was my cue to ask the question.

"Would you like to be my friend?"

I did this with all the heroes and heroines who attracted me, George Sand, Bonaparte, Colette, Sarah Bernhardt, Eve Curie, and Eleonora Duse.

If there was no answer to my question I did not insist, but when I heard a positive reply within me, I would tell my new friends the quality I admired most about them, then confide my confusion and unhappiness. Once they had agreed to help me, our interior dialogue took place at my will. In my mind's eye I visualized myself transported, becoming a part of their activity in the past.

Joan of Arc, at that period of my life, was my favorite. At night I would turn my back to my sister Chantal and secretly kiss

Joan's image, which I had cut out of my history book. She too had heard voices which guided her destiny.

The night before my first communion I experienced a revelation of great consequence. Isabelle had just finished the last touches on my gown, and the small pleats of my coif stood upright like a halo. I went to sleep happily, a smile on my face, my new white leather Bible tucked under my pillow. Sometime in the middle of the night I was awakened by a soft wind, followed by a chill running up my spine. Floating in the air at the end of my bed was a candle flame without the candle. It moved gently, like a finger, inviting me to follow. After putting on my bedroom slippers, I followed the flame through the hall and down the stairs. Set up in the entrance hall was a familiar scene. The men sitting around the table had long hair and beards, and wore robes.

Everyone was either talking in measured tones or listening attentively to someone else. The mood was joyous. The table was covered with nuts and fruit, bread and wine. The flame disappeared as I stood in front of an empty stool. I had dropped my eyes. An intense light emanated from across the table.

"Sit down; you are one of us."

I sat down and looked up. The man who had spoken was dressed in a white robe; he was beauty incarnate. I felt a joy I had never known. I was filled with ecstasy, a sense of belonging, as if great tenderness was being extended toward me. I smiled and talked easily. I recognized these persons as members of my real family. I felt that I had been separated from them, but time did not matter; our flow of conversation and intimacy went on as if we had always been together.

I have no recollection of returning to my bed. The next morning I was awakened to take my bath. The luxury of the water filled with perfumed bath salts gave me a delicious sense of well-being. When Isabelle came, she was inquisitive.

"When did you go downstairs?"

"Why do you ask?"

"Because I found one of your bedroom slippers down in the entrance hall, that's why."

So it had really happened. It had not been a dream.

Before going to church we stopped at the photographer's. He commented on my beauty.

"She looks like a bride," he said. Pleased, I looked in a mirror, smiled at myself, and thought, yes, I do look like Jesus' bride.

My experience in church was anticlimactic. I had had my real communion the night before.

I never lost the hope that some day, somewhere, I would meet those people in the vision who I felt were my real family. The love, purity, and joy I had felt in their presence stayed with me always as a reminder to reach my goal. I had to stay pure and truthful.

I was nine years old. It was a week before Armistice Day, commemorating the end of the First World War, and the chauffeur had been very quiet as we drove home from school. When we arrived, suitcases were piled in the entrance hall. Everyone was moving rapidly and silently about. I went to find Isabelle, but she was not in her room, so I snuck out the back way into the service staircase, closing the door gently behind me. I tiptoed down the dark, steep, staircase to the kitchen door one floor below. Using the special knock we had devised, I let Lucy, the cook, know that it was me. Lucy and Isabelle had words sometimes, so I moved carefully between the two of them. Lucy was a heavyset woman who squeezed me against herself when no one was looking, and gave me cookies and chocolate when I had been punished and sent away from the dining room.

"Lucy," I whispered, when she came out of the stairwell carrying some garbage. "What's going on?"

Her finger went to her mouth, silencing me.

"Your Maman's headaches are very bad, and they've decided that the country air of Metz would be better for her. So you're all leaving for Aunt Marguerite and Uncle Lucien's house tomorrow morning."

"How about school? We're not on vacation for another week."

"Isn't that wonderful? You'll have a few more days of fun." Her hug flattened me against her damp bosom, which collapsed slightly like a wet, inflated life preserver.

"Go back up," she said, "and don't tell anyone I told you."

"I can't. I closed the door behind me." I remembered the illicit manner in which I had passed from Isabelle's room to the servants' stairs.

Lucy looked annoyed for a minute.

"All right, wait a minute."

Lucy went back into the kitchen. I could hear her voice through the closed door.

"Everybody out for fifteen minutes. I can't hear myself think with all this going on. I have to make my sauce. Out everybody, and I also mean you, Miss Nanny, with all due respect, of course."

They all vacated the kitchen, including Isabelle.

"Okay," Lucy said. "Go on through the dining room, and have a good vacation. I'll miss you." She patted me on the head.

We left in two cars the next morning. Papa drove the first, with Hughes in the front seat with him, Christiane riding in back with Maman. We followed in the second, the chauffeur driving, with Isabelle, Colette, Chantal, and myself in the jump seat. It was fun. We were playing hooky, and giggled happily as we watched children walking to school loaded with books.

It was noon when we stopped and put down blankets for a picnic lunch. It was like a dream come true when I found myself sitting next to Maman, my calf touching her thigh in the midst of the trees of the forest that bordered the road. I felt intoxicated, eating automatically. I closed my eyes to savor the rapture of the moment. Suddenly Maman stood up.

"Come," she said to me, "let's walk a little deeper into the forest."

I jumped to my feet. Maman took my hand. I was trembling. Her flesh felt warm, a warmth that sent waves of heat into my heart. She was singing softly, a little song about an elf in the forest. She stopped abruptly and dropped my hand, reaching at the same time for her forehead.

"I have to relieve myself," she said, squatting behind one of the larger trees.

"Me too," I imitated her.

The golden autumn leaves covered the ground like a blanket, and the moist scent of their decomposition entered my nostrils like a powerful balm. I heard a soft thump. It was Maman. She had lost her balance and was lying on the ground. The fear in her eyes sent me into a panic. I stood frozen. After what seemed like an eternity she spoke very softly.

"Corinne, come and help me get up. You're such a clever girl. I don't want you to tell anyone that I lost my balance." She was brushing the leaves away from her clothes. "This is our secret, you and I. Help me."

Her hand on my shoulder was the weight of the world, and at

the same time I felt ten feet tall, a giant of inner strength. My arm hardly reached around her waist. My wonderful, gorgeous, queen of a mother thought enough of me to entrust me with a secret. Not even torture would get me to violate her trust.

On our way back to the cars, my brother Hughes was walking somewhat apart from us, following the embankment along the road.

"Papa!" We heard him cry out. "Come here. Look what I've found."

My father went to investigate. A short while later they both returned with a pillow case full of old-fashioned pocket watches. None of them were working, and they had all stopped at different hours.

"Why would anyone throw them away? Here of all places?" I wanted to know.

"Maybe someone robbed a jewelry store and dumped everything that wasn't pure gold," Chantal suggested.

"May I have one?" I begged.

"No," said Hughes. "Some of them need keys to wind them up. Here Maman, look at this one. It must go on a chain around the neck."

My mother took the watch in her hand.

"How strange," she murmured. "Twelve-fifteen, that's when I was born."

My joy was complete when Maman told Christiane to go and ride on the other side of the car; she wanted me with her. When we resumed driving, my mother looked at me, smiling. I saw a small leaf that had been caught in her hair when she fell. I reached up and carefully removed the golden treasure. I hid it in my hand. Maman gently pried my fingers open, and then closed her hand on mine with a trusting squeeze. She winked at me confidentially.

That night my pillow was my Maman. I was in total bliss. My lonely calvary was over. My mother and I had a secret. I was very special. She had shown me her love.

Toward morning Christiane and I were awakened by a frightening sound we had never heard before. It was some sort of a chant. Like an eerie song the melody slowly changed tempo, and was replaced intermittently by the sound of someone gasping for air. I went to investigate. It came from my parents' bedroom.

Isabelle, with tears in her throat, caught me and directed me back to my room. I resisted.

"What's that horrible noise?"

"Don't worry about it," she answered. "Go to sleep. We'll talk about it in the morning."

I lay stiffly on my bed all night, drifting in and out of sleep, only to be awakened again and again by the crescendo of haunting laments coming through the walls. In the morning when the children came down for breakfast Uncle Lucien, Isabelle, and Aunt Marguerite were standing at the bottom of the stairs, looking pale, as if they should be in a wax museum. My aunt spoke.

"Maman went on a long trip last night. We're not going to see her for a long time."

"That's impossible," I screamed. "She wouldn't leave without me, not after yesterday."

"What happened yesterday?" Isabelle's voice was menacing.

"She made friends with me."

Left to stand with Chantal at the bottom of the stairs, I remained bewildered.

"What do they mean, she has gone on a long trip?" I asked my sister, who was four years older than I.

"She's dead," Chantal stated.

"Dead?"

"Yes, we'll have to bury her, and she is going to join Grandpa and Grandma. I wonder who is going to get her jewels?"

To my surprise I slapped Chantal with a force unknown to me. With my eyes wide open from the shock of what I had done I could see a red welt appearing on Chantal's face. She was screaming at the top of her lungs. I ran up the stairs to my parents' room. It was empty. Papa was not there. I grew bold, slid into the open bed, and pulled the covers over my head. First I cried softly at the impossible injustice of my fate. After nine years, when at last I had received the closeness I yearned for so desperately, I was now deprived of it forever. My mind was in turmoil. I wondered if I was responsible for my mother's death by keeping my secret oath not to reveal that she had fainted in the woods. My nose searching like a puppy dog for the scent of its owner, I crawled under the covers until I found that place where Maman had lain as she died.

"Maman," I whimpered. "Why did you leave me? I need you

so . . . you've abandoned me just when you recognized me." Shaking my head violently against the reality facing me, I heard Isabelle in the hall.

"Corinne? Where are you?"

Afraid of being discovered, I stretched my body stiff as a corpse. When Isabelle gave up her search I felt I was floating on a calm lake. Then I became the lake, vast, bottomless, lifeless, as I drifted into nothingness.

Chapter 2

As the decade continued its relentless drift toward war, I gradually learned the facts of life. As might be expected, my sexual education was left to chance. At the age of ten I covered my ignorance of such matters by bragging to my closest girlfriend that I had it all figured out. I had unlocked the secret of life in my own imagination.

"Paulette," I said, "do you know where babies are kept in mothers when they get big?"

"No," answered Paulette, her eyes widening.

"Well, it's simple. In the two breasts. You know how when you lie down on your bed your head and feet stick out higher than the rest of your body? That's why women have those bulging mounts." I envisioned the child lying crosswise across the mother's bosom.

"Wow!" said Paulette. "I wonder if my sister is going to have a baby. Her breasts are starting to look that way."

It was too good a story for Paulette to keep to herself. All the girls in our class heard about it. So did one of the parents, and inevitably I was called in to the headmistress. Waiting outside her office I was trembling with fear, but she was very gentle, and told me that a baby grew in the mother's tummy, not in her breasts. The breasts were there, I was informed, to make the milk the baby would need when it was born.

"Don't talk about these things with other girls, Corinne. If they want to know, tell me, and I'll tell them myself." With a good-natured pat on my behind, I was sent back to class. For a time that explanation had been sufficient, but about the time of my twelfth birthday, my curiosity was aroused again.

Tucked behind innocent-appearing books in my room there was a small volume I had taken in panic one day from a locked cabinet of my father's library. The key had been left in the glass door that protected these mysterious tomes from the elements, not to mention prying children with impressionable minds.

No one was home, and the opportunity for illicit exploration was too great to resist. Carefully I removed one of the books after unlocking the cabinet with the obliging key. Opening its pages, I discovered myself in the midst of a volume of erotic literature, profusely illustrated with pictures of grown-ups in the nude, in all kinds of positions I had never seen before. I felt no sense of sexual arousal from what I saw. I was not curious about the depiction of male genital organs. They all seemed to look the same. The breasts of the ladies, however, were of considerably more interest in their multitude of dimensions and shapes. Mine had already started to swell, and as I looked at various specimens I speculated on how they would appear in their full fruition. I was particularly attracted to a colored picture in one large book. A beautiful long-necked lady stood naked on a conch shell, floating on a peaceful green sea, her long blonde hair flowing in the wind. It was the Venus of Botticelli, her arms stretched languidly upward, reaching for a cloudy sky that was breaking into sunlight overhead. The warm rays streamed down about her, highlighting her alabaster body in tones of golden peach. I thought she looked like me.

The lady was not the least bit concerned about the activities going on above her head. Her smile betrayed confidence that she would receive what she was reaching for. Her breasts were neither large nor small, but extraordinarily round. Her navel was high, and sunk deep within the soft pillow of her belly, her legs slender, the muscles attached high on her hip bones. Yes, she is beautiful, I thought. That's the way I want to look when I grow up. I patted my body, which was still short and straight. With a sigh of anticipation I closed the book and returned to my search.

Lying flat on the bottom of the cabinet was a book with a plain cardboard binding. As I was about to investigate its contents I heard a key in the front door. I had been deriving considerable elation out of living dangerously, but I did not want to be caught. I closed the glass door to the bookcase as rapidly and as noiselessly as I could, and took the book quickly to my bedroom, where I concealed it beneath my mattress. I then grabbed a school text, and pretended to read, just in time to see Isabelle enter the room.

It was not until after everyone was asleep that I felt safe to go back to my investigations. The book contained exquisite black and white engravings. The characters were dressed in period costumes, and I saw it was a story set at the carnival in Venice, with gondolas, the Grande Canale, and all the elegance of the fifteenth century on every page. I opened at random and began to read. The words described a lady asleep, only partially covered, on a silky bed. Through her window a dashing cavalier entered the room. He caressed her gently until she awakened from her slumber in surprised delight. Following a series of declarations of romantic love, the gallant young lover throughly aroused the desires of his loved one to the point at which she pleaded for him to join her in the luxury of her bed. The story unwound through all descriptions of sensuous play. Exhausted and satisfied, the lady finally fell asleep. Upon awakening, she reached for the body at her side as the first rays of dawn streamed through the window, and discovered to her confusion that the beautiful young man in bed with her was not a young man at all, but a stunningly handsome young woman.

My surprise upon this revelation was easily equal to that of the fifteenth-century lady herself. I was intrigued. How could one mistake a woman for a man, and why would a woman want to make love to another woman? Maybe I missed some important details, I decided, before starting to read the romantic story again. It was dawn before I put the book away, safely hidden. I was always aware that it was there, arousingly sinful and intriguing in its mystery, and it was not until the following summer that I found new pieces to fit into the puzzle.

Shortly before my mother's death my father discovered that his business partner had misdirected the company funds and absconded to South America. My father had hidden our financial ruin from my mother as her chronic headaches grew worse. After her death there was no longer any need for pretense. We moved into the top apartment of a building near St. Germain-des-Prés that had been put in the childrens' names, and both the house in Passy and the villa in Normandie were sold. We were reduced to spending summers in the small house at the beach which had been the servants' residence.

Nevertheless, it was once again a glorious summer at the seashore, despite the deteriorating international situation. In France, the Popular Front Government of Léon Blum had given way to the weak administration of Daladier. Democracy in Spain was imperiled, and Hitler had swallowed another giant meal in Czechoslovakia. These were the topics of conversation at our dinner table. I suddenly felt I had nothing in common with the little girls I had played with the year before. They seemed stupid, playing their games and clinging to the proximity of their mothers, putting on silly superior airs. The boys were no better. They would ride their bicycles at full speed, ridiculing the girls and laughing at them.

I found myself attracted, however, to an older group of boys who seemed to be interested in something else.

My own bicycle was now too small. It was a further confirmation of the loss of status and financial position my family had suffered, a fact already much bandied about. My brother Hughes, however, was now too old to ride around on a bicycle just for the fun of it. Sailing and reading were his activities that summer. His bicycle, covered with dust, became mine. A little water restored its shiny black frame to glory. It was a tall bike, and it was really impossible for me to sit on it and pedal at the same time. I could not have cared less. Pedaling in a standing position may have demanded more balance, but it gave me more strength and more speed. It was difficult at first to get the boys with whom I now wanted to ride to accept me as part of their group, but my exploits on the large bike impressed them. Soon they were willing to make an exception. The fact that I was a girl was overlooked.

Even so, I was accepted with reservations. I was not invited when the boys gathered in their clubhouse, an abandoned cabin on the sandy beach with its door facing the ocean. It was a sore sight to the vacationers, its dull green paint nearly peeled off. In fact, there had been a motion by the proud owners of all the freshly painted cabins on the beach to have it removed. One day at the dinner table I suggested that instead of getting so upset about the matter, the families should take up a collection and have the offending cabin painted themselves. There was a predictable moment of silence followed by some hard looks of disapproval, and then the conversation resumed as if I had not spoken. Like a record player that keeps playing the same song with only a brief moment of silence, they fell back into the same complaining old groove.

So there the boys' clubhouse stood, unpainted and still, the mysterious lair that held male secrets. The boys had found the key to the place hidden beneath a floor board. They made certain that I did not come too close. Once they caught me leaning against the cabin wall, trying to hear what I could of their clandestine rituals. They all screamed, telling me I would be banned from the group if they caught me snooping again. Sometimes they remained closed in the cabin for almost an hour, and somehow always looked guilty and sheepish when they finally emerged into the sunlight.

One of the boys, Michel, liked me. I could feel it. My mind was full of questions, but one in particular stood out in importance. One day I blurted it out to him.

"Michel, how do . . . how are babies made? I mean where do they come from? What are they made of?"

He looked at me a moment almost tenderly, then giggled and pedaled off to join the leader of the group. I retreated, embarrassed at my forwardness, ready to turn around and go off to brood in my favorite hiding place, the attic of our house. To my surprise, the leader of the group joined me. He announced that they had decided to admit me to the cabin. My heart was beating with expectancy when I entered the boys' secret domain.

When the door was closed we were surrounded by darkness. With Michel present at my side I felt protected. Soon my eyes grew accustomed to the dim light. On the hooks hanging on the side walls were poignant reminders of two summers ago, two sad and shapeless bathing suits.

I could vividly remember the people to whom the cabin had belonged, two children, a boy and a girl with dark hair, very quiet. They had never seemed to want to play with the other children, but remained sitting at the side of their heavyset mother. Only once had I seen their father. He looked different, full of life. That day the children seemed to have awakened from their lethargy, and with a certain envy I had watched them splashing, laughing, and running in the water with their father. While they cavorted in the surf the woman watched, her fat body hidden under a floral housecoat, a content smile coming to her lips.

Now in the darkness of the cabin I was overpowered by the smell special to the seashore, salt-laden humidity mingled with the dry odor of long decomposed fish scales. My reflections were interrupted by the lighting of a candle. As I saw the half-lit faces of the boys around me I knew that the time had come for me to learn the secret of their meetings.

"I'm told that you have some questions about sex," said the leader.

"I want to know about babies," I replied innocently.

The raucous laughter that followed distressed me. What was I doing here? I made a move toward the door, but the reassuring hand of Michel held me back.

"Look," said the leader, pulling his pants down. "Did you ever see a penis this close before?" He walked toward me, his body close to my chest.

"Sure," I said bravely.

"Yeah? Where?" said the leader.

"In books and things," I muttered.

"Well, take a good look. You don't have anything like that, do you? What you have down there is just a hole. Now, let me show you what happens."

Instinctively, I pulled back against the rough wood wall. The boy who had exposed himself now started a rapid motion up and down with his penis in his hand. The boys around me were giggling uncontrollably. In a few moments his penis was sticking straight up.

"Feel it," he demanded.

"No, I don't want to," I answered fearfully.

"Feel it!" His voice was still more commanding.

My hand moved reluctantly forward, touched him, and quickly pulled back.

"You see," the leader said triumphantly. "It's big and hard, and look below. There are two sacks, one and two. They are both full of stuff that makes babies. Now if I put this in your hole and move it in and out, the stuff will come out and make a baby inside of you."

"The stuff? What do you mean, the stuff? What is it made of?" I asked.

"I'll show you." And with a fast movement the leader was again moving his hands.

There was an eerie silence in the cabin. The hand of the leader was now going so fast that I didn't want to look. I wanted to cry. I was frightened.

"Here I go," the leader exclaimed triumphantly. "Look, look!"

I looked. A strange kind of white liquid came out.

"Bravo, bravo!" the other boys were screaming.

"My turn, my turn."

"No, it's my turn."

"Michel, it's your turn," the leader said.

"No, not today. I don't want to."

"OK. Then you, Louis."

Standing in a corner Louis, a skinny boy, dropped his pants and started the same crazy motion with his hand.

"I'd like to see her hole," Louis suggested.

"Yes, yes. Let's take a look at it," the others agreed quickly.

A growing trepidation took hold of me.

"No," said Michel. "That wasn't part of the deal. We've accepted her in the clubhouse. Her initiation was to see what we had, that's all."

"Why should she see what we have and we not see what she has?" Louis protested.

"That's right," the leader echoed, reaching over to lift my skirt.

"No," said Michel, pushing him back.

The leader fell over the candle. Everyone was screaming. Michel took my hand and we made our way to the door.

We were out. I was safe. The fresh salty air filled my lungs. It was so fresh, so clean, so pure. I ran to my brother's bicycle without looking back, and pedaled away with all my might.

For days my feelings of embarrassment and fear at what might follow now that I had been "initiated" kept me cloistered in our house. Finally, at the insistence of Isabelle I ventured into the garden. The boys rode past the gate, stopping, looking in at me over the fence, calling to me. But I hid behind the bushes.

One afternoon Michel came by himself. I was watering the flowers.

"Corinne," he said. "Don't be afraid. They won't do it anymore. Come and ride with me."

"No."

"The sea is very rough today. They all went up to the lighthouse."

I had missed our bicycle riding. I particularly enjoyed doing one stunt that required a great deal of dexterity. So I accepted Michel's invitation. Every few blocks the boardwalk was broken up by steps leading down to the streets that ran on into the sand. Here fishermen and vacationers rolled their boats to the edge of the water. Alongside the steps were little paths of hardened sand packed down over the years by bicyclists who did not want to carry their bikes down the steps. My friends and I, however, shunned these paths. We would ride straight down the steps standing up high on our pedals, then, going full speed, lift up our front wheels and climb the steps on the other side of the roadway to the continuing boardwalk.

It was good to be out again and perform this particular maneuver with Michel. The wind was blowing hard, the air was wet. It was difficult to breathe, but it was exhilarating. We were approaching the row of cabins that included the boys' clubhouse when suddenly a flurry of activity caught our eyes. The cabin of iniquities was being hoisted onto a trailer. They were taking it away. On the boardwalk the man of two summers ago, who had been with the children and the obese lady in the flowered housecoat, was standing alone. He was dressed in black, his face set against the elements. We stopped close to him. He did not turn. He was looking from the cabin toward the sun.

"Monsieur Colton, please let me present my feelings of deep sympathy," a gentleman was saying. "What a terrible tragedy. Burned in a fire, all of them. There's nothing one can say. Is there anything I can do?"

"No, thank you," Monsieur Colton replied in a voice empty of love, empty of life, empty of feeling. I wanted to cry. I wanted to cry for them all, people I didn't know. As I pedaled away on my bicycle the tears rolled down my face, opening the gate for the flood of sadness and hurt I had been holding back. I felt that the boys in the cabin had tainted the memory of that happy family. I was overcome by a familiar deep longing for my mother's love, my father's love, or anybody's love. I was overcome with self-pity. I wanted to hide this display of emotion.

I pedaled ahead. The steps of the boardwalk were in front of me. I pulled on the handlebars and my front wheel went up. I pushed hard on the pedals. The bicycle overturned. I felt an excruciating pain knife through my body. I was down on the ground. I reached between my legs where the pain seemed to be centered. There was blood on my hand where I had touched myself.

"Are you hurt?" Michel had caught up with me and was concerned.

"No, it's nothing."

The bicycle was a mess. The slender racing saddle was no longer in a horizontal position, but was sticking straight up.

"I'll walk you home. Are you all right."

I could not walk. It was too painful.

"Get on," Michel said, motioning to his bike. "I'll bring yours later."

Sitting sideways on the handlebars with Michel's arms encircling me, I was numb. Like an automaton I got off the bike, stumbled into the house, on to the bathroom, and looked at the damage. My loose panties were torn and bloodstained. I rinsed myself off. Hiding the panties in my hand I walked to the bedroom and flung myself on my bed. Burying my face in the pillow I wanted to cry. But the tears would not come. When the pain stopped and I quietly fell asleep, escaping into a deep slumber, I was unaware that I had lost my virginity, not to a boy, not to a man, but to the saddle of a racing bicycle.

The summer of 1941 found us still at the beach. We had been away from Paris since the winter of 1938–39. Now, the Parisians were returning for their annual vacations. Beaches were not popular because of the threat of mines, and only the state beach was monitored for this hazard. Consequently, it was a glorious year for the tennis club. Everyone was there. The kids mixed with the young, the young with the mature, and the mature with the old. In the clubhouse, at the pool, in the garden, in the restaurant, and in the gameroom, one could forget the war, for no German ever attempted to join our club.

I had grown during the last two years. My breasts were full, my waist small, and my hips curved seductively when I walked. I was new game for the sophisticated young men of the tennis set. They were all charming and polite as they competed with one another for my favors, which of course I had no intention of giving anyone.

The attention of one boy, Carlos, was the envy of all the

ladies in our summer crowd. I wanted to experiment with my newfound power. So I coaxed him away from the group into the orchard, and perched in an almond tree from where I could tantalize him with my charms. As I was eating fresh almonds he caught my dangling legs.

"Carlos," I said. "I like you very much. You are handsome, and it's flattering that you find me so attractive. Most girls would be so weak they could not refuse you. They're naïve, and haven't had any experience. I've had lovers before," I fibbed. "I've found out that nothing really excites me more than a man with a full-grown beard. I don't know why, but it weakens my resistance. I just have to give in."

"Is that so?" he said, with a mixture of belief and skepticism. "All right. I'll be back after you in a few weeks. I'll grow a beard, and I'll be here to collect on that weakness of yours."

The race was on. It was such a good line that I used it on most of the other boys.

The following weeks were glorious. The beards sprouted around me like weeds. From the veranda of the club I could see all my aspiring beaus in various stages of growth. Carlos, with his Spanish ancestry, had proudly produced a thick, slightly sinister black beard much sooner than I thought possible. He was even more handsome than before, like a noble Spanish pirate.

I did not know how dearly I would pay for my little game.

Fall found us back in Paris. One day Isabelle informed me that a certain Lucien Berger had called and invited me to play bridge Sunday afternoon at three o'clock.

"He said he got to know you at the tennis club in Hermanville," she added.

Lucien . . . Lucien. . . . It was taking me a moment to fit that name with a face. Oh yes, I giggled, remembering to myself, he's the one with whom I played a very liberated woman who could not follow through on her sexual attraction for him because she had contracted a disease. I had told him that by the time his beard had grown I would be cured. It was now four months since the summer and my games at the tennis club. I had not expected to see any of the boys until the next year.

"I don't want to go," I said aloud.

"But you must," said Isabelle. "It's a very important family.

They live in Passy, and Chantal is very fond of Roger, Lucien's brother. You have a chance to open up our social life with them." Chantal's mood was one of morose depression. She was hiding her loneliness through an exaggerated stiffness toward everyone. I knew she was afraid of ending up an old maid at the age of twenty. To be twenty-one and not engaged was at that time in France considered a sure sign that one was lacking in charm.

"Well, at a bridge party he can't ask me to. . . ." I was thinking out loud, and stopped speaking, shaking my head as I speculated.

"You're mumbling again, Corinne. It's really very impolite," Isabelle admonished. "Call him right now and accept. Here's the number."

It was a cool, beautiful crisp day. The autumn leaves were carpeting the street. The colors were a feast to my eyes. Because shoes were impossible to buy, I was walking in a pair of boots that had belonged to my father, enjoying kicking the humid layers of golden leaves. The boot toes were stuffed with paper and were getting wet, but I didn't mind. My good shoes were in a shopping bag. I planned to change before I arrived at the bridge party. With a heavy sweater underneath the jacket of Isabelle's old suit I felt warm and joyous. I always liked to return to Passy and walk the streets of my youth. Even during the occupation the flowers in the window boxes, the elegance of the concierges, everything pointed to the abundance of this upper-class district. This is where I belong, I thought. I'll live around here again one day.

My hand was caressing a wrought iron fence that protected a well-manicured front garden from intruders. I had arrived at the address of Lucien Berger. The doorman lifted his cap.

"May I help you, Miss?"

"I'm expected at the Bergers'." I was holding my head high, forgetting my strange attire.

His eyes fell on Papa's boots.

"Is that so, Miss. . . ?" He waited for me to supply a name.

"Wait. . . ." I put my hand on his arm. Balancing on one foot, I started to unlace a boot. "I have my good shoes in the bag." I attempted an explanatory smile.

"Yes, Miss. . . ?" He looked annoyed.

"Miss Dibos."

"Here, sit down," he said, deploying a little folding stool.

"Thank you very much."

"Take the elevator on the right. It's the sixth floor."

"What number?"

"There's only one apartment per floor."

They must be huge apartments, I thought, enjoying the slow ascent of the elevator that shook sideways everytime it passed a weight on the rope I had pulled to set it in motion.

Lucien opened the door all smiles.

"How nice to see you, Corinne. And how are you today?"

A sense of oncoming danger seized me. I stepped back toward the elevator.

"Please come in, follow me," he said. "We have the bridge tables set up in back."

As I followed him down a long hallway I attempted to control my mounting nervousness.

"Whom did you invite to play?" I tried to sound light-hearted.

"Oh, I think you'll know everybody," he said, opening the door and flattening himself against the jamb. His hand on my shoulder moved me in. I heard the click of the lock behind me. I felt like a frightened doe with no escape. I suddenly knew that I was about to pay for the games I had played last summer.

Four other boys were there, Paul and Henri, who still had beards, and Claude and Armand, now beardless. There was no bridge table anywhere to be seen. I was in a locked room with four virile, angry young men. In a panic, I chose to display bravado.

"How wonderful to see all of you at one time."

"The pleasure is all ours," said Lucien.

Paul giggled.

"And what a pleasure it's going to be," he added.

They all laughed. What are they going to do? Are they going to rape me? Oh no. What am I going to do?

Claude grabbed a chair with a magisterial gesture and placed it in the middle of the room. With his hand he indicated that I should move to it and sit down.

"The chair of the accused," he said, and then continued, "it has come to our attention that this person, Corinne Dibos, has many personalities, and it is our intention to discover which of us she has made a fool of."

Help, I asked Joan of Arc silently. And Sarah, please help me. . . . I was addressing myself to the great Sarah Bernhardt.

"The defendant will be given the opportunity to speak for herself," Lucien said. "Will the first injured party state his case?"

Jean-Pierre walked over to me, sniffed around my head, then turned toward his friends who were now sitting in a row on the bed.

"It was in July, 1941. I had just finished a set of tennis. I was hot, I went to lie on the grass to rest, minding my own business, when this creature came up to me, slid on the grass, lying alongside of me, then put her arm across my chest, passed her hand in front of my nose, and asked me how I liked her perfume, which by the way she is not wearing today. She then told me that it had been given to her by a paraplegic lover whom she made love to because no one else cared. She then mentioned how she appreciated my beautiful muscular legs." With one foot on the bed he was flexing his leg muscle.

"At least she was right about that," Paul said.

"Then she proceeded to tell me that her lover was leaving the shore in a few weeks. When I asked her how she could have had sex with him, she mentioned that he had a beard, and that she couldn't resist a man with a beard. 'The way I feel about you,' she told me, 'it would be impossible to resist if you had a beard.'"

"I didn't say I had sex with him," I protested. "I just said he was my lover, not my sexual partner." The words tumbled out of my mouth.

"Anyway," Claude went on, "I had never seen myself with a beard, and it was all right with me, since the reward for growing one made it tempting. By the time my beard had grown, and I called her, she started making excuses for not meeting me and keeping her promise."

"May I speak now?"

"No," they said in unison, "you'll have your turn."

"As for me," said Paul, "I was happily engaged in a flirtation with Renée. You all remember Renée?"

"Oui, oui, oui," acknowledged Lucien.

"When Miss Dibos here started to moralize," Paul went on,

"about the evil of man's inconsiderate behavior toward women. She told me how she had been taken advantage of and made pregnant. She was crying, everyone in the club was looking at us. I took her behind the clubhouse. There she described the horror of her abortion. I have no reason to live, she said. I felt sorry for her. I wiped away her tears with my towel. She was sobbing hysterically. I took her in my arms and rocked her gently. She made me fall in love with her, and told me a wierd story about a dream she had in which a bearded man had come and purified her with his love. 'I thought it was Christ,' she told me, 'but now when I look at your face and your kind eyes I know it was you.' Then she asked me to grow a beard so that her dream would come true. The rest of my story is the same. Once the beard was grown I never saw her again."

"I never said that I would make love to you, that's what you demanded of me. I said that you looked like the one who could save me."

"Silence, the accused must refrain from speaking," Lucien ordered.

With a handkerchief stuffed in my mouth, a scarf tightly knotted over my face, my hands bound in back of me, I was quickly rendered helpless. But I was Joan of Arc, facing her accusers.

"My turn," announced Henri. "Did you tell me that your parents wanted you to become a nun and you desperately wanted to experience being loved by a man before you entered the convent?"

I nodded affirmatively.

"You really made me feel sorry for you," Henry continued his indictment. "And then you told me that you made a promise to the Virgin Mary that you would wait until the right man, and that you would recognize him and give yourself to him. Have you found him yet?"

"No," I shook my head.

"Well, here he is," he said angrily, putting his bearded face next to mine. "I'm here to get my payoff."

I was damp with fear. His hand reached for the zipper of my skirt.

"Just a minute," Armand interrupted. "I have not told my story yet." He looked at me with regret. "I would have done anything for you. You spoke to me with such assurance. I was so shy. The tales of your affairs with other men excited me. I couldn't sleep at night. My beard didn't want to grow. You kept tantalizing me, and then rejecting me, telling me that I had to wait because my beard was too thin. Corinne, I want to know why you were playing those games." He was untying my gag.

"I don't know," I was crying. "I guess I was trying to find out what kind of woman I would be most comfortable being. I guess I was trying out different roles."

"Great," said Paul, moving toward me, reaching for my skirt again.

"Let me give you the experience of a very hot man."

"Oh, please, no. . . . I beg you don't do that. I really have never had any sexual experience with a man."

"This calls for a conference. Come into my room," Lucien said to the other boys.

I was left alone.

"I need help. Sarah, what am I supposed to do?"

The voice which answered seemed to come from behind me. I could not turn around. My arms were still tied behind my back to the chair.

"They're angry because each one of them believed you. You're a great actress," the voice said.

When they came back into the room in silence I knew that they had decided my fate.

"We're going to teach you a lesson," said Claude. "You're just a kid, a bad kid, and we're going to spank you just the way you treat a bad kid."

I was petrified. They untied me from the chair, keeping my hands tied behind me. Claude grabbed me and placed me over his knees.

"Let me help," said Paul, lifting up my skirt and exposing my panties. "Go ahead, Claude. My turn next."

Jean Pierre hit me. I screamed.

"Get the gag back on her mouth," Paul ordered.

"Listen, I'm sorry. I'm just an actress, and I'm a good one at that, otherwise you wouldn't. . . ." The handkerchief shoved into my mouth caused me to gag.

I had given the cue. One after the other they passed me from knee to knee. I was spanked while they were shouting, "That's for being an actress, that will teach you to act. So you want to be an actress?"

I resigned myself to the pain. I was not in my flesh anymore. I was floating out into a green meadow. There were flowers everywhere. On a hillside the yellow daffodils were spelling out my name, Corinne, a great actress. I slipped into unconsciousness, and went lifeless. They stopped. When I revived Armand was sitting next to the bed where I was lying on my stomach.

"I'm sorry, Corinne," he said. I'll accompany you home."

"Where are the others?"

"I think they went to get drunk."

Of course our social connection with the Bergers never materialized, and I did not tell anyone about my experience there until one day in Hollywood when I was asked by a magazine reporter about the exact moment in my life when I knew that I was going to be an actress.

Papa, on our return to Paris, thought the nuns at the convent school would be able to restrain what he now perceived as my precocious behavior.

Across the street from the convent in which I was now enrolled was a boys school, a monastery. One boy followed me discreetly when I went home. He was different from the others; his clothes were expensive, and he had a mournful look on his face. One afternoon the Mother Superior came into our class and informed us that some of the students at the convent and in the monastery were being forced, starting tomorrow, to wear the yellow Star of David on their breast pocket. She said that the school accepted pupils of all races and religions, and that it was our Christian duty to help our less fortunate brothers and sisters through difficult times.

"If you see anyone with a star," she said, "talk to them. Make them feel that you are not afraid to be seen with them."

I did not see the boy from the monastery for a few days, but one morning I saw him running toward the school with his head down, his hand holding his books over his chest pocket. He bumped into me. My books fell. He dropped his arm, and there it was, the star.

"I'm sorry," he said. His head seemed to be drawing back into his shoulders.

"Wait," I said. "I've missed you. Would you like to walk home with me after school?"

"Do you really want me to? I'm marked, you know."

"I know, and it's all right. I would not be ashamed of you. What's your name?"

"Sam," he said, smiling pitifully.

In the next month he told me the horror of the fate of his family. The Gestapo had come to their luxurious apartment, and without any time to pack or phone friends, they had been taken away, put in a cattle car on a train. From inside they had worked day and night to break one of the door locks. Sam and his sister were chosen to be the first ones to jump off the speeding train. Sam went first, his sister second. When he picked himself up and walked to join her he found her dead, her head smashed against a huge rock. He fled, and found his way back to Paris. He was now living with another Jewish family who had taken an assumed name. The family ran a perfume store, and thought they were safe. The Germans were among their best customers.

Sam would often tell me of his fears for his family. He talked at length, but his voice sounded empty. A part of him had already died. I wanted to comfort him.

One afternoon we were sitting in the park watching the pigeons playing the love game. The misery of the curse the Nazis had set upon him was written on his face. Large tears rolled down his cheeks.

"Sam, look at me," I said. "I love you very much. You're not alone. I'm your friend."

I wiped away his tears. His head dropped and snuggled in my neck. I pulled it back and held it lovingly in my hands. I kissed away his tears. They were salty. I had never tasted the tears of a man before. There was a powerful force in that taste that filled me with a strong maternal instinct. I kissed his lips gently, again and again.

"Come," I said. "Maybe you can come home and have dinner with us. Come home with me and I'll ask."

"No, I couldn't do that. That would endanger you. I'll never forget what you just did for me, Corinne."

For the next ten days I was in bed with a sore throat and a high fever. When I returned to school Sam was gone. No one answered the phone and the perfume store was closed. No one at school could tell me anything. I never saw Sam again.

The nuns who taught in the convent seemed to take a special interest in me. I blossomed under their attention. When the school year was over I was tempted to stay with them, to join their order and bask in its warm security. One day I told the Mother Superior of my vision at the age of seven that Jesus had called me one of his own.

"Few are blessed by the call from Jesus Christ himself," she said. "My child, you are blessed. You have received the call. Pray and listen to your soul. Tell me when you're ready to announce the decision to your family."

Every day I went to the early sacraments and contemplated the decision I had to make. On the one hand, giving up materialistic pleasures and what people called the carnal joys of life or the luxury of beautiful clothes would all be easy, I decided. On the other hand, living a life without the experience of motherhood would be more difficult.

"When you take your vows you will be Jesus' bride," the Mother Superior had said.

Being Jesus' wife would be perfect for me, I knew, for he had already been my childhood friend and confidant. And as far as motherhood was concerned, I could love the children that I watched play in the garden of the orphanage. There were no obstacles between me and my vow, so why did I feel that something was very wrong?

In the peaceful chapel I lit a candle with a silent prayer. Dear God, give me a sign so I will know what to do.

I knelt in front of the image of the Virgin Mary. Through the stained glass window the orange rays of the sun streamed onto my folded hands. I heard a sound like the wind rustling in the trees. Listening intensely with my inner ear I began to distinguish words forming a high-pitched melody.

"Now is the time for the work of God to be done out in the world. Being cloistered behind a convent wall was right in the past, but now your destiny is to go out and be Christ's bride in view of the whole world." Feeling grateful, I answered silently, Thank you, dear God.

Chapter 3

After I made the decision not to take the veil, the pendulum of my interest swung back to the hidden wicked book in my room, and I avidly read it again. I was also attracted to the unorthodox behavior of a certain girl at the convent. As soon as she was around the corner from the school she would transform her prosaic uniform by covering it with a flowery sweater she always carried in her school bag. Approaching her, I suggested that she follow me into the bathroom. There, in the privacy of a closed toilet stall, I opened the forbidden book which I had carried with me to school and read her a particularly enticing passage. Our friendship grew, and time permitting, every day we would read with our bodies close, our heads joined, repressing the giggles of self-consciousness, until the fateful day when I was called into the office of the Mother Superior. To my surprise I saw my father there with a frown on his face. As I was asked to sit down I wondered why he was there and not Isabelle. The nun spoke.

"Monsieur Dibos, an extremely grave situation has been discovered. This was found in your daughter's desk." She held forth the infamous book in its plain wrapping.

Papa turned to look at me, not severely as I expected, but with an eyebrow raised in question, a twinkle in his eye.

"Someone had left the key in the door," I whispered.

"Did I do that?" my father said. "How old are you, Corinne?"

"Going on sixteen," I answered, in wonder at his friendly tone.

"Monsieur Dibos," the nun interrupted. "We cannot have perverted literature tarnishing the minds of these young, pure, beautiful souls who are in my care. I must suspend your daughter."

"Mother Superior," Papa said, "that will not be necessary. I'm taking her out of the convent. Will you permit me to make a contribution to the church?" he went on, laying a large bill on the desk. "May Corinne gather her belongings now? I'll be waiting outside. And now, the book please."

Speechless, the Mother Superior pushed the depraved volume in his direction with a letter opener.

Walking home at my father's side I was awestruck at the quiet strength he had displayed.

"Papa, thank you. I love you," I said, adjusting my step to his.

"Well," he was coughing to hide his embarrassment. "You must learn to keep your physical life separate from your spiritual aspirations. Everything in its place."

When we arrived home he spoke with Isabelle.

"It's time for Corinne to go to a normal school," was his only comment.

I entered the lycée Victor Drury, an immense high school, in the middle of the semester, and cliques had already formed, so I felt like an outsider. I was grateful when a small, dark-haired girl, Florence, suggested that we could walk together. Since Florence lived on the way to school, we became inseparable. Her mother, a widow for ten years, had devoted her life to spoiling her children, particularly her son, André. André was handsome, with dark soft curly hair, very white skin, and almond-shaped brown eyes. It was not long before I had fallen in love with him.

We soon became very involved. When I got out of school André would surprise me by being there waiting. He had dropped out of college, but still kept his friends. Being accepted by them made me feel flattered and sophisticated. Florence and I plotted the future, when we would become sisters after I had married André.

Eventually, André and I decided to arrange a weekend together. I told my parents I was invited to go to country for the weekend when actually we wanted to be together in the city. The day finally arrived, and I went with André to Montmartre—the center of the Parisian underworld, a vast sink of prostitution, pickpockets, petty thieves, lowlife, and cheap hotels where questions aren't asked.

We had gone to see a movie that afternoon, a beautiful love story that left us in stunned silence.

"Watch out," André said, as he helped me over a puddle of

slime. Someone coming out of a bar, no doubt, had thrown up right in the middle of the sidewalk.

"What do you want me to do?" I whispered to André.

"I'll tell you. Where we have to go is about two blocks from here."

Around the corner the crowd was dense. The neon signs of a flashy nightclub made us squint for a moment. The market of showgirls was blinking its lights at us in blatant invitation. I stood in awe at these displays, and André finally grabbed my hand and led me away. I resisted being pulled. In my mind I was thinking back over the heroine of a book I had read a few months ago. It concerned a love affair in Japan in which a woman, out of respect for a man, walks behind her lover. With my head thrown back, my lipstick all but erased by our passion in the movie theater, I felt my body still ignorant, but in need of the experience that awaited me. Not wanting to walk behind anyone, I moved forward, proud and intrepid, like the emblem on the bow of a ship on the high seas.

The females selling their charms called out to André as we made our way through the crowds.

"Hey, petit," one of them said. "I'm tired of those old bastards. If you have twenty francs come on, I'll let you off easy."

Another, an overly made-up blonde, interrupted our stride. "Hey! *beau gas!* Would you like to try me and my best friend? I bet we could call it a night for both of you."

André just laughed at them. His laughter was reassuring. He wanted only me.

The strong man of the *boîtes*, like the barker at a carnival, stood in front of each club, taunting passersby.

"Girls, girls for the taste of everyone."

We passed a pimp dressed in a violet velvet jacket and a washed-out pink satin shirt.

"Maybe even you, young lady, can find one that attracts you," the pimp said.

André pulled me protectively to him, and hooked his arm in mine. We walked silently the rest of the way. Around the corner the street was dark, lit dimly by gas lights. Stopping suddenly, André grabbed me in his arms.

"Do you love me?" Pushing me adroitly against the wall, he

did not wait for my answer, but kissed me passionately. When he stopped, I felt needed.

"Now look. You see that hotel over there?" André pointed to a building across the street. "You just have to go in and say that you're a freelance and you have a customer who has promised you five hundred francs for a night, and that you'll give them one hundred of it as commission, and on top of it your client will pay for the room. Got it?"

"Yes." I answered, my voice trembling. "I go in and say that you'll pay me five hundred francs and I'll give them one hundred commission. Is that it?"

"Don't forget to tell them that I'll pay for the room."

A couple was passing by. The man was pawing the abundant derriére of his willing companion. A shiver went up my spine.

"Do you think they'll believe me?" I whispered.

"Well, if they don't, since all the hotels are occupied by Germans, I'll just have to go back and make my mother happy by spending the weekend in the country."

"They'll believe me. I promise," I said, falling for the threat.

I rang the bell, the door opened, and a tired old man stood before me.

"Yes?"

"I want a room please."

"We don't have any rooms to rent here. I suggest you try the Hotel Bonaparte down the street."

"You don't understand," I said, affecting a giggle. "I have a customer. I'm a freelance. I'll give you one hundred francs and he'll pay for the room."

The tired eyes of the elderly man behind the desk looked me over from head to toe.

"How long have you been doing this? How much is he giving you?" Without waiting for an answer he added. "I don't want you here. You're too young and pretty." He looked at me hard. "But I can see that if I don't you'll do it anyway, and you might end up where you won't be safe."

His hand reached toward me and pinched my breast. I jumped back in horror.

"Where's your customer?" he asked.

"Outside."

"All right. Pay me two hundred francs in advance. Here's the key to room eleven. First floor on the left. Now I don't want any noise. Don't come crying to me for help."

"Oh no, sir. Thank you." I almost shouted.

On an impulse I went up and kissed the elderly man on the cheek. He stood stunned as I ran out to the street.

"André, André, it's all set," I shouted, waving the key.

"Shhhh. Be quiet, ma cherie. Do you want everyone to know?"

We went up to the room silently. Cherie, he had said, ma cherie. I had never been called cherie before. Not knowing what to do I sat shyly on the bed looking around. A large mirror was hanging on the wall, reflecting in its length the yellow chenille bedspread that had seen better times. The picture on the wall facing the window depicted a fat monk drunk with wine, his hand groping between the enormous legs of a heavy, laughing waitress.

"Look here," said André. "Look at that pink bathroom."

The old tub was deeply encased in mosaic tiles. It was the most luxurious bathroom I had ever seen.

"I wonder if there's any hot water?" I said.

"But of course," André answered, whirling me around. "That's what we're here for. In a place like this, hot water is the most important necessity."

I didn't like the sarcasm in his laughter as he tried to pull down my skirt. Where was the tenderness? I knew it was foolish, but I had hoped André would carry me over the threshold and declare his love like those love stories I had read. I suddenly felt that I no longer wanted to be with him. I pulled away.

"Why don't you take a bath? I'll go and get a bottle of wine and some sandwiches."

He was gone. I went to the window and watched him walk away, turn the corner, and pass from my view. It did not feel right. I heard a voice whisper in my ear. "Get out of here," it said. I grabbed my purse and then stopped.

"I can't do this," I spoke softly. "He won't understand. He'll be furious." I must always think about how my actions affect others, I thought. He'll be hurt and disappointed. I've committed myself. I can't back out now.

I went to turn on the bath water. It was steaming hot, not like the tepid water of our weekly family baths at home. Anticipating the luxurious pleasure of the hot bath I mechanically folded my clothes. When André returned I was still in the tub. Embarrassed, I prudishly covered myself with the wet towel. In a very joyous mood, André handed me a glass of cool, white wine, and returned carrying two dozen open oysters. The wine warmed my blood. My skin was immersed in warm liquid, and the freshness of the oysters sent me into ecstasy. André was suddenly Marc Antony, his shirt and undershorts turned into a toga. We were in ancient Rome, at the baths, and I was one of his concubines. One of his concubines? I frowned. I wanted to be his one and only wife. To chase the thought away I sank my head under the water.

"Look at your skin." André was holding my hand, which had turned into a network of white furrows. "Out, mademoiselle, it's my turn." He handed me a towel.

Wrapped in the bedspread I sat next to the bath serving him wine and small pieces of cucumber sandwich and blushing as I glanced at his body. He was almost hairless, except for his forest of pubic growth. His organ was very much smaller than the illustrations I had studied. It wavered slowly in the water like an undersea plant.

"Your turn again," said André, standing up in the tub. I walked into the bedroom, dropped the bedspread, and returned naked. I felt his eyes piercing my veil of modesty. I ran to the tub. As I lifted my leg to get into the water André grabbed me and held me against his nakedness.

"André, let's get in the tub together," I ventured, wanting to escape from my naked vulnerability. I sat in the bath water presenting him with only my back. We splashed and tickled. It was an orgy of hot water, a contest to see how hot we could stand it.

Exhausted, sweaty, and dizzy, we lay down on the bed, our strength sapped by the hot tub. It was close to noon the next day when I woke, surprised for a moment at my nakedness, and at the strange room. I quickly grabbed my slip and covered myself. André was still asleep, his mouth in a pout like an unsatisfied child. What a beautiful body he has, I thought, but as my eyes traveled down to his feet I remembered that when I was twelve I imagined a man in bed with me. I had made a wish, that my man would not have any feet, because feet are what people use to walk away and leave you behind. Just as I had watched, the day she shared love with me, maman's feet going up the stairs to the bedroom where she died, deserting me, André woke up.

"Come here," he said.
. I sat down beside him. He rolled me on top of him, then over and over until I was covered, completely entwined. I tried to push him away, but it was hopeless. "André, cheri, please! We haven't had breakfast yet." He was moving up and down on me. Then he planted a kiss on my forehead before he got up and said, "We can go and have breakfast. That was a good idea." I felt like a grown-up woman sitting with André in the cafe. The coffee was warm and its aroma filled my nostrils, the bread was crisp and freshly baked. I looked at André's profile and felt exalted and happy. André had kept his promise to respect me. He had played a little rough that morning, but since I didn't feel any pain I thought I was still a virgin. My heart was singing inside. I could trust him, therefore I could love him.

It was a beautiful day, the sun shone brightly, and I was proud to be walking arm in arm with André, just like every other married couple on a Sunday afternoon.

In the months that followed I started to skip school in the afternoon so I could spend a few hours alone with André before his mother came home. But I was always busy talking to Florence in her room when their mother returned home. She suspected nothing. One day she asked me if my parents would allow me to come with them for a weekend at their country house.

"Sure they will," I said eagerly.

Soon we were all together in the country. I felt as if I had a new family. Florence and I decided that the time had come to let her mother know of the love André and I felt for each other. It was decided that I would look at André adoringly, and be apprehended by the woman as we held hands, just enough show of affection to break the ice and let her know gently of our regard for each other. Whatever I did must have been very convincing. That night when André snuck into my room, she was not far behind. She caught us in an embrace and began to scream.

"Tramp, you're just a tramp, trying to attract my son into your bed. Out, get out, out of my house at once. André," she screamed, "get her out of here."

She was crying and screaming at the same time. André

grabbed my shoes and coat, and without letting me change from my pajamas to my clothes pulled me down the stairs and out onto the street.

"André, what's happening? Why is she so angry? Where am I going to go?"

"I'll take you to a hotel in the village."

With André carrying me on his bicycle handlebars we arrived at the hotel. He registered me, took me up, and sat on the bed watching me silently. I was crying.

"Cheri, why was she so mad?"

"I have to go," he said.

"You're going to leave me here alone? Please, no, stay with me." I kissed him, trembling.

"Stop," he said. "I have to go and take care of my mother."

"André, tell her that I'm a good girl. Tell her that I'm still a virgin."

"That you're what?" André looked at me incredulously.

"Well, I *am* still a virgin," I said, a little shaken. "It didn't hurt, it never hurt. Please tell me that I'm still a virgin."

By now I was alarmed. André started to laugh. He moved toward the door. He could not stop laughing. I dropped to my knees and grabbed his legs.

"Oh André, please. Please tell me that I'm still a virgin. Don't laugh at me. Please."

Choking with laughter mounting into hysteria, he pushed me away and was gone. The door closed. I lay flat on the floor, faced with the enormity that there was only one way to interpret that laughter, laughter I heard diminishing as André pedaled away on his bicycle. Even when he was far away the laughter still resonated in the silence of the night. He was walking away from me. Abandoning me.

It wasn't fair. I didn't deserve it. Just because I believed that you were still a virgin until you felt pain. Now I realized the significance of the bicycle accident. I should have gone to the convent. But it was too late. I was forever banned from becoming a nun. They didn't take girls who weren't virgins, I thought.

Tears finally came to wash away my pain. Exhausted, I fell into an uneasy sleep broken by nightmarish dreams. After a while I awoke, got dressed, and waited for André. I had a solution. We had to get married, right now. Then everything would be all right.

André arrived with my suitcase. He was tense, prepared for a scene with tears and recriminations. Surprised at my self-control, he accepted my request that we go to a mass. Kneeling next to him I prayed to God and asked him to forgive me and help me become an honorable woman.

The sun was blinding, bright and blazing when we walked out of the little dimly lit Gothic church. We stopped at a cafe.

"André, we have to get married."

"Get married?" he said. "That's impossible."

"Why?"

"Well, cherie, I'm too young. I don't want to work. Who would support us?"

"Maybe for awhile we could live with my parents, or your mother," I suggested.

"Forget it. She never wants to see you again."

"André, you can't do this to me." My voice was determined. "At least we can become engaged. Then we can explain to her how we feel." André looked sheepish.

"Engaged? I guess that would be all right. But it has to be a secret, a complete secret. Our secret. Promise?"

"Yes, cheri, our secret, but for how long?"

"Only a little while."

Life went on as before. I would skip school and join André in his mother's bed. But André did not want Florence in our confidence any longer. So I left just before she came home from school. The clandestine nature of our relationship added a new dimension to my feelings. I had been wondering why I did not feel any of that ecstatic joy that I heard went with love-making. André had started to make a lot of noise, breathing heavily, whimpering, and finally screaming, a strange scream, raucous and deep. I decided that if I breathed like him, if I whimpered, and even screamed a little bit, it would help me feel what I was supposed to feel. Having an orgasm they called it. In fact, whenever the subject of a woman's pleasure was discussed, orgasm was never mentioned. Instead, the boys would brag that they had brought the girl to a climax five or six times before they had their orgasm. Well, my whimpering and screaming did not bring on the desired result, not ten, not five, not even one. Nothing! But it did develop a passionate reaction in André that I had not expected. It became what André expected from me. So to please him I was caught in the trap that so many women then fell into, pretending to feel more than I did, and by that action removing any chance to experience pleasure.

André pointed out to me one day that my period was late, that it should have begun sixteen days ago.

"Oh really?" I said. "I wouldn't know."

"Well, I know. I've been keeping track. Maybe you're pregnant."

"Oh André, that would be beautiful," I beamed. "Then your mother couldn't be against our getting married. I hope I'm going to have a baby, our baby. What do you want? A boy or a girl? Papa and Isabelle like you. It'll be all right." I was talking to myself. André was already on the phone.

"All right doctor, thank you. We'll be there in an hour."

"I feel fine, cheri," I protested. "I don't need a doctor, not yet."

"We'll just go by his office so he can make a test. See if you really are going to have a baby."

After the doctor confirmed my pregnancy it was a few days before I saw André. He was busy putting together a business deal, he said over the phone.

"Don't go to school," he told me. "Come over right away, cherie. My mother is leaving soon. We can play as if we're married."

I felt elated. A blanket of snow covered the streets of Paris. With each step the crystal snowflakes yielded the beauty of their structure as they were crushed underfoot. The sound was like a statement of love. Cherie . . . cheerie . . . cheeeerie . . . cheeeeerie. Extending my arms wide, I offered my face to the falling white lacework, my mouth open, my tongue burning from the icy cold wetness. I was happier than I had ever been before.

André's mother was there to greet me when I arrived. She made me sit down in the living room and brought me a cup of tea. It was strangely formal.

"Of course Corinne, you are both too young to get married. André has promised to wait a year or two. You do understand."

"Well, I'm . . ."

"Yes, I know. The baby. Well, it is still a little early yet. Sometimes in the beginning of pregnancies women have miscarriages. So we shall wait and see. Come have dinner with us next Friday, will you? Good-by now. I have to go to work."

As soon as the door closed André picked me up and carried me into his mother's bedroom. Cajoling me, he undressed me and took me shivering to the bed.

"Hurry up and get under the covers. It's cold," he said.

I felt glorious because his mother had accepted me, and had invited me to dinner. André's love-making was forceful, he made the usual sounds, and when it was over he remained on top of me. Soon I felt something moving inside of me again. It was hurting me.

"Stop," I screamed. "It hurts. Stop." I put my hand down and discovered that he had put something inside me. My God, it was a large carrot.

"Are you crazy? What are you doing? Stop it."

"Look," he said. "I don't want a baby now. If I do this a lot to you I can bring on your period. Then we can get married and have a baby later."

"But I want this baby," I said, struggling out of bed.

"I have something to say about that, you know, he's mine too," André stated.

He managed to keep me in bed most of the afternoon. He approached me constantly. Each time I started screaming, and pushed him away.

After that I did not see him for several days. But he continued to telephone and ask about my period. Friday the four of us, André, his mother, Florence, and I had a most pleasant evening. Finally it was getting late. I wanted to go home, but André's mother suggested that I could stay with them if I liked. Sleeping here with them, with André, with her approval. It was too good to be true.

"Thank you," I accepted triumphantly.

This was certainly a sign of total acceptance. I slept like a baby in André's arms. My dreams were like fairy tales. My Prince Charming adoring me forever and ever.

After breakfast the next morning André handed me my coat. His mother was already dressed to go out.

"Come with us, Corinne. I have to go to the doctor, and André is taking me."

I sat by myself in the waiting room at the doctor's office. André and his mother were behind a door marked "private." The three of them came out at once.

"Well young lady, I've been told you're pregnant. Since you're here let me check and make certain everything is all right." The doctor spoke with a squeaky voice. He was bespectacled and gray-haired. His puffy jowls dropped over a straggly, sparse beard.

I was hustled into the examination room.

"Take off your clothes and put this robe on," the doctor ordered before leaving.

He returned in a few minutes.

"Sit up on that table."

André was at the door.

"Please stay with me, André," I pleaded.

The position I had to assume on the table was humiliating. With my legs up and spread apart, I gazed at André's face while he held my hand firmly in his.

The doctor examined me quickly, and then left the room, leaving André behind with me.

"Can I get dressed now?" I asked.

"Not yet," André said. "Not before the doctor tells you."

The doctor was back.

"I'm going to give you an injection," he said. "It will relax you and in a little while I will complete my work. We'll take care of this problem." He left again.

"André, what problem? What does he mean?"

"Shhhh. He knows what he's doing." André was caressing my hair.

When the doctor returned he was wearing a mirrored band on his head.

"Relax now, take a deep breath." He was putting something inside me. Soon the pain was excruciating. I tried to move away.

"Keep her still, damn it," the doctor said to André. "Keep still, young lady, in a few minutes it will be over."

I had to be helped off the table and into my clothes. I could hardly walk.

"How often do I have to go through this kind of examination?" I asked André's mother, who was waiting in the outer room.

"Only once," she replied. "Well, good-by. I'll see you later, André. Here you are." She handed him the shopping bag she had been carrying.

"I want to go home," I said weakly. "I don't feel well."

"I'll tell you what," André said. "I have a friend who has a hotel room not far from here. He's away for the weekend, and he gave me the keys. We can go there for awhile so you can rest."

I had difficulty walking out of the office and into the street. When we arrived at the hotel André helped me into bed. He placed the shopping bag on a night table nearby, and gave me a pill.

"There's no outside line in this room. I have to go out and make some calls, cherie, so you should try to take a nap." He kissed me on the forehead and left.

I woke later with excruciating abdominal cramps. I must have slept for several hours, because it was now dark.

"André?" I called out, and turned on the bed light. I was alone.

I reached for the bag and examined its contents. In it I found sanitary napkins, a vial of pills, a sandwich, a thermos of coffee, and a note. Sobbing with pain, I read its contents:

There was no other way out. Don't worry. The doctor is very good. Take two pills every three hours. Don't try to get up before tomorrow. One day you'll forget all about it.

P.S. Don't tell anybody you just had an abortion. You could get in trouble with the police.

Automatically, I took the pills. The hot coffee burned my mouth. I was in a state of shock, too terrified to think. My body began to shake. I threw myself back on the bed, my head hitting the wall. My conscious mind was leaving my body. I felt that I was looking down on my wretched form lying on the bed. I became a detached observer with the responsibility of taking care of this human form which was now hemorrhaging on the bed below me.

In a dreamlike trance I began to hallucinate. I could see my mother as she went up the stairs for the last time, the night she died and left me. I could see her grave. I saw myself enter the gates of the cemetery as I had done so many times, and, making sure no one was watching, I lay down on the marble slab covering her grave and hugged the cold stone.

"Maman?" I was holding back deep sobs. "Why did you leave me? Where are you now? Is the earth cold down there like this stone? I know you did not like the cold. You were always wrapped in furs. No, you cannot be down there anymore. Are you? I know you're in heaven with God. Maman, Maman, Maman!" I called out.

A ripple of leaves answered me and a shiver entered my body.

"Maman, are you here?"

And then I heard her voice:

"Has Corinne been a good girl?"

In the morning I awoke with no tears, no self-recriminations, no judgments. It was a question of doing what had to be done. A voice inside me resonated in my mind like an echo: "Go home, no need for revenge. You had this experience so you could grow." I'll never trust anyone again, I thought without emotion. "You will, you will, again . . . , again . . . , and again," the voice said within me.

"I'll never want a man close to me again," I said.

"You will, again and again," said the voice.

When I left the hotel the winter sun on my face felt like the kiss of an old lady, reserved and full of loving recognition. I was not the same person I had been before. Something had died in me. I would leave André and his mother on the shore of my childhood. I would set sail into the future. No need to wave good-by, no need to cry, no need to . . . , no need . . . , no need.

Chapter 4

It was 1943. Slumbering France was beginning to awaken. The forces of reaction, led by Laval and Pétain, continued to work out deals with the Nazis. Some were willing to accept this passively, but more and more were not. The Resistance was organized in the hills of the countryside and the hidden corners of the cities. Slowly the nation awoke. The underground network spread, enraging the Germans with sabotage and espionage, building liaisons with our British and American allies, softening up the Nazi war machine, making it vulnerable to the inevitable invasion.

As a young woman I too was coming awake. I joined the atelier of Monsieur Canard, a painting instructor in Montparnasse. Study with him was a prerequisite to entering L'Ecole des Arts Décoratif. Charcoal sketching and stylized drawing opened up a new world for me, and in this class I made a new friend.

Suzanne had short, curly, naturally light blonde hair. Her nose, slanted at the bridge, bulged slightly over her thin nostrils, her green eyes reflected a cool elegance. Perfectly drawn lips broke easily into a condescending smile, disclosing the sign that the French attributed to those destined for wealth, a small space between her two front teeth. She was only five feet tall, her breasts were small, and her waist seemed naturally cinched over the roundness of her hips, while her slender ankles distracted attention from her muscular legs. She attached herself to me, showering me with compliments.

Suzanne was a year or two older, and wore fuzzy angora sweaters her sister made for sale at a high price on the black market. With Suzanne, money was no object, and wonder of wonders, my affluent new friend owned two beautiful bicycles. How come? I wanted to know.

"Last Christmas," she explained, "both my mother and father

61

heard that I wanted a bike. Since they're not on speaking terms, I ended up with two. Which one do you want? The blue or the green one?"

I was speechless. My impossible dream had come true.

"My eyes are green and yours are blue, so I guess this is yours," Suzanne said, rolling the blue bicycle toward me. We became inseparable, and we relished the freedom the bicycles gave us.

Suzanne's gift had given me back a part of my pride. I found myself becoming devoted to her. To me she was a beautiful, kind, and clever friend, even though at school she would sit close to me and lift my ideas, executing them in her own meticulous style. But I didn't care. I was even flattered when she won high grades with my designs. After all, it was nothing compared to the joy I received from the bicycle.

In good weather we pedaled happily together through the streets of Paris, pursuing our interests and curiosity from L'Ecole des Beaux Arts to L'Ecole des Arts Décoratif, to Monsieur Canard's atelier, from the Sorbonne to the movie on the Champs Elysées.

The streets were often filled with German soldiers. Guiding my bicycle with my hand, I walked through the crowd of Frenchmen who showed their contempt by paying absolutely no attention to the German show of strength. Whenever our path crossed that of a German, we would turn our backs like many other French, and look into the window of the closest shop until he had passed.

The movie lines outside the theater were long. People were jumping up and down in place to keep warm. Noses were red and running. One of my pleasures was to see as many acting performances as I could. I wanted to learn what it was the star did to create that magic attraction. Suzanne always had a purse full of francs, so money was not a problem, but I could not see us waiting in line three hours in the cold to see one movie.

"Follow me," I said to Suzanne as we approached the cashier.

I glanced at the poster for the film, turned my head sideways, and without bending down to speak in the round hole of the glass cage, I said to the woman selling tickets, "Do you have any passes for me?"

"I don't have any passes," she answered, looking in her drawer.

"Do you mean my father didn't call in yet? I'm Nicole Marchand, the daughter of the producer. When my father calls tell him that we're already in, and that we'll see him when he picks us up after the movie is over."

Smiling, the cashier handed me two passes.

"It's an excellent film, Miss Marchand. I really enjoyed it."

In the darkness of the movie I clasped my hands together and prayed.

"Forgive me, Father. Is acting a lie? I wish I was Marchand's daughter, or the daughter of someone else who could help me. So dear God, forgive me. We'll give them the money when we come out."

When the lights came back on, my eyes were still moist with emotion. I asked Suzanne for some money, and approached the man checking the tickets.

"Found this under the seat," I said, handing the astounded man the bills. "Someone might come back for it."

We were out on the street, both laughing so hard we had to stop. Suzanne put her arms around me.

"You ought to be an actress. You would win all kinds of awards."

Suzanne and I also double-dated, and she always had an array of boys she wanted me to go out with. When I had finished with one of them she would pick up my discard, who immediately fell madly in love with her. It was all a subtle game that I only later comprehended. The boys would learn my faults while Suzanne displayed opposing qualities, and even while they were going out with me they would be falling in love with her. I was Suzanne's bait.

At the studio I had difficulty making friends, and the other art students knew me only as a quiet, shy, small, slightly overweight girl who was getting high grades for her charcoal sketches.

"Lots of strength, good line, Corinne, you're good," Monsieur Canard would typically comment when looking at my work. I was getting the recognition for which I longed.

Noticing how the class reacted to my success, however, I was disturbed by the whispering all about me. I did not hear anything specific, but I imagined that some of them thought I didn't deserve accolades. I was disappointed. I wanted the whole world to accept and admire me. Suzanne was there, however, with her smile of approval, her hand squeezing my arm. At other times she would even pass a congratulatory note written in the corner of her own drawing.

It was now the spring of the year, and during Easter vacation Suzanne proposed that I accompany her to the country for a few days. She described a castle that had been converted into a hostelry. There was a peaceful lake where we could go boating. It sounded very attractive, and very expensive.

"It's a gift from my sister to both of us," Suzanne smiled. "She wants to get rid of me so she can have the apartment to herself over the weekend."

Soon we were on our way.

We made our escape from the bustle of Paris into the countryside, and in an idyllic setting we enjoyed each other's company over dinner, chatting about our friends. As it neared the time for us to sleep, Suzanne became more reserved. Our room had a double bed. Without warning, Suzanne suddenly snuggled into my arms. I didn't know what to do. She felt my stiffness.

"I sleep with my sister every night," she said. "I have to hold on to someone before I can go to sleep."

She is just a little girl, I thought tenderly. She was soon resting peacefully, her head heavy on my shoulder. I had a terrible cramp, but did not want to move and disturb her. Hours seemed to pass. Finally she moved involuntarily away from me and stretched out her body like a languid cat.

"Kiss me, give me tenderness," she mumbled just audibly in her sleep.

I moved, turned my body away, and fell asleep.

Some time later I was awakened by someone kissing my left breast. My God, no, I thought.

"Suzanne," I said, trying to laugh. "What are you doing? Are you crazy?"

I felt her mouth on mine. Her hands were on my body, caressing me. The kiss was gentle, her tongue was very small. This is the way a woman's kiss feels to a man, I thought.

"Suzanne, please. Don't."

"All right, you do it to me then." Her green eyes pierced me with the challenge, even in the darkness.

She rolled over and lay with her legs apart, her body beginning to undulate. She closed her eyes, her hands touching her own body.

"Caress me," she said. "Look what I'm doing to my nipples. Do that for me and kiss one of them."

I turned over and rested my elbows as I stared at her. Her firm, athletic body was magnificent. Its perfectly rounded dimensions were firm and supple. I bent my head over her and kissed her. Her mouth devoured mine with desperate hunger. She was trying to push my head lower on her body.

"Kiss me down there."

"What? No. I can't."

"Do it. I'll tell you what to do," she ordered.

The tone of her voice was empty of tenderness. I broke away from her and ran into the bathroom. I locked the door. My whole body was shaking. I turned on the bath.

With more questions in mind than answers I came back to our room. Suzanne had gone and left a note. The room was paid for, for the next two days. I should enjoy it. She would see me back in Paris.

When we met again at the atelier she looked at me reproachfully, and I felt embarrassed. Things were never the same between us. I wanted to return the bicycle, but she would not let me, even though we never went riding together again.

I spent many days hanging around the Deux Magots, the famous cafe with the odd name. The place was frequented by some of the leading thinkers in France, and was an oasis of hope in occupied Paris. I would go into this sanctuary and choose a table near the one where the most notable intellectuals congregated, listening quietly as these philosophers and poets talked of the future. Final German victory did not figure in their scheme of things, nor did they count on American airplanes and Russian tanks to bring about a decisive result. Rather, they hoped for a rebirth of France, and for them my generation was of utmost importance. Jean-Paul Sartre was the leader of this group. In his novels and plays he had written of commitment, cowardice, freedom, the individual's struggle to make life a thing of authenticity and value, and now there was talk of a monumental philosophical work he had in preparation. Jean Anouilh, the playwright, was often in the cafe. Cocteau would be there, and many painters and actors. Much of the discussion was on a high plane. I would sit drinking in their words. I did not understand everything that was being said, but it made little difference to me. I recognized their genius.

Cocteau particularly intrigued me because he had made a famous and highly personal film, *The Blood of the Poet*. He was always sketching while the others talked. I was fascinated by the way he drew. His gaze would be concentrated on his subject, and he never once looked at the paper or tablecloth he was using. Once the sketch was begun his pencil was not lifted until it was complete.

One day I had come in early and sat down at the little table next to their corner, knowing that they would begin to appear about three o'clock in the afternoon. I ordered my favorite raspberry ice cream, and sat there alone somewhat uncomfortably, imagining that all eyes were upon me. I got out my sketch pad and started to draw in the manner of Cocteau, who always signed his drawings with a star. The result was interesting but terribly unbalanced. One of the eyes of my figure was on top of his mouth. Nevertheless, I liked it, and sat staring at the finished product in front of me.

I felt someone tap me on top of the head, and a hand picked up my sketch to examine it.

"Not bad. It's a good beginning," my critic said. "What you need is to look intensely at the contour of your subject first, and make your paper become a photographic plate. Use your eyes like a camera. Project what you're seeing. Notice the width and height of the paper, and with the side of your little finger you can sense the edge while you draw. It will help with the sense of proportion. And always start drawing from the left.

"I'm Jean Cocteau," he introduced himself. "What's your name?"

"Corinne Dibos," I answered.

By now the others had gathered at their usual table.

"She's got talent," Cocteau said, passing my sketch around.

"Come and sit with us," Sartre invited. He introduced himself and the others. I was seated between Sartre and Cocteau himself. I tried to appear calm.

The level of energy generated by this group was incredibly high. I felt so elevated by their words that I seemed to be floating on air. It was all a vast irony. I, with a shy and distant father, was now surrounded by five or six men, each old enough to be my father, who seemed to care about my presence, turning to ask my opinion when their conversation had reached an impasse. The cigarette butts and saucers accumulated on the table.

I lived each day in anticipation of their dialogue and their rich camaraderie. Their exchanges were alive and real, pungent with meaning, like a stimulant. I vowed that like them I would embark forever on the same search for truth. There were no accidents, and nothing was to be taken for granted. Everything was to be scrupulously examined, turned over and tested until nothing remained but the brilliant, glistening core of objective actuality.

My place was now secure at this table, and my mind continued to expand through my association with these luminaries. Quite often Cocteau came with a tall, blonde, strikingly handsome man, an actor named Jean Marais. His beauty was breathtaking. He kept looking around at the crowd, and seemed bored with the conversation.

The habit of reflective inquisitiveness soon took hold in me. I was becoming an existentialist, thinking about the choices I made, realizing the importance of my intentions and projection in everything that happened to me. With my thoughts I created my world. I protected my freedom of choice at all times, and I had the same abhorrence of being a mere pawn on the chessboard of life expressed by my new companions.

One morning after a few days of rain the sun came out. Everything seemed shining with joy. When I arrived at the Deux Magots I sat down quietly and listened to the conversation proceeding at a fevered pitch. I had an Indian filagreed silver compact my sister Colette had brought back from her honeymoon in Switzerland three years ago. Something was in my eye. I took out the compact, opened it, and was looking for the cause of my discomfort. Sartre was engrossed in making some grand statement and suddenly jumped up to emphasize the point. My compact went out of my hands and crashed on the marble floor.

"Oh, I'm sorry," Jean-Paul said.

He reached down to pick up the errant item. His expression changed. He looked like one of those cartoon figures with a light bulb on top of his head to indicate the presence of a sudden inspiration. He was looking intensely at the mirror in the compact.

"That's it. It is. That's what we're talking about."

The mirror had split, but under the first surface was another split mirror, and under that still another. The Swiss made thinner mirrors than those in India, so we could only presume that the compact had been sent from India without a mirror, and instead of cutting a piece of cardboard to hold the thin mirror in place, the Swiss had found it more convenient to put five thin, plated mirrors in place of the one for which the piece had been designed.

It was an amazing sight to look at oneself in this mirror, and it was eagerly passed around. The reflected face was reproducing almost infinitely, separated into portions, eyes projected on cheeks, mouths on foreheads, whole faces in the background, images piled on images, split, separated, and yet all visible as one concrete reality. There was much speculation on what was illustrated, the seemingly absurd way in which things are related, and the infinite regression of reflection. It was as if an artist had set out to produce a visible expression of Sartre's book *Being and Nothingness*.

The talk at the Deux Magots drifted again and again to the question of youth, their need for hope, and how young people could develop a sense of identity. They needed a way to recognize each other. It did not require a uniform, exactly, but a style. New clothes were a problem. Clothes that were for sale were outrageously expensive. The hand-me-downs that most young people wore often came in outrageous color combinations. If everything were black, clothes would have dignity and elegance. There would be no make-up, no artifice. The hungry young generation took up the idea with fervor.

The time I spent in the Deux Magots gave me confidence. I felt more articulate, more intellectual. I continued my art studies, and during the yearly reunion party at the atelier of Monsieur Canard I discovered my talent as an orator. Having absorbed much of the thought and expression of all my illustrious new friends, I was feeling superior and secure in my mental powers.

At the party I was standing at the head of the room, a glass of white bordeaux in my hand, on the slightly elevated platform reserved for our illustrious professor. Everyone stopped talking as my voice became stronger and clearer. I was embroiled in an argument with a pimply-faced boy who had been jealous all year of the attention paid me by Monsieur Canard. He had a totally closed mind on the subject of existentialism, on which I was now holding forth. His negations forced me to add greater precision and strength to my views. The room had become silent. As I won the debate, applause burst forth from my fellow students. I looked for Suzanne. She was looking at me from across the room, an expression of surprise on her face. I smiled back at her, but she dropped her eyes and looked away. Monsieur Canard approached and asked me to follow him into his private room through a door at one end of the atelier, right where the huge skylight joined the wall. The door was painted red, and was off limits to students. Walking behind him through the crowd I felt myself growing taller. At the door I could not resist turning around. Everyone was watching. Without hesitation I blew kisses to my audience, then turned and followed Monsieur Canard through the door, pushing it closed behind me with my foot.

Monsieur Canard was a medium-sized man, the shiny elegance of his bald head tapering to the ornate, finely trimmed, classic goatee of the Montparnasse artists. He was looking at me as if he had never seen me before.

"Corinne," he said, "I always saw strength in the stroke of your work, but when you stood up and made that speech I saw how you handled everyone in the room. In no time they were all, if not convinced, at least thinking. That's a rare quality. Have you thought about studying law? Such a capacity is a necessary element in the courtroom. It's what makes a successful attorney."

"I have fantasized about politics. . . ."

"Well, if you decide to investigate law, let me know. I have a friend who is a professor at the Sorbonne. I would be glad to give you a recommendation for his class."

As I walked home I could see myself defending the guilty rich for extravagant fees so that I could help the innocent poor for nothing. I could become the Robin Hood of the courts.

I was making new friends, painters and artists in the cafés of Saint Germain-des-Prés. I felt more totally at ease with them than with my own family. Among this group, love took the form of admiration and support for each other's work, for a canvas or a sculpture, a poem or a new thought. It was a world in which I felt accepted for who I was instead of falling short of what others expected of me.

In September I found myself in a musty, damp classroom at the Sorbonne. I had decided to pursue Monsieur Canard's suggestion and begin the study of law. As the year progressed, however, the tremendous amount of data I was required to commit to memory made me begin to doubt this choice of career. I wanted to get in front of a judge and a jury, not sit for hours and days with my head in a book. I wanted to speak on behalf of my client. I wanted to be onstage.

Toward the end of the second semester I got an opportunity to test my courtroom skill. Mock trials were a regular part of our curriculum, and every student had to play a role in one of these proceedings. I was one of the first to sign up, and consequently I was able to choose the part of a defense attorney.

Standing in front of the accused I looked at him intensely, moved theatrically over to the jury box, and started my argument.

"Ladies and gentlemen, in the same exact circumstances as the defendant," I began, "how many of us would have found ourselves reacting in the same manner. I want you to keep in mind . . ."

The words poured out. I watched the impact they were making on the jury, and it became clear which of the jurors I must convince. I was totally in charge of the situation. All eyes were on me. I experienced power, and with it the thrill of intense fulfillment.

The class was spellbound. I decided that this was indeed for me, that my passion as a speaker would make me a superlative attorney.

The next few months found me secure within myself. I had grown up; my attitudes had changed. The shape of my body also began to change miraculously. Gone was the baby fat. I grew several inches taller, my waist narrowed to a petite eighteen inches, my face displayed high cheekbones, and my eyes seemed to grow larger. Like a butterfly coming out of a cocoon I became beautiful. As I looked at myself in the mirror, I smiled. They would never hire me as a defense attorney but my path was obvious. I would become an actress.

Jean Marais, the intimate friend of Cocteau, had come from an acting school run by Charles Dullin, a director and producer who was responsible for putting on the best plays of the period, including those of Sartre and Camus. Marais' belief that I had the necessary qualities for acting was the final factor in my giving up law. I joined the Dullin studio, which numbered among its graduates many successful stars like Simone Signoret and Gérard Philipe.

It was not long before I heard of a new school that would be entirely devoted to motion pictures. Called, appropriately, L'Ecole du Cinéma, this new school was run by the French government, and was an innovation of the Pétain regime. Most of the great French directors who had carried French cinema to creative heights before the war had gone into exile. The people of talent who had remained behind had chosen to present muted criticism of the Nazis in the form of romantic and historical films with allegorical messages. The new school would lay the foundation for the postwar reawakening of the French film industry. It was devoted to every aspect of the making of films, from screen acting technique to technical studies in directing, cutting, lighting, makeup, and so forth.

At the outset I was the subject of photographic tests which turned out to be very revealing to me. There appeared on the screen an intriguing, pretty, powerful, and sexually alluring female. On the basis of these tests I was immediately enrolled in the school, and my life took a new turn. I was now surrounded by others committed to the same vocation as I, and I constantly found opportunities to express myself. Every day there were rehearsals with different actors playing different scenes. It was like playing with love instead of getting caught at it.

I had not been at the school long when one day I saw walking toward me in the hall a man I recognized from the day before when I had bumped into him in my haste to get to a class on time. He looked older than the other young men at school, with a large forehead framed in dark brown hair, heavy, well-shaped eyebrows, and large, round, brown eyes. His eyes were particularly striking, like hazelnuts with sparkling gold specks. His moustache seemed to hide a positive but rather sardonic smile. His lower lip was full and sensuous, his jaw was square but softened by two matched dimples. His hands had been strong when he caught me, and his stature made him look taller than what was probably a little under six feet. I could tell that despite his slender appearance his sweater and pants were filled with a muscular body. My beret had fallen off when we collided, and the gentleness with which he picked it up and placed it on my head was kind and considerate. Even more remarkable, he had known the precise angle at which I wore it. He had been watching me, I concluded. Now, when I saw him again, I felt a twinge of excitement. He stopped, and we began to talk. His name was Jean-Pierre.

"Would you like to do a scene with me? I've found this play with a part that is perfect for you." He was holding the script in his hand.

Ill at ease, I reached for the play.

"I don't know. Let me read it."

"Why don't we go out in the garden and read it together?" He was guiding me in that direction with his hand on my elbow. "We're not due for our next class for forty-five minutes."

Outside we sat on a stone bench hidden by a row of bushes. I instinctively trusted this man. From the beginning, our affection and respect for each other grew.

On the day that Jean-Pierre and I were due to give our reading I was engaged in a curious maneuver to do something about the lamentable state of my wardrobe. Many of the girls in the school were from wealthy families, and in any sort of clothes competition I was running a poor last. I felt odd about being concerned with my clothes, and I knew the impact of seeing myself on the screen was disturbing my values. Part of me was still imbued with the existentialist commitment to being unaffected in matters of dress, but to appear to be a successful actress I needed a more colorful wardrobe.

The school had taken down some old draperies that had been hanging in the hall where the studio was set up. There were miles and miles of beautiful flowered material all thrown in a pile in a little storeroom under the staircase. Was this sumptuous cloth going to be thrown out? For weeks it appeared to have been abandoned.

At night I dreamed of the gorgeous gowns that could be made of this material. I had dyed it many different colors in my dreams, and had become the best dressed woman in the world. I was Scarlett O'Hara coming down the stairs at Tara for the grand ball, all eyes on me while I remained distant and aloof. They would never miss it if I took some of the material home. After all, it was only going to be thrown out, I reasoned, and devised a plan for taking the cloth, rehearsing the details carefully in my mind. After lunch, when no one was walking around, I brought my bicycle near the side entrance of the building where the little storeroom with the drapes was situated. I felt very excited as I executed this little caper. I folded one of the drapes into the smallest volume I could manage, and stuffed it under my coat. I hurried back to my bicycle, concealed the cloth in the covered basket that was attached to the handlebars, and parked it back in the bike rack. It was time to get to class. A fine sweat covered my body as I ventured into the classroom. I almost collapsed with guilt when the professor called my name.

"You're late, Mademoiselle Dibos. I do not permit interruptions in my class. If you can't be on time you needn't bother to come. I'd prefer that you stay away altogether and forfeit your turn to do a scene."

In my excitement I had almost forgotten that I was scheduled to do the scene I had rehearsed with Jean-Pierre.

"Are you ready, Mademoiselle?"

"Oui, Monsieur."

As I stood on the set ready to do our dramatic love scene in front of my class, I felt an inner tremor, common to many actors.

"Silence on the set!" the professor said. "Action!"

Jean-Pierre started his first line. I fell into a state of total blankness. In moments another entity took over within me. I didn't recognize the voice that came out of my mouth.

"Excellent," said the teacher when we had finished. "It was really good."

Jean-Pierre bent down and kissed me on the cheek. Shivers were running up and down my spine. My eyes were moist from excitement. During the remainder of the class I was in a dream world, in some other time and place.

When it was time to go home that evening Jean-Pierre held my hand in his. He picked up my books and walked with me to the bicycle rack. By now I had forgotten about the drapes. Jean-Pierre opened the bicycle basket to drop in my books, and there was the contraband material. I snapped the lid closed and blushed. Jean-Pierre acted as if nothing irregular had transpired.

Perhaps he didn't remember the material from its former place in the studio hall. Whatever the case, I didn't care. I just wanted to go home with my treasure.

"Corinne," he said. "Could we do another scene next week?"

"Well, I don't know. We've been told to change partners," I said without conviction.

The intimacy that Jean-Pierre and I had acted together had added a dimension to my understanding of what kind of relationship could exist between a man and a woman. We had played a scene involving a couple who had been married too long and were now guilty of not listening to each other. During the ten minutes in which we played this scene I felt as if I was really married to Jean-Pierre, and the feeling was so real and so gratifying that I now felt frustrated when we had to relapse into our true roles.

As the days passed, Jean-Pierre began to take on greater and greater importance in my life. Without in any way intruding upon my existence he began to direct me in my growth as an actress. Through his research into the repertory he had discovered brilliant scenes for us to do together. Other actors in the school were still approaching me with mediocre material in which the female part was always secondary. Jean-Pierre was cleverer, and found parts that gave me confidence and made me feel important. Gradually we became inseparable, and he assumed a protective attitude toward me.

The winter of 1943–44 was an especially rigorous one, and my knees were giving me trouble. The problem became so severe that at times my knees locked and I would almost fall over. Perhaps it was the excessive demands we made upon our bodies as we cycled incessantly through the cold streets of Paris but whatever the cause, I gained relief from Jean-Pierre, who patiently massaged my knees every day. At first it hurt, but the warmth that emanated from his hands would soon spread a glow throughout my body. I felt that he was healing me, not just my knees, but all of me, from all that I had suffered with André.

Jean-Pierre's thoughtfulness toward me took other forms as well. Chocolate was at a premium, and our coupons gave us only a very small bar per person each week. Bread and chocolate had always been the traditional teatime fare for French children. The habit had been formed, and longing for that taste always gripped me when the time came for tea. Jean-Pierre gave me his ration.

To me it was as if he had given me his most valuable possession. No one had ever treated me with such kindness, or been so generous. His eyes seemed always on me. I had loved, but I had never been loved before. Jean-Pierre had not pressed physical attention on me, and I felt that he was loving me as a person, not as an object. It gave me a tremendous feeling of well-being. At last I was loved and respected.

We were alone at my home one afternoon when I confided my experience with André to Jean-Pierre. Afterward, Jean-Pierre's kissing and petting went beyond the point of play. While we were making love I whimpered, made various noises, and finally screamed as I had with André. Jean-Pierre stopped and moved away from me.

"What's wrong?" I said.

"Don't pretend with me. Don't ever pretend with me." He pulled me close to him again. "I don't know how long it will take, days, months, or years, but we'll find a way for you to take real pleasure in bed with me. If I ever catch you playing these games again I'll spank you, or worse, we'll be finished. What started you playing this game?"

I lay naked in his arms, and with his hand gently stroking my hair I told him the details concerning my loss of virginity and my experiences with André. All of the fear and pain I had felt then returned vividly. When I finished, Jean-Pierre was crying.

"You poor baby," he said gently. "I'll take care of you. No man will ever be able to hurt you again."

I knew that he meant what he said, and I wanted to believe that it could really be so.

Jean-Pierre sometimes worked as a movie extra to make needed money.

"I only work in mob scenes," he told me. "That way I'm not noticed. It won't hurt me in the future when I'm a star."

I registered in the union and joined him in this work mainly because I didn't want to be without him for even one day. My first work day as an extra was exciting. We were to comprise the audience in a theater.

"Let's go sit in the balcony," Jean-Pierre said. "The farther away from the camera the better you are."

I thought that curious. How can you be discovered if you hide? After we took our seats I excused myself to go to the bathroom downstairs. Afterward I went and stood near the camera crew.

"Hey you, Mademoiselle," one of the assistant said to me. "Go and sit there in the third row right behind the principals."

I was going to be seen on the screen. Maybe they'll even give me a few lines, I thought. I looked at Jean-Pierre and waved at him proudly. His gesture in return indicated exasperation and annoyance. I felt rejected. All through the shooting I sat lonely and bored. I kept looking up at the balcony, and I didn't like what I saw. A beautiful dark-haired girl was now sitting next to Jean-Pierre. I could see her flirting with him, and he was smiling back at her. I saw them laugh, and the demon of jealousy took possession of me. I asked to leave for a few minutes and tried to get up to the balcony, but there was a man blocking my way.

"No traffic," he said. "We're ready to shoot again."

When the day was over I ran to the man who was to sign our release cards, and waited there for Jean-Pierre. He soon approached, the beautiful tall brunette practically leaning against him. I was angry and embarrassed but carried on as if nothing was wrong.

"I'll wait for you outside, darling," I said.

"Don't bother," he replied. "Why don't you go home? I'm going to be busy."

I had been rejected in front of the creature who was hanging on his arm. I was stunned.

"What do you mean? You're not going home with me?"

"No," he said laconically.

I stood there in shock, the blood draining out of my face, my body trembling. Letting out a cry, I turned and ran out of the building. Why would he treat me like that? I couldn't bear it. I thought that I would kill myself. I've had it, I thought. What did I do wrong? Why is he punishing me? Is it a crime to have ambition? I want to be discovered. Doesn't he? Is that what he does as soon as I'm not with him? Flirt with another girl?

I found my way to a park only a block away beneath the Eiffel Tower. I walked despondently over to the pond where Jean-Pierre and I had spent many happy moments together. Next to this charming pond that had seemed so romantic to me in the past was a small hill with a path leading up to its summit. From the top one could look below into the water and see the rocks just beneath its surface. I walked to the top of the hill and stared down into the pool below. The thought flashed through my mind that I could simply leap into the water and dash my head on the rocks. In a moment I could put an end to all my misery. I began to cry miserably, trying to get the courage to make that leap. Then someone handed me an open paper bag.

"Would you like some chestnuts? They're good and hot." It was an old lady, looking at me with sympathy and understanding.

"Oh thank you," I said.

"Come, let's sit together. Why are you crying? Tell me. Maybe I can help."

"No, you can't. Nobody can."

She lead me solicitously to a bench. I took a chestnut. I felt her concern for me, and between bites I told her my sad tale. She listened intently, nodding as if she had long been familiar with such situations.

"You're working here tomorrow, are you not?"

"Yes."

"All right. I'll tell you what to do. Just don't pay any attention to him. I know it's going to be difficult, but keep yourself busy, and talk to the people sitting next to you as if you had no concern about him at all, not to make him jealous, but so he'll get the idea that his behavior has had no effect on you, that you're indifferent toward him."

"But I'm not," I protested. "I love him."

"You must not let him think so. He won't be able to stand your indifference. I wouldn't be surprised to see you here with him tomorrow if you do as I say."

"But I hate deception."

"Alas," the old woman said sagaciously, "none of us likes it, but we are caught. No one knows who started, Adam or Eve, but somehow it seems that men react in the way we want when we play little games. It shouldn't be that way, but it is."

I said nothing.

"You don't want to end up like me do you? A lonely old woman?" she said a bit wryly. "You see, I learned too late that playing a little game now and then is not too much of a price to pay to keep the man you love."

I hated the idea that this might be the only way I could keep Jean-Pierre. Nevertheless, I resolved to try it.

That night I did not hear from him, and it was hard to keep from calling him. The next morning when I arrived at the film location, I did what the old lady had suggested. I took my seat as before, and never even looked toward the balcony. Once during the lunch break I let my gaze wander in that direction and got a quick glimpse of Jean-Pierre. There was a man sitting bside him. Where was the girl? I felt a rush of joy. I left the auditorium and walked quickly down the street to a park to eat my sandwich. Jean-Pierre came walking briskly after me.

"You're not going to say hello?" he said.

"I'm still waiting to say goodnight," I answered sarcastically.

He walked away. I had not been able to follow the old woman's advice.

For two days we did not talk to each other. At school I began to rehearse a scene with someone else. Then one afternoon I was sitting by myself. Jean-Pierre walked over and without a word put his hand on my painful knee, which I had been rubbing, and handed me a bar of chocolate. I felt the warmth of his touch. I knew what it meant. The ordeal was over.

"Darling," I said with great passion, "don't ever play games with me again."

Jean-Pierre took me in his arms.

"Don't worry, it's over," he said tenderly. "I never want to be without you again."

"You mean you want us to get married?" I don't know why I said it, but it had been building inside me. I could not believe what I heard him answer.

"Yes."

"When?"

"Soon."

"Can I tell Papa and Isabelle?" I was suddenly happier than I had ever been in my life. I could not contain my joy.

"Of course, if you want to."

For the next few months I was in heaven. Papa and Isabelle had at the end of the summer quietly gotten married—they were happy to advance some money to Jean-Pierre for an engagement ring. I designed it myself, a golden bow with a diamond caught in the knot. Of course at the time there was no money for a diamond, and I had to settle for a less expensive stone. But I didn't care. On my finger I now wore the mark of my future.

The last winter before the liberation was one of great hardship. Allied bombs began falling around Paris with great regularity. The Germans were now in retreat on the Russian front. Their constant declarations that the Allies would never successfully invade Fortress Europe took on an increasingly hollow ring. The conditions of the occupation itself became more repressive. Reprisals against civilians increased, the Germans announcing that for every one of their number killed by the Resistance they would execute one hundred French. Food was in desperately short supply. The rich French cuisine was but a dim memory. When available, meat and vegetables were reserved for Germans and for French collaborators.

As the fortunes of war turned slowly and inexorably against them, the Germans became ever more fanatical in their hatred of French Jews. Many had left for the free zone where they secured reasonably safe hiding places. In Paris the situation was more difficult. Only Jews who were already known to the Germans wore the yellow star; others tried to remain inconspicuous or out of sight. They hid in cellars and warehouses. My friend Suzanne, who never wore the yellow marker, was now living with a wealthy older man. The few times I saw her there remained a deep but uneasy feeling between us.

About this time I got an opportunity that I felt might be very important in furthering my career as an actress. The director Henri Clouzot has seen me do a scene at school, and now wanted me to do an audition. Clouzot was famous for his film *Le Corbeau,* which some denounced, however, as Nazi propaganda because it had been produced by a Nazi film company. After the war it was banned for two years and Clouzot suspended for six months by the French film industry.

On the appointed day I was very nervous. Jean-Pierre was waiting downstairs to take me to the address Clouzot had given me. To our surprise it turned out to be a small hotel next to the Champs Elysées.

"Jean-Pierre, I don't want to go in there."

"Don't be silly. You'll be all right. Call me when you get home."

I knocked on the door of Clouzot's room, and was greeted by a hirsute, dark-haired man with lively deep eyes. It was Clouzot himself.

"My secretary had to go on an errand; please come in," he said.

"Why do you have your office in a hotel?" I asked without entering the room. My eyes traveled rapidly, taking in a sofa bed with a shabby red bedspread and a small table with an unopened portable typewriter on it. The sofa was pushed against a mirrored wall.

Clouzot laughed. I backed further up against the hall wall.

"Please come in. We'll leave the door open if it will make you more at ease. I've set up an office here because it's the only place where you can get heat, room service, and hot water twenty-four hours a day." He was smiling widely at my obvious distress.

"There are no residents here, only lovers coming in for a few hours, and a few German officers." He started laughing.

"You're making fun of me and I don't like it." I turned to leave. I thought he must be a collaborator. I wanted to get away as quickly as I could.

"Forgive me." His hand reached out to stop me. "I was merely smiling in appreciation of your candor. Most people have the same questions, but they never ask them aloud. I've ordered some tea and pastries. Please stay and have some with me."

I softened a little and came into the room. The waiter arrived with the tray and closed the door as he left. Clouzot was very charming, playing the host and inquiring courteously about my background.

"The part requires a girl who has no fear," he said. Opening his briefcase he pulled out a script and dropped it on the bed. "The scene I want to test you in deals with a girl who goes to a detective's apartment to recover her pimp's address book." Pulling a small notebook out of his vest pocket, he continued, "The police found this in a murdered girl's apartment, and in a previous scene her pimp had seen the detective put it in his back pocket like this." He put the small volume into his hip pocket and waited for my reaction.

"What's the dialogue?"

"I'm fairly happy with it, but I'm still rewriting it. Let's play the scene and see what comes out." He showed me the place in the script and gave me a cue.

"Mademoiselle Renée," he said. "That's your name in the film," he noted. "I didn't expect to see you so soon again."

"Do you know who killed her?" I spoke the line automatically.

"Do you care?"

"She was very kind to me." My voice choked with the appropriate emotion. "She gave me all her discarded clothing. She was the only friend I ever had." I was sobbing. The tension and fear I felt in my own immediate situation enhanced my reading of the script.

Putting his arm around my shoulder, Clouzot moved me gently toward the bed. "Sit down, Renée. Did you see her? It was such a brutal murder. The killer carved her face up with a razor."

Without answering I buried my face in a pillow. It's only a scene, I told myself. I'll get the part. Clouzot moved his body close to mine. With one hand he stroked my hair.

"Tell me about your relationship with this girl. Let yourself go. I'm your friend." His hand slid smoothly around my waist.

"That's enough. It's going too far," I said, departing from the script.

"Let me see," Clouzot continued, ignoring what I had said. "How are you going to get the book out of my pocket? It's a decisive action for whoever is going to get the part."

"Some other time," I said, pushing him away.

"No, right now." He had me pinned against the mirror. I could see his mouth searching for my jugular vein. He was sucking on my neck. With one foot on the mirror I pushed back with all my might. He toppled off the bed, falling backward onto the floor. I grabbed my purse and ran to the door. Halfway out I turned back and looked at him.

"I thought you were a serious director."

"I am," he said, laughing. "You just emanate so much sex I couldn't resist. You're very good." He was getting up. "But you didn't get the address book."

He was still making fun of me. I slammed the door. Walking home, I swore under my breath at every man I saw.

I was getting restless about my future. Somehow Jean-Pierre's lack of real ambition was worrying me. I thought it might be infectious. I had been at l'Ecole du Cinéma for eight months, and I did not seem to be moving any closer toward my goal. A few directors had come to watch us do scenes, but they all had obscure names. I began to question whether or not this was really the life for me. Maybe I should get married right away and have a family, forget about my big ideas for making a better world. Jean-Pierre vetoed the idea, however. Children were not for him right now. He had confidence in my talent, and was always reassuring me.

"Look at the reaction of people when they see your screen test. You've got it. You're going to make it big."

Make it big? I was bored, bored with myself and what I was doing, tired of this stupid war. My attitude toward life became disturbingly negative until the Allied landing in Normandy, not far from the family villa, brought back a ray of hope. However, I contracted a severe case of yellow jaundice and spent the next two months in bed. Malnutrition and anxiety about the future had worn me down.

By the time I recovered, the summer was almost over and the Americans had liberated Paris. De Gaulle marched in triumph down the Champs Elysées as the Germans burned their archives and fled to a new line of defense. It was like a De Mille spectacular. Women behaved with abandon in the streets, joyously kissing the American soldiers, jumping on trucks and tanks with garlands of flowers. A few snipers remained on rooftops taking pot shots at the crowd, but no one seemed to care. The soldiers of Free France were going into buildings to clean out the last of the Germans, shooting their cornered quarry without questions. Women who had consorted with the enemy were stripped bare, their heads shaved, and forced to walk naked in the streets like captured animals while the excitement of the watching crowd rose to a fever pitch. I wondered about the men. Why didn't they suffer the same punishment?

One morning I got very sick to my stomach, and the sickness continued each morning for the next several days. I went to the doctor. I was pregnant. In my excitement, I couldn't wait to tell Jean-Pierre. I was not prepared for his hesitation. Part of him loved me, but the other did not want to get married and shoulder the responsibility of a family.

One day Jean-Pierre would say he wanted the baby, the next day he said it was impossible. For three weeks he vacillated. Finally he told me that he had reached a conclusion. He wanted me to have an abortion the next day. I was crushed. Somehow I had thought this time it would not end that way. But I was not courageous or foolhardy enough to have the baby against his will.

A part of me was going to die with this embryo. I knew that. It was like facing a funeral. I was despondent as I bicycled behind Jean-Pierre to see the midwife who was going to be the accomplice in this murder. Going up the stairs of the building I was almost overwhelmed by its stench.

The woman who opened the door was a typical crone. Heavy layers of make-up could not conceal the fact that she was nothing but a witch. I was taken into a bedroom. She put down a plasticized cloth on her bed, and instructed me to lie down. She inserted some kind of black-looking object in me.

"That's it. Here," she said, turning to Jean-Pierre. "Do you know how to give shots?"

"Yes," he answered, almost inaudibly. "My mother is a diabetic."

"Good. Here's some morphine. If she gets too much pain give her some. Now I need my money."

Jean-Pierre handed her some notes, and she counted the money carefully.

"I need some more for the morphine."

We were out of the apartment and on our bicycles. It was excruciatingly painful to pedal. We had two miles to go before we arrived at Jean-Pierre's apartment. It was torture. I was sweating profusely when we finally reached our destination.

"Where's your mother?" I asked.

"She's spending the night at a friend's house."

He put me to bed and brought me some hot soup, telling me how much he loved me. He rubbed my back, gave me a pill and stayed with me until I fell into a forgetful sleep, obliterating what had happened from my mind.

It was not long before I woke up with a scream, a scream that sounded as if it had come from some disembodied presence, not myself. Jean-Pierre was there, holding me.

"It's all right darling. It's all right."

It was hell. I was going through the pain of damnation. If I was not dead I wanted to be. The pain was unbearable. I became hysterical, intolerant even of Jean-Pierre's solicitude. He went to get the morphine and gave me a shot. I moaned. And soon I was taking a trip through the inferno, as if it were some vast, eternal, murky sea. I felt myself going up and down, reaching a culmination of pain, and then a rapid descent into slight relief. I became incoherent. I felt I was slipping into death.

In the middle of the night Jean-Pierre reached a point of total panic. He carried me downstairs where I recognized, of all people, our family doctor. We drove to the hospital.

I woke up the next day in bed. Jean-Pierre's glove was next to me on the pillow. It all came back to me. I'm not dead, I thought. My God, why? I don't want to live. I was crying when the doctor came in.

"You're a very lucky girl, Corinne. If your friend had waited much longer we could not have saved you."

"How long do I have to stay here?"

"Three or four days. I want to keep you under observation."

"What about my parents?"

"They've been told that you were in an accident, and that I'm keeping you here to make certain you haven't suffered any internal damage. I told them to wait until tomorrow before they come to see you."

"Thank you doctor. Thank you so much."

Jean-Pierre was there all day and evening. The possibility of my death had awakened in him feelings of guilt and remorse.

Two weeks later when I went back to the family doctor for a final checkup he looked at me with an odd expression on his face. During the four days at the hospital I had idolized him. He had saved me from death, given me a second birth.

Now his hand moved on me in a way that it had not in the hospital.

"What are you doing?" I said.

"I'm taking my pay," he answered.

"You're what?"

"Who do you think is going to pay me for my troubles? Your friend? He doesn't have any money. Your family doesn't know about the operation. That leaves you. It's all right with me. You're a very appetizing young lady."

"Get away from me, you . . ."

"You'd better be a good girl, or I'll tell your parents."

"Why don't you?" I challenged him. "I don't care anymore. I'll tell them about you."

I walked out of the office with an energy that would have flattened anything that stood in my way. Nothing was said. Nothing was ever done, but I'd had my first taste of blackmail. It would not be the last.

The war was over. I had become a woman. I looked back on what had happened with a mixture of sadness and pride. I had confronted a number of difficult situations. Yet I had emerged stronger. I had survived, and a new liberated world lay before me. I wanted to love and be loved with all the other creatures of this universe. The idyllic summers at the beach were behind me. The carefree days of prewar Paris were part of a world that had vanished.

"There is nothing to do but to look forward, to see where and what we are, and make the best of it," Papa said.

"What do you mean, make the best of it?" I asked.

"That's what a good scientist does," he replied, tapping my cheek gently.

I was no longer the naïve little schoolgirl who wondered where babies came from. I no longer believed that being born a countess gave me special rights, and I was still longing for a mother's love. I was not going to be a nun, a painter, a lawyer, or an architect, but I had no doubt that I was destined to be recognized all over the world. I was going to become a star, a Hollywood star.

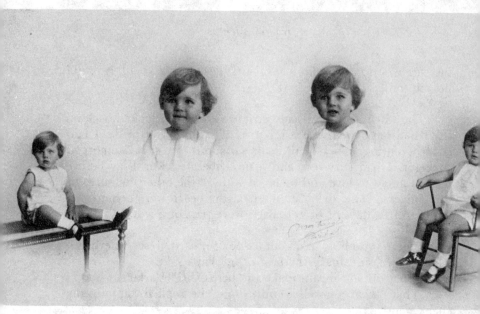

Above: My first sitting. *Below*, *left to right:* Hughes, Colette, Maman, Papa, Christine, and Chantal. I'm sitting in front.

My mother,
Juliette Munier Dibos.

My father,
le jeune comte Pierre Dibos.

Papa and Isabelle taking
their daily stroll on the
Boulevard Montparnasse,
1950.

I was born in the room behind the large balcony at 3 Avenue Montmeurency Auteuil, Paris.

The top two floors of this building became our home when I was six. My mother held her weekly salon here.

The little bride of Christ.

Left to right: Papa, Maman, me, and Chantal.

Left to right: Papa, Isabelle, Colette, Corinne, Christine (in back), Chantal, Maman, Uncle Lucien, Altros the dog, and Aunt Marguerite at Hermanville in Normandie, 1928.

On our daily walk to and from the Bois de Boulogne: Chantal, Isabelle, and me, 1936.

A Sam Levin photo for the pinup series. I was about eighteen years old. *Sam Levin*

More pinup shots by Sam
Levin. Have racquet, will
travel. A l'espagnol. *Sam
Levin*

These two Sam Levin photos became very popular and scandalized my family. *Sam Levin*

When I saw this photo I realized that I could be a star. *Sam Levin*

One of my favorite photos at the time. *Sam Levin*

A Rita Hayworth look. *Sam Levin*

Modeling for Claude Dauphin in my first film *We Are Not Married (Nous ne sommes pas marier)*.

This is the hat I wore when I met Ray Milland.

Chapter 5

There had to be a way to make my career begin. For many restless nights I twisted and turned in my bed, my sleep disturbed by the gnawing sense that I had to take my destiny into my own hands to make something happen soon. My room was filled with issues of *Cinémonde, Ciné Clair,* and many other publications devoted to the motion picture industry. I immersed myself in these and dreamed about my name appearing in their pages.

My bedroom was minuscule, almost completely taken up by an overwhelming armoire, a vestige of our days in Passy. One side was employed as a closet, the other taken up by family photo albums, spare linens, old letters, and boxes of gifts, opened but never used. There was also a middle section on which stood a beveled mirror. Behind, squeezed between some of my father's clothes, was my meager wardrobe hung on five hangers, a tweed skirt and jacket cut out of Papa's old suit, the black suit Isabelle wore at my mother's funeral, my pride and joy, the pale green dress made of the infamous flowered material, and a couple of other odd pieces that had seen me through the war years. There was my bed, and my childhood desk.

One night very late I sat at this desk and made a list of all the things I had been doing, and all the possibilities I had neglected. One word appeared on the list of things I had not been doing. Pray. The word leapt out at me. I had not prayed in a long time. I had wanted to put distance between me and my impulses toward becoming a nun. I had succeeded, but perhaps I had gone too far. I knelt down near my bed and began to speak with God.

"Oh God, forgive me, for I have neglected you," I began. "Please forgive me for the baby, for everything. I'll do penance. I'll go every Friday to church for three months if you'll give me one thought on what I should do."

I felt I was reaching deep within myself. There were no more words, no thoughts. I stopped the workings of my mind and waited for the inner quietude necessary for hearing the voice of God. A pile of magazines was perched precariously on a bookshelf overhead. One fell off and landed on the floor, open to a page with an article about a director, Marc Allégret. Allégret, the nephew of André Gide and brother-in-law of Simone Signoret, was a very important director at this time, and had discovered many famous stars in France, including Simone Signoret, Michèle Morgan, Jean-Pierre Aumont, Danièle Delorme, and others. Later, he would play an important part in developing the careers of Jeanne Moreau and Brigitte Bardot. According to the article, Allégret had been chosen by RKO Pictures to do a film about an American soldier who spoke only English and a French girl who spoke only French. During the rest of the evening the name Marc Allégret kept ringing in my ears.

At three in the morning I asked information for Allégret's number. Something in me compelled me to call him. I dialed the number with trepidation. I heard a groggy voice answer.

"Hello? Am I speaking with Monsieur Allégret?"

"Yes. What time is it?"

"Three. My name is Corinne Dibos. You don't know me, but I know I'm the right girl for the picture you're doing for RKO."

"Really? Did you have to call at this hour?"

"Yes sir. I just received the message. I had to call."

"What kind of a message . . . never mind. Are you an actress?"

"Yes."

"Come at two tomorrow afternoon to my office. Thirty Avenue des Champs Elysées. Bring your pictures, even if they're just snapshots."

I had taken the first step. I knew everything was going to be all right.

My meeting the next day with Allégret was interesting. I think he expected a candid country girl who had just come to Paris and was behaving in a typical starstruck and vaguely neurotic fashion. He acted very surprised at my professional demeanor and training. I could tell that he was impressed. I left his office feeling secure, knowing I was going to get this part.

The next day Allégret called and said he wanted me to meet
the representative of RKO in Paris, who turned out to be a very
sweet man who looked like a heavyset Sherlock Holmes. He, in
turn, invited me to join him and his friends Mr. and Mrs. Robert
Taylor for dinner at Maxim's. I couldn't believe it! Dinner at
Maxim's with Robert Taylor and Barbara Stanwyck! It was completely beyond my imagination. All because of a prayer and a
phone call, I thought. I was floating on air. It could be said that I
conveniently overlooked the fact that I had the face and figure,
and had worked training myself for this moment. But so had
many other talented young actresses.

The man from RKO was waiting with Robert Taylor at the
bar in Maxim's when I arrived. As soon as we sat down at a table
they began busily conversing in English. I could hardly understand a word. What little English I had learned from Isabelle was
completely inadequate for comprehending the American dialect.
I wondered what had happened to Mrs. Taylor. I felt that all eyes
in the room were on me, the women envious of my position beside this famous American star. Taylor was even more handsome
in person than he was on the screen. I had an immense crush on
him. I felt like a little girl. Where was his wife, I kept thinking.
Where was Barbara? Dinner was now drawing to a close. Couples
were beginning to move gracefully on the dance floor when the
representative of RKO excused himself and left us alone. Something in me froze. I didn't know what to say. Taylor was looking
straight out at the dancers, seemingly as shy I was. He was
breathtaking almost to the point of being unreal. I wanted to
touch him, pass my hand over his forehead and strong chin. He
turned around and looked at me, smiling.

"Would you like to dance?" I said.

"No, Mademoiselle. I don't think so. My wife, Barbara,
caught a chill on the boat coming over from the States, and is
spending the night at a hospital. I don't think it would be fair for
me to enjoy myself that much. Dancing with you would be too
much of a pleasure."

I blushed at the compliment and immediately placed Robert
Taylor high in my pantheon of heroes. I was being turned down
by the kind of man I admired more than any other, a loving and
considerate husband. Years later in Hollywood, I was disap-

pointed when I heard that he and Barbara Stanwyck had divorced.

Apparently I had been accepted. I was set to do the picture with Allégret. I was going to get my start in American films. Each time I thought about it I became so excited that I felt as if I were choking. I was in that state, lying on my bed one day, when the phone rang. It was Allégret.

"Corinne," he said, "come to my office. There's been a change of plans. RKO has canceled the picture. They've decided the time is past for doing war movies. I'm going back to the picture I was doing before RKO approached me. Come around this afternoon at three-thirty. Maybe I can find something for you to play in it."

Allégret's office was on the fourth floor. Instead of taking the elevator I decided to walk up and breathe deeply on each step in order to deal with my nervousness and disappointment. Between the third and fourth floors a group of men were standing on the stairs deep in conversation.

"Could you come down to earth long enough to let me pass?" I said briskly.

Like the Red Sea they parted. I walked by in my most regal fashion.

"Hey, that's the kind of broad we need," one of them said.

"You're right, she is," said another.

I turned around.

"Whatever it is you want me for, gentlemen, I'm not available."

With that I walked rapidly into Allégret's office. I hadn't been there for more than a few minutes when one of the men from the stairs stuck his head in through the door.

"Yes, she's here."

"Let me go and see what this is about," Allégret said, getting up from his desk.

The men outside turned out to be the producer, director, cameraman, financier, and film cutter preparing to start shooting a film in Italy in forty-eight hours. They had just finished looking at tests for one of the parts, and were totally dissatisfied with what they had seen. My fiery attitude had struck a responsive chord. They decided that I was just what their picture needed.

The next day I was having lunch with the director and producer of the film in question.

"Incidentally, what's your name?" It was Gilbert Lafitte, the director, speaking.

I thought for a moment before I answered. The night before, when I told Papa what was happening, he had told me not to use the family name. I had not been able to think of a satisfactory film name, but I knew there was luck in double initials, like Danielle Darrieux, Simone Signoret, and Michèle Morgan. So it had to be Corinne C. As I sat with Gilbert Lafitte my eyes traveled around the room looking for inspiration. I gazed at a bottle of wine on the table. The vintner was Calvet.

"Corinne Calvet," I said.

"That sounds very good." Lafitte was enthusiastic.

The producer recognized the name from the wine he had chosen.

"It sounds like a brilliant, light yet deep wine that can only improve with age. You could not have chosen a better name for a career that is going to be very promising. Very promising indeed," he concluded, winking at Lafitte.

"Let's drink to that," Lafitte suggested. "You have to get packed tonight. Can you do it?"

My smile was my answer.

Jean-Pierre took me to the train. He had tears in his eyes.

"It's your big chance, darling. Take advantage of it. And remember, I'll be here when you return."

Cinema in postwar France was just beginning to find itself. The industry was keenly concerned with competition from other countries, particularly the United States, and a quota system limiting foreign film imports was instituted. There was also much encouragement to coproduce films with neighboring European countries, hence the particular venture with which I was involved. Turin, a large industrial city in Northern Italy where the film was being shot, was still under the tension of war. Handfuls of Fascists in hiding in the mountains refused to accept the demise of Il Duce. They came down and attacked cars coming and going from the city. Consequently we were given a military escort to and from the studio.

The title of the film was *We Are Not Married.* It starred Claude Dauphin and Louise Carletti. In the script, Claude, a painter, and

Louise were living together. Both of them had outside love interests. My part was both simple and difficult. I was to play an artist's model who was always appearing in a state of semiundress. My lines were limited to yes and no, and each time I said the wrong word some contretemps ensued. I was embarrassed by my attire. Dauphin had been one of my childhood idols, and when at last I was in a film with him my part was virtually nonexistent. I felt intellectually insulted. I had been signed for twelve weeks. They had told me that I was in almost every scene, but I had had no time to read the script before accepting the part. When I finally did I was crushed. How could I display my talent as an actress?

Half-naked, I was little more than a prop. I decided to find some way of making the audience laugh, and so I devised a system. I would shake the top of my body every time I said no, and the lower part whenever I said yes. During the shooting no one noticed what I was doing.

Gilbert Lafitte, the director, was very sweet and attentive to me. The producer had his wife with him, the financier his girlfriend, who was playing a small part in the film, and Claude Dauphin had his pick of the Italian women. Louise Carletti had her daughter and a maid, while Roland Toutain, the wing-walking acrobat, was accompanied by a certain Shirley with whom he was passionately in love. Gilbert had no one, and I had no one.

After we arrived in Turin his days were occupied with preproduction arrangements, and right from the beginning the whole French contingent spent their evenings together. Gilbert would politely kiss me goodnight in front of the elevator door at the hotel.

On my first day of shooting the set was extremely cold. It was winter. Icicles had turned the Italian countryside into a fairyland, and I was a fairy princess slowly turning into an ice sculpture as I stood shaking in a transparent, extremely short black slip. In order to deal with this problem I was placed on a platform and surrounded by eight electric heaters. This had the curious effect of making me feel like Joan of Arc at the stake. My feet and legs slowly went from warm to hot, while my nose remained as cold as a snowball. I was in extreme discomfort and I had stage fright, but I also enjoyed it like the anticipation of a powerful pleasure. A controlled excitement ran through me when the director said the magic word:

"Silence."

It went well. The scene was completed almost before it was underway. It was perfect, without a hitch.

That evening I was in a celebratory mood. I had gained the respect of the crew, the producer, and the director himself.

When Gilbert suggested a little dinner for two and a bottle of champagne to celebrate my first successful day, I accepted without a thought. When he held my hand at dinner it seemed natural. Afterward, when he came to my room, I was still floating on air. When I came out of the bathroom in my pajamas and saw him lying under the covers without any clothes on, I couldn't see any reason why I shouldn't join him.

For a moment I did not think of Jean-Pierre. All of my life in Paris seemed distant and remote. But when I started to react to Gilbert's caresses with pleasure I began to come back down to earth. I could not let myself climax. That would have really been unfaithful, I felt. Letting myself experience that pleasure would have been too much for Jean-Pierre to forgive, since it was his skill and patience that had awakened my sensuality.

"No, please, don't," I said. "Stop." I started to cry softly.

"Too much excitement for one day," Gilbert said with resignation, and started putting on his clothes. "Sleep well, my beautiful angel. I'll see you in the morning."

Gilbert was thirty-six years old to my twenty. Perhaps it does not seem like such a great difference, given the rapid maturation process that now takes place, but at that time Gilbert to me was very much a father, and I was in awe of him. He was kind and understanding, and tolerant, even amused by my mistakes. In his arms I felt incestuous and I would have preferred not to have sex with him; being in his company was enough to make me happy. I listened to him talk at meetings, and I learned a lot about the intricacies of film-making. I accepted his love-making because it seemed to make him happy. Afterward, I always felt like cuddling with him.

I managed to keep all thought of Jean-Pierre out of my mind until one day a letter that had been considerably delayed arrived from him. I felt quite devastated as I read between the lines:

Do not feel guilty about what you have to do. Before, you were only playing at being an actress. Now that you have started, you need to concentrate toward that goal. I don't want you to feel that I'm in your way. We may go our separate ways in the future. I love you, and I always will. But if you still feel the same way about me when you return I have a lot of love-making saved up for you.

Love,
Jean-Pierre

What was going on? Had someone gossiped about Gilbert and me in Paris? Did he hear about it, or did he just feel it? Why did he tell me it was all right? Is he guilty of the same thing? No, that can't be. He tells me that he has a lot of loving saved for me. Oh my darling Jean-Pierre, I love you so much.

There had been uncertainties in my relationship with Jean-Pierre revolving around his mother, an ardent member of the French Communist Party. His political tendencies followed hers, and deep down I knew that was a potential source of difficulty for us. His mother resented the fact that he was considering marriage to someone who did not belong to the party. He would have to go against her wishes in order to fulfill the bonds of our engagement. I decided to take him a gift to show my love and expunge my guilt.

It was not difficult to choose a gift for Jean-Pierre. Italy did not suffer from the shortage of leather we had experienced in France, and the stores were full of luxurious shoes. I had just that morning bought myself a beautiful pair. These shoes had taken a week's salary, but I was walking on a cloud. What a change from Papa's brown boots in which I looked like a clown, with the toes flapping when I walked. During the milder months I wore shoes carved out of wood, with sandal straps made of material nailed to the wooden blocks. I had become very good at making these, and even had a few customers. But now all this improvisation was behind me. My feet were encased in a thick, embossed, soft leather of natural tone, with heavy and pliable soles. In the same shop I had noticed a pair of men's brown suede shoes, with delicious cream-colored, crinkled rubber soles. They were stylish and casual at the same time. I went back to the shop and bought a pair for Jean-Pierre, and kept them in my suitcase. Everytime I came into my hotel room I would look at them and hug them, breathing the new leather smell with delight.

I told Shirley, Roland Toutain's girlfriend, that I had bought new shoes to take back to Paris.

"You'd better wear them so they look used. Otherwise they'll be confiscated at customs," she had said.

I abandoned the thought of wearing them myself, and was thinking about the problem while Gilbert was on the phone. I began to play with one of his shoes. I dangled it on my toe, and then slipped it on. I realized that Gilbert and Jean-Pierre wore the same shoe size. But I can't tell Gilbert who they are for, I thought. What if I told him they're for my brother? It might even turn out to be true, I rationalized, for if I find out that Jean-Pierre has been seeing another girl I'll give the shoes to Hughes. Gilbert was agreeable. He would wear the shoes for a few days. He even liked them.

The film was finished. We went back to Paris. There I found Jean-Pierre more loving than ever, and on him the shoes looked just as I had imagined. I confessed to Jean-Pierre about Gilbert. I tried to explain exactly what had happened. Jean-Pierre interrupted.

"Darling, look. You were gone three months on location. I don't want to know about it. Now you're back in Paris. Here you belong to me, to no one else but me."

"Oh yes, to no one else."

Despite the limitations of what had transpired between Gilbert and me, he had taken the affair more seriously than I thought. It was not easy to make him understand my true feelings, but I needed to. I met him a short while later in his office.

"Gilbert, you know I told you I was engaged?"

"Yes, to what's his name. Jean-Pierre?"

"I told him what happened to us in Italy."

"You did? What did he say?"

"He said that he understood, but now that we're back in Paris I'm to be his and no one else's."

"Is that what you want? You mean you don't want to see me anymore?"

I was distressed. My connection with Gilbert was very important to me. Through our association I was experiencing rapid professional growth. I learned from him constantly. I wanted Gilbert to value our friendship enough to give up the sex part of our relationship, but I was afraid that without it my association with him on professional grounds would vanish. Sex was the trap that I was rapidly growing to understand and face.

"No," I said, "I love you too much. I don't want to stop seeing you, and meeting all the important people you know."

"Well then, what do you mean?" His voice was like ice.

"I'll see you, but we won't make love."

"Never?"

He looked sad. I was afraid I would lose him. I compromised.

"Well, let's say never when we're in Paris."

"Do you mean if I take you out of Paris it will be all right?"

"Well, if we're at least a hundred miles outside Paris it would be like we were on location again." I was half joking, but he took me seriously.

"*Mon petit lapin,*" he said. "I love you. I love that strange logic of yours. I guess I better make sure my next picture has a lot of location shooting. Run along now. I'll meet you later."

I left, and waited for Gilbert at a tea shop around the corner from his office, a place I had chosen because they had those irresistible, hot, melting croissants I couldn't resist. Gilbert would join me later and take me out to dinner. Jean-Pierre was then to pick me up at the restaurant on his motorcycle and take me to the theater where we both played small parts.

In the play, I was a young, stupid maid who was always dropping trays and creating a commotion. Jean-Pierre was a butler who was having an affair with the best friend of the mistress of the house. I had taken the part mainly to be with him, but also because I was understudy to the second lead. After the play, Jean-Pierre would take me home, come up to the apartment, and wait until I was ready for bed. He would then talk or make love to me, or read to me, and when I was getting sleepy he would turn out the light and leave. In the morning I would be awakened by his phone call. I basked in his loving concern and attention.

One day Gilbert was working late and called me to join him at the office. From there we went to our accustomed restaurant, but there wasn't time for dinner. Jean-Pierre was due to arrive imminently to take me to the theater. Gilbert told the doorman to ask him to join us in the bar. My expression of mock surprise made him laugh.

"It's about time I met this man you love, *petit lapin,*" Gilbert said playfully.

Why not, I thought. I had been honest. I didn't see any reason why the three of us couldn't be friends.

I stood up when Jean-Pierre walked up to our table. I linked arms with him and Gilbert as I introduced them. We all sat down, a low cocktail table between us. Jean-Pierre did not seem to be at ease, but the Pernod ordered for him induced him to take off his scarf, open his jacket, and to my horror, cross his legs. Bouncing to the beat of the piano music filling the bar was the shoe, the brown suede with the crinkle rubber sole. I wanted the earth to open up and swallow me. Gilbert would see the shoes I had said I was giving to my brother. I blushed beet red.

"What's the matter, Corinne? Are you all right?"

"Yes, of course I am."

Gilbert's eyes traveled from my face to my trembling hands and from there it was only a short distance to the bobbing shoe.

"I recognize those shoes. Are they the same ones, Corinne?"

I nodded. Gilbert looked at Jean-Pierre, who didn't know what was going on.

"Corinne brought them back from Italy for me," he said proudly.

"You have beautiful taste, Corinne. I'm glad you gave them to Jean-Pierre instead of your brother."

"Oh, Gilbert. You understand." I blurted out, putting my arms around him. "You're not angry, you're not hurt?"

"No," Gilbert said, looking at his watch. "You'd better hurry, you two. It's not long until curtain time."

I hoped that I had established my relationship with Gilbert Lafitte in the way I wanted, but new complications were in store. One afternoon in the tea shop next to his office I met an elegant young woman who came up to my table and asked me if she could sit with me while waiting for her friend. She said she was shy and embarrassed about sitting alone. She wanted to know all about my family, my loves, my occupation. She seemed to have a genuine interest in my life. I babbled on without reservation until I was summoned to the phone. It was Gilbert, telling me he would be delayed. He had to wait for one of his relatives who was stopping by his office.

"I'll wait for you here," I suggested.

"No, *petit lapin*, I don't know how long I'm going to be.

Maybe it would be better if I just talked to you tomorrow. I'll call you."

"But Gilbert," I protested. "Tonight the theater's dark, and Jean-Pierre is busy doing something for his mother."

"I'll tell you what. Just go home and I'll call you later." I heard a certain sharpness in his tone.

"Maybe I will, and maybe I won't," I returned in a rather nasty way, and hung up.

When I got back to the table I realized that I didn't have enough money to pay the bill.

"I'd better call him back and have him come and pay the bill," I said out loud, not really speaking to anybody.

"Don't bother," said my newfound friend. "Please be my guest. My friend is so late I don't think she'll come, and since we both seem to be at loose ends, why don't we go back to my apartment. I want you to meet my young son. He's four. The maid will fix something to eat and we can have a quiet dinner. Incidentally, my name's Louise."

Why not? I thought. Jean-Pierre is busy, Gilbert is busy, and it will do him good if when he calls I'm not there waiting.

Louise's apartment was luxurious. We picked up her son at a neighbor's, and her maid fixed us a delightful dinner before she left. The evening was very light and gay. The phone rang a few times, but Louise did not answer.

"My husband's away on a business trip. I don't answer the phone when he's gone."

She could have told me that apples grow on beanstalks. I wouldn't have cared. I was fascinated.

"He's in the film business," she went on. "I'll have to introduce you to him someday. Who knows? Maybe he can do something for you."

It was getting late. I was yawning. It was time to go.

"Corinne," said Louise, "please stay here with me tonight. The reason I didn't answer the phone is because there's a man I'm afraid of. He's made advances toward me and I made the mistake of flirting with him a little. Now he won't let me alone. He works with my husband, and swore he'd get to me the first time my husband was out of town."

It was a thin story, but the wine I had drunk made me gullible. Besides, the idea of going out into the cold and waiting for the subway was not appealing.

"Sure," I said. "I'll stay if you need me."

She gave me one of her nightgowns, a transparent pink second skin. We were soon in bed. The bedroom was large, a cold room without any warm color.

"My feet are freezing. Let me feel yours," Louise requested.

She moved her body close to mine and felt very warm. The thought of my encounter with Suzanne flashed through my mind. I tensed. Louise laughed softly.

"Don't be nervous, Corinne. I love my husband very much. I don't want to lose him. I would do anything in the world for him. Now relax and get warm."

The tension left me. I was almost asleep when we heard the front door opening. Louise held me in her arms.

"I'm scared," she said. "It could be him."

"Louise. Where have you been? Why didn't you show up at the office?" It was a man's voice.

"That's . . ."

My voice was stifled. Louise's mouth was covering mine.

"What's going on here?" The man walked into the room.

"Oh, you're home, darling," Louise said dramatically. "How wonderful. Why don't you come and join us? Corinne, you know my husband, don't you? Gilbert, don't stand there like an idiot. We've been waiting for you."

"How did you . . ." Gilbert started.

"Your wife and your mistress together in bed. Isn't that appealing to you? Come my love, you can have us both."

Gilbert was silent. He was frozen. I had gotten out of bed and had to walk by him to the chair where my clothes lay.

"I'm sorry, Corinne," Gilbert whispered.

I ran into the living room. Shaking uncontrollably I got dressed. What was I supposed to do? By now the subway had stopped running. My house was all the way on the other side of Paris. I didn't have any money for a taxi. It would take me hours to walk home.

They were fighting in the bedroom. Gilbert was slapping her, she was moaning. Then it was Gilbert moaning. What was happening? Were they making love? Had they forgotten me? Did they think I had already left? Gilbert came into the living room, his head lowered.

"Come on, Corinne," he said. "I'll drive you home."

Louise's swearing was loud enough to wake up the whole neighborhood. "Here's a present for you," she said, throwing a handkerchief in my direction. "You want my husband? Take his come. I just spat it out. I don't know what he's said to you about me, but don't believe him. I know all about him, everything there is to know, and I know how to excite him."

What was happening? I felt covered with filth. I ran out of the apartment and all the way down the stairs. Gilbert followed.

In the car we were silent. It was the silence of death, the death of our relationship. In front of my door Gilbert finally spoke.

"*Mon petit lapin,* forgive me for not telling you about Louise. I've been trying to figure out a way to leave her. Our marriage is no good, it never has been. Now I love you, and I want to be with you."

"What about your little boy?"

"Oh, he'll be all right. His grandparents will take care of him. Louise doesn't love him. She only had him to pin me down."

He bent over to kiss me.

"No, Gilbert. I cannot. You've lied to me, and I feel as if I'm going to be sick to my stomach."

"Now listen here," Gilbert snapped. "Don't be so high and mighty, you and your Jean-Pierre. And those rules of yours. I cannot make love to you unless we're one hundred miles outside of Paris."

He was imitating my tone of voice, mocking me.

"Why do you think I accepted that situation? Did you think I played with myself, or that I don't need sex? If you weren't so selfish and stupid you could have figured out by yourself that I was married."

I ran out of the car and up the stairs. I threw myself sobbing on the bed. There was a note on my desk informing me that Jean-Pierre had called twice. I went to sleep, grateful for his love.

A month went by. After a few attempts Gilbert gave up trying to revive our relationship. Then one day the producer of *We Are Not Married* called to say that it was going to be previewed. I fidgeted in the reserved section of the theater with Jean-Pierre at my side. Everyone involved with the film was there. Gilbert came over with a smile and I let out a gay hello.

"It's a big day for you, *petit lapin*," Gilbert whispered. "Nobody likes themselves on the screen, but if you watch the other people reacting you'll be able to see how much they really like you."

Jean-Pierre took my hand. The lights in the cinema dimmed. Then it was dark.

"I love you." Jean-Pierre's breath was hot in my ear.

And there it was, that new name of mine being projected on the screen. "Introducing Corinne Calvet." I held my breath with anticipation, squeezing Jean-Pierre's hand.

"Hey, take it easy. You're breaking my bones."

About ten minutes into the picture, each time they cut to me the audience started to titter. Now that the picture had been edited, there was no doubt that I was very important to the tempo of the comedy. When it was over I felt shy. Everyone was looking at me when I walked out of the theater.

"Here she is," someone said.

"You're very good," said another voice.

"What's your name again?"

I wanted to run. I had become a public person. I was not ready for it. They had seen me practically naked.

Gilbert called the next day.

"You're a hit, Corinne. We've had calls this morning from people who want to know if you're under contract. Please drop by my office this afternoon. We want to sign you for three more pictures."

No sooner had I finished talking with Gilbert than the phone rang again. This time it was Marc Allégret.

"Corinne," he said, "I'm doing a picture with Fernandel and Simone Simon. It's called *Petrus*. There's a good part in it for you. Why don't you drop by my office this afternoon. I'll show you the script."

Another picture right away with Allégret directing. I was really getting excited when the phone rang a third time.

"Mademoiselle, you are ravishing. I'm extremely impressed by your beauty. Would you have dinner with me?"

I recognized Jean-Pierre. He was speaking with a Russian accent.

"Oh yes. Let's go to some romantic restaurant."

"I'll pick you up at seven," he said, sounding lighter than I had ever heard him.

I then called Gilbert and canceled my meeting with him, rescheduling for the next day. Gilbert complained a bit, and asked me if I was going to be ungrateful. After all, they had given me my first opportunity. I said of course not, and left to see Marc Allégret.

The picture *Petrus* was to start shooting in Switzerland in three weeks. I asked Marc if he thought I should sign with Gilbert.

"No, I don't think so, not yet. This is a good part. Do my picture first, and I'll sign you for two others. Then you'll be in a stronger bargaining position when you sign with Gilbert."

Everyone wanted me. I couldn't believe it. Allégret showed pictures of all the stars he had worked with. It almost seemed that he was trying to sell himself to me by showing me what he had accomplished.

"Thank you, Marc," I said, kissing him squarely on the lips, "I have to run now."

I was a success. People were talking about me in the industry. What is it they see in me, I asked myself. I knew that in the film it was the contradiction between my body and my words, that I had turned what seemed an unimportant gesture into an element of characterization that had captured the attention of the audience. I began to get an inkling of what was to come when I thought about the possibility that I was being seen as a young, pretty girl with a gorgeous body and not many brains, rather than as the person I really was. It crossed my mind that despite my reservations the goal might justify the means, and that being seen as a body might be the price of success. If that's what they want, I thought, I'll use my sex appeal on the screen, and by the time I'm a star the public will know who I really am.

I got an idea as I studied the pictures being used on the covers of the most popular movie magazines. The French print

media had discovered the pin-up, that Hollywood invention designed to keep up the morale of American soldiers hankering for
the female companionship they had left behind. From Betty Gra-
ble in her famous white bathing suit to Dorothy Lamour in a
sarong, a host of the famous and not so famous lent themselves to
the pin-up craze.

I made a decision. I would become the number one French
pin-up. I would go to all the newspapers and magazines and challenge the space they were giving to American women, saying that
I could prove that French women's bodies were better than Americans'. I had no doubt in my mind that it would work. The only
problem I had was money. How was I going to pay for the photos
I needed to back up my claim?

I went to a photo shop and asked the shopkeeper to tell me
the name of the photographer he most respected.

"Sam Levin, of course," he told me. "He's not only the best
for long shots, but for close-ups also. In fact, he's been in here
buying new lenses and a new type of film that's been developed in
America the last few years."

"I would like him to photograph me," I said. "But I know it'll
be expensive."

"Maybe you could offer to pose for him to test out some of
his new equipment, and instead of paying you he might agree to
give you some prints," the shopkeeper suggested.

"Do you think he will?" I was very excited. "Thanks for the
idea."

Levin's studio was near the Place de la Concorde, in the famous Boulevard St. Honoré. My heart was beating irregularly
and my feet barely touched the ground on the carpeted stairway
up to the fifth floor. I rang the doorbell. Levin himself opened
the door. He was a medium-sized man with a receding hairline
covered with a layer of sweat. His sleeves were rolled up and his
brown eyes shone in his ruddy face.

"Come in," he said. "I'm in the darkroom. Look at the photo
books on the table. I'll be out as soon as I can."

I felt shivers as I looked at the pictures that covered the walls,
big stars like Jean-Louis Barrault, Michèle Morgan, Fernandel,
René Simon, Claude Dauphin and many others. Will mine soon
be there with them? I wondered. The pictures seemed to be looking at me. I hoped they were welcoming me as one of their kind.

When Levin came out, wiping his hands, my face was flushed, my eyes wide with ancitipation.

"What can I do for you, Mademoiselle ..."

"Corinne Calvet. I've just done the film *We Are Not Married,* and I've decided that I want to crown myself French pin-up number one. I need your help. I'll pose for you every day; you can try out all your new equipment and films and things. You don't have to pay me for posing. I'll do it free if you'll just give me some prints of the pictures I like." I said it all in one breath.

He smiled, looking at me appreciatively.

"You don't have to worry about the costumes. I'll take care of them."

Levin accepted my proposal. The play had closed, so every evening for the next two months we met in his studio. It was a game for me to find appropriate outfits for the number one French pin-up.

Sam would start with long shots, but always moved in for some close-ups. I was under an array of spotlights, and could feel their warmth on my face. I developed an instinct for judging the heat, knowing just where the shadows started. There was a strong rapport between Levin and myself. He encouraged me to talk during these photo sessions. I trusted him. I was totally malleable. Looking at the results of the sessions, I discovered the many personalities I had within me. The costumes I borrowed varied from bathing suits to furs, from bear rugs to period apparel, always displaying a good deal of skin. When I had photos in about two dozen different costumes I approached my first magazine. The editor's response was so positive that I soon had my pictures lying on the desks of the most important film publications in Paris. Pictures of me began to appear everywhere. Nobody challenged my title as the number one pin-up. Soon, close-ups of me became popular, and I became France's new sensation, Corinne Calvet.

One day, leaving Sam's studio, I walked toward Notre Dame on its densely populated island in the center of the ancient city. Deep in thought about my future, I passed the quais bordering the river Seine. Hundreds of pigeons were flying around the main steeple of Notre Dame. I stood and watched, fascinated. A small formation of birds broke out of the main group and flew in my direction in a wide curve over my head, then flew back to join the rest of the flock above the cathedral.

The majestic carved portals expressing human weakness suggested to me that I leave my own behind as I entered the sacred place. Dipping my finger lightly in the blessed water, I crossed myself and walked quietly to my favorite alcove. In a niche was a statue of Mary before she became the mother of Jesus. I lit a candle, placed it alongside the altar, and asked for her help.

As I walked out of this peaceful retreat, the pigeons on the steps did not scurry away at my approach.

I reflected on the horror of the German occupation, the hysteria of the liberation, and the Americans' greed as they infiltrated French society. I squinted in the glistening summer sun as I moved into the sanctuary of the chestnut trees by the river. Their shade formed an umbrella over the bookstalls lining the edge of the Seine. They contained a treasure of wisdom. A finger of sunshine broke through the heavy foliage. It fell on a small volume in one of the bookstalls, directing me to pick it up. I opened it and read.

Learn to put into action the universal force of creation, and your desires will become realities.

One day Sam invited me to have dinner with him before our nightly session in the photo studio. I was apprehensive. It was clear to me that his devotion was getting more than friendly, and I could feel the energy of his desire, even when he was under his black cloth, looking through the privacy of his lens. Inevitably, Sam approached me with his sexual needs. I tried to laugh him off.

"One shouldn't mix business with pleasure," I said, when he began making advances toward me.

For the time being, he did not insist, and he was making himself indispensable by acting as my unofficial agent.

The release of the picture *We Are Not Married* reconfirmed without doubt that the public accepted me as a promising star. I had now given myself a goal. In one year I would be a success in Hollywood. I was positive. Twice each day I visualized a future in which I was the star of a big Hollywood premiere, spotlights converging on me as I stepped out of a limousine, raised my eyes, and saw my name in lights on the marquee, "Starring Corinne Calvet."

The phone rang one rainy morning just after I had finished my visualization exercises.

"Did you see in the paper that Paramount is looking for a leading lady to play opposite Ray Milland?" My ex-schoolmate from the Dullin school, Martine Carol, was bubbling with excitement.

"I'm invited to the studio cocktail party. I know it's a big chance, and I'm scared to death to go alone. Please, Corinne, come along with me."

"What if they choose me?" I teased.

"Well," she hesitated for a moment. "I'm not the only one they've invited. If they choose someone else it may as well be you. But don't count on it."

I searched through some movie magazines and discovered that Mr. Milland was definitely no longer a juvenile, but a man comfortably settled in his forties. I decided that if I was going to be his leading lady I would somehow have to make myself look more mature. My problem was solved by a friend, a small, gentle boy who, to the despair of his mother, spent more time at home making hats than he did outside playing football.

"The answer," he said, "is a black velvet hat with a cluster of shiny black plumes on the left side."

I watched in amazement while with a few pieces of material he fashioned such a creation, and two hours later handed me the most magnificent chapeau I had ever possessed.

On the day of the cocktail party I wore Isabelle's black suit, the hat, and some borrowed high-heeled shoes.

When I walked into the living room to glance at myself in the full-length mirror I saw a very grown up young lady with no visible traces of the wild, spiritual, unconventional existentialist who was still inside.

The party had been arranged for Ray Milland by Mr. and Mrs. Frank Farley. Farley was the representative of Paramount in Paris. Milland had gained world-wide recognition for his interpretation of an alcoholic in *Lost Weekend*. There was a sharp atmosphere of competition when we entered the elegant reception room decorated in classic Napoleonic style. There was no one at the door to welcome us.

"Look over there," Martine whispered to me. "It's him. I think I'm going to faint. Well, here I go." Grabbing my hand, she shook it. "All's fair in love and war. May the best woman win. I'll talk with you tomorrow." She was gone.

A young man approached me and asked me my name, checking his list.

"It's not here," he challenged.

"C-o-r-i-n-n-e C-a-l-v-e-t," I spelled, unperturbed.

"Wait here," he said. A man carrying a glass of champagne moved toward me. A camera was hanging from his shoulder.

"Aren't you the queen of the French pin-ups? Yes, you are," he concluded as I smiled. "Here, have some champagne."

"No thank you," I answered. "Maybe some tea."

"Over here," he said, putting the glass down, and passing his arm through mine he guided me up to the serving table. Cup in hand, the photographer moved me to the corner of the room where Ray Milland was surrounded by anxious females. Martine was there, and Gaby Andrew, Florence Marly, and a number of others. Several of them later became quite popular.

"Mr. Milland," the photographer said, "This is Corinne Calvet."

In response to the offer of his hand, I absentmindedly handed him my cup.

"Non merci," he laughed. To my surprise he could express himself quite well in French.

I blushed.

"How do you like Paris?" I asked, regaining my composure.

"Marvelous city. . . ."

The other women were hanging onto every trivial utterance, smiling provocatively. I wished that the floor would open up so I could disappear. Someone pushed me. The tea spilled. I retreated to the back of the room where I noticed a silver-haired woman sitting alone. I went and sat by her side. Her smile was kind, and it gave me courage to test my poor English. Before long, through a combination of my English and her French, we found ourselves in a discussion of Cocteau's recent film, *Beauty and the Beast*. Following Sam Levin's advice, I was careful not to overstay my welcome. Soon I prepared to leave, and went back to say good-by to Milland before I departed. At first he looked perplexed, as if he did not remember who I was. Then, recognizing my hat, he asked me where I had been.

"Right over there," I said, tossing my head in the direction of the white-haired lady.

"Oh, really? Well, good-by."

As I was leaving, the young man who had questioned my right to be at the party informed me that Paramount Pictures wanted me to come to their office the next day and fill out a questionnaire.

When I arrived at the Paramount office I found myself once again facing the same anemic young man. He handed me a two-page form and a pen. I started filling in the answers, but soon the questions began to probe into my private life, asking for details in personal taste, my thoughts on marriage and children, my sleeping habits. Did I wear pajamas or a nightgown? What was my preference in men, short, tall, fat, skinny, hairy or bald? All of this under the pretext of collecting biographical information. It seemed more like the kind of questionnaire a madam might use in selecting girls to work in a brothel. By the time I got to the second page I was furious. I got up from the ugly black sofa on which I had been sitting, walked over to the young man, and opened my mouth to say something. Then I decided that words would be futile. Instead, I simply tore the questionable questionnaire into shreds, laid them on his desk, and started to walk out.

"Mademoiselle, Mademoiselle," I heard the young man calling behind me, but I just kept walking.

Later I discovered that the woman to whom I had been talking at the cocktail party was Mrs. Ray Milland, and I'm sure she helped my cause, especially after the mistake made by Mr. Milland's first choice, Martine Carol. The day after the cocktail party, while Mrs. Milland was visiting a famous couturier, Milland had a rendez-vous with Martine to discuss the picture and get to know her better. Everything had gone smoothly, but Martine made the mistake of talking later with the French press about her meeting with Ray Milland.

Before I learned of Martine's mistake, Sam Levin arranged for me to go to the Riviera for a color test with the new Technicolor process. It was a big opportunity. Technicolor was rapidly being perfected, and the test would put my image in front of all the producers and directors who wanted to work in this medium.

"They want me to come also," Sam added.

I had never been to the French Riviera. When we arrived, I
told Sam I wanted to buy a mascot to bring me luck.

"What kind of mascot?" he asked.

"A toy animal of some kind. Something I can hug at night."

"How about me?"

"Sam, you're not cuddly."

"I guess I'm not, but you are. Listen Corinne, I know I'm a
lot older than you, but even though I keep telling that to myself,
it hasn't stopped me from falling in love with you. I see your face
everywhere I look. I can't work on other pictures. I beg you. Let
me take you in my arms, make gentle love to you, and cuddle up
all night."

Sam Levin had confided in me. His family had died in a con-
centration camp. He had narrowly escaped with his life. I owed
Levin a lot, and I would never be able to pay him for his time and
effort. Despite my thoughts, or perhaps because of them, I just
stood there with a frozen smile on my face. Sam took my silence
as tacit agreement. He started jumping around like a little boy,
and then kissed me on top of my head.

"I'll see you later," he said. "I'll pick you up at six this evening. We'll drive up to the mountains, have a romantic dinner,
and maybe go dancing. Then you'll be mine."

He was gone. I had said nothing, and yet I was committed. It
was the same trap, a business association with a man was being
pushed inexorably toward the boudoir. Was it I or the society I
lived in? I was indebted to him, and I did not think I had anything to give that he wanted but myself. Obviously, men were not
interested in my brain. My body was what they wanted. But Sam
didn't appeal to me, and I didn't like it when he approached
closer to me than three feet. I would then notice his mouth, which
was too full, his moist skin and shiny skull. I will have a few Per-
nods during the evening, I thought; maybe if I'm a little drunk I
won't mind so much.

We drove out of the city and had dinner. When we returned
to our hotel he opened the door of my room and there, lying on
the bed halfway under the covers, was a toy duck, a beautiful
Disney Donald Duck with immense eyes and a long orange beak.

"Oh Sam, he's beautiful."

I was kneeling by the bed, hugging my new toy. The duck
would stand up on its own, its wide webbed feet supporting it.

"He's going to bring me good luck, Sam. I know, I can feel it. I'll keep him with me always. How did you put it in my room?" "I arranged for the maid to tuck it in your bed when she brought the champagne and the caviar, which is right over there for your pleasure, your majesty."

When I added the champagne to the Pernod I had consumed at dinner I was soon giggling and tipsy, hanging on to my duck. Sam was feverishly pulling off my clothes. It was somehow funny. I gave in and let myself go limp in his arms. As he caressed me I was overcome by a feeling of nausea.

"Sam, stop, I'm going to get sick," I said.

"No, no, not now. Just relax, don't fight it. I love you. I'll be gentle, I promise. You want me, don't you?"

"No, I do not. I don't believe I want you at all, Sam."

"How can you know before I make you feel good? Do you know how good I can make you feel?" The ordeal was over quickly.

As I came out of the shower where I had scrubbed myself clean Isabelle called from Paris.

"Corinne, you have to come back immediately. I just received a call from Paramount. The big boss from New York wants to see you, and he's passing through Paris tomorrow on the way to Sweden."

I hesitated before answering.

"I don't want anything to do with those people. I want to see the projection of the color test I did yesterday."

Isabelle was shocked that I was not interested, but she knew better than to try to convince me to return immediately. An hour later a Monsieur Segonzac, the second man in charge of the Paramount Paris office, called me directly.

"Miss Calvet," he said, "Paramount wants to sign you to a seven-year contract. Mr. Russell Holman, the New York executive, is passing through Paris. He'll have to give his approval, and it would save time if you could come here immediately."

"Monsieur Segonzac, from the questionnaire I don't think my values will fit what Paramount expects of me."

"What do you mean?" he asked.

"I don't think it's anybody's business what I sleep in."

"Don't pay any attention to that silly questionnaire; it's not important. What is important is your chance to become a world-wide star, but Mr. Holman has to give his approval."

A seven year contract! It was incredible. It was more than what I had wished for.

"I'll be on the night train," I said. "It arrives at nine tomorrow morning."

I soon discovered that it was too late to make a reservation for a sleeping compartment on the train, and that I would have to stand in the corridor for the entire trip. But I was not sleepy, and my mind raced ahead of the whistling train. I found a place near the bathroom where I could sit on my suitcase, hugging the Donald Duck doll on my lap. I only had a toothbrush, no make-up to repair my running mascara. Hurrying to make the train, I had fallen down, and the rip in my stocking exposed my entire knee.

When the train arrived Isabelle met me with a fresh dress, stockings, and a new glitter in her eyes. But there was no time to change. Mr. Holman's train was leaving almost at once from another station. In the car, Monsieur Segonzac was almost as nervous as Isabelle and I. In a few minutes we arrived. A man looking more like a banker than a film mogul was pacing impatiently in front of his compartment. I knew that it would be impossible for me to impress anybody in my present attire, so I became defiant and walked toward him like a proud soldier, holding my duck under my arm. Holman's eyebrows shot up into the air, and I spent the next precious four minutes before his train departed explaining that Donald Duck was my mascot, and that I hoped he would bring me good luck, all in French, of which Mr. Holman did not understand a word. From the steps of the train he turned and asked me if I would be interested in coming to Hollywood.

"Yes, sir." These were the first and only words of English Holman heard from me.

It all happened so quickly that Isabelle and I waved as the train left the station, and then stood transfixed. I expressed myself loudly about the stupidity of having made me return for this ridiculous meeting. Later I discovered that my behavior was what had impressed Mr. Holman. He reported to the studio in Hollywood that I was a refreshing personality who spoke English quite well.

Jean-Pierre was at the apartment waiting for us.

"How did it go?" he asked.

"Terrible, look at me."

"You look beautiful. What's that?" He was pointing to the duck.

"It's Donald, my good luck charm. Isn't he cute?"

Jean-Pierre picked me up and carried me into the bedroom. "I'll fix us a cup of tea," Isabelle said. "We all need it. Too much excitement for one day."

Jean-Pierre, the bedroom door closed, looked deeply into my eyes.

"I love you," he said, before kissing me.

I love him too. How can I leave him, I thought. Maybe if we got married he could go with me.

"Jean-Pierre," I said, breaking his embrace. "If they give me a contract it means we'll be separated. I don't want that to happen. What can we do?"

"They will give you a contract." His voice had an added dimension of admiration. "You should be grateful, and do exactly what they tell you. It's the chance of a lifetime, and you can't let anything interfere, not your family, your temperament, not me, nothing. Do you hear, mon amour?"

"We could get married. Then you could come with me."

"No, they'll want you to date movie stars, and I'm sure that if you were married they would hesitate to sign you."

"Don't be silly," I said haughtily. "My personal life has nothing to do with my qualities as an actress."

"I'm not so sure," Jean-Pierre said skeptically. "Do you remember, who was it? Jean Harlow? Anyway, one of their big stars in the first years of the talkies. They canceled her contract because she got married without their permission."

"I don't know," I said with concern.

"Listen Corinne, they know how to make stars. You just have to do what they tell you."

"What about integrity?" I was shocked at his thinking.

"What about it?"

"I can't let them destroy my integrity. That's my self-respect."

"Corinne," his voice was sharp. "You're talking like a bourgeoise. You're talking about rules and regulations that the church and your upper-class upbringing taught you. But you're not stuffy like them at all."

When I was with Jean-Pierre it all seemed so simple. It was only when I was alone that I felt contradictory impulses, and matters did not seem so clear.

A few days later, swept by the tidal wave of Paramount's offer, I was walking in a trance. During the next few weeks Jean-Pierre's position never changed. He was not going to stand between me and my future. It was noble of him, but I could not help feeling deep resentment that he was being so stubborn. I knew he loved me, and I was right in thinking so, for he stayed single for twenty years. The embers of our love would flare up briefly during our occasional reunions, but neither of us wanted to rekindle the flame. It was a love that would never again burn brightly, nor would it die.

When the contract came I had no agent in Paris, and no one to negotiate its terms on my behalf. Mrs. Farley, the wife of the Paramount executive who had arranged the party for Ray Milland, and who had hired me to pose in the new Paris hat collection for the London *Picture Post,* had long aspired to be an agent, and took over this task for me. She drove a hard bargain. No wonder. At the other side of the table sat her husband. The terms were particularly good, seven hundred and fifty dollars a week, fifty-two weeks a year, plus three hundred dollars per week expenses and the use of a car. For an unknown in America, in 1947, it was a tour de force.

Mrs. Farley took me in hand. She was a beautiful woman, and very conscious of fashion. I trusted her completely. She took a look at my wardrobe, which was mostly black in keeping with my existentialist ties.

"This will not do. This will not do at all."

"It will have to do," I answered, "because it's all I have, and my parents are in no position to buy me anything else."

She left the apartment, muttering.

The next day Mrs. Farley called to say we were going shopping. She had obtained the enormous sum of three thousand dollars for the purpose of buying me a wardrobe. I was very excited. Gone were my father's cut-down suits. The idea of going to a real couturier made me dizzy. But I was soon disappointed. There was nothing I liked. It was all too elegant and sophisticated, or too décolleté and dressy. I was lost. I suggested going to a dressmaker where I could design my own clothes, but Mrs. Farley explained that we had to buy from famous houses in order to impress the studio with the names on the bills. So Lanvin it was, and Christian Dior. Mrs. Farley's taste overrode my indecision. My straight, long hair was now shortened and set in curls. Who was the stranger I faced in the mirror? The exquisitely made up young woman who stared back at me had no past, but she was told she had a future.

It was a new me who emerged from the taxi at the Gare du Nord the day of my departure. Photographers recorded my farewells. I was a beautiful, sexy, elegant girl, hugging Jean-Pierre, my love, and my friend Gilbert, who had insisted on being there, as well as Isabelle and Papa. We all had tears in our eyes.

"Good-by, *sale gamine*," Isabelle said, her voice cracking.

I was saying good-by to France, her poets, and my loved ones. A part of me wanted to scream, wishing someone would ask me to stay. Didn't they understand that I was just a young girl, frightened to be alone, in a panic over men's desire? Couldn't they see how vulnerable I really was, afraid to wake up the next morning without the protection of someone who loved me? Jean-Pierre, my eyes begged silently, tell me to stay. I'll give up the whole thing, get married and have a family. I'm scared, I've never really been alone.

The train started to move slowly. My emotions were like a stretched rubber band. I was hanging out the window, gazing at the slowly diminishing people of my past. As the train gained speed, the tension on the elasticity of the rubber band reached its limit and snapped. I was released of my attachments, and as the train jerked, I was thrown back into the compartment. Mrs. Farley, an extremely well-organized woman, was changing from her high heels to slippers. Looking out the train window, I thought it was amazing that I felt no pain, no regrets, only exhilaration about the future. This is the feeling Maman must have had when she died, I decided, when her life energy had been stretched to its maximum and she was released from her body. She must have felt no pain.

"Corinne," Mrs. Farley spoke softly. "I'll stay with you until you're safely on the *Queen Elizabeth*. And for the next four days we're going to be very busy. I've arranged many interviews, photo layouts, and a few dinner parties." She was smiling with concern.

"Thank you. That will be nice. I'm all right. I think I'll lie down and close my eyes for a while."

In London the press was cordial and warm. They accepted me as a movie star, and it felt good and natural. I was on my way.

Then I found myself alone in my luxurious cabin on the ship. The press, the photographers, the guests, Mrs. Farley, and the butler had all left. The ship's horn blasted the last warning of departure. My excitement turned into apprehension of the unknown. The stateroom was filled with flowers. I walked into the bedroom and was overcome by the rich fragrance. I lay down on the bed, my eyes burning with dry tears, the pungent smell of the bouquets reminding me of my mother's funeral. Taking a deep, long breath, I passed into oblivion.

When Sarah Bernhardt arrived in the United States, there was a band playing the "Marseillaise," but there was no band for me when my ship pulled into New York. Even so, the French march was echoing in my head. Helped by patriotism, I raised my head high and smiled for the barrage of photographers.

On an upper deck I was told to sit on the railing. I was bombarded with a series of questions and demands.

"Let's have some cheesecake."

"Pull your skirt higher."

"How soon do you intend to have an American lover?"

I felt like a doe in the forest surrounded by hunting dogs. I was confused and insulted by the imbecility of their impertinent questions.

"I don't know, I don't know," was all I could utter.

At last the ordeal was over. Hiller Innes, the Paramount representative, accompanied me in a limousine to the Hotel Pierre, where a majestic suite had been prepared for me. Before Innes left he handed me some newspaper clippings announcing my arrival in the United States. My name was mispelled Corinne Calvay.

"That's not how I spell my name," I said.

"Yes, I know. The publicity department came up with a slogan for you, 'Calvay is Okay.'"

"Calvay, okay? What does it mean?" I inquired.

"That means you're okay," a woman who was with Innes began to explain in French.

"I don't understand."

"The studio felt that the American public wouldn't know how

to pronounce your name. They would see Calvet and say Calvette, so we changed the spelling so they would pronounce it correctly."

"But . . ." I began to protest.

Mr. Innes interrupted. "Have a rest. We'll be back at one o'clock to take you to lunch with Mr. Holman. It's now ten. That gives you three hours."

They were gone. I was outraged. They had renamed me without my consent. It was bad enough that my father had denied me the right to use my true name, and now this. Yet I remembered the words of Jean-Pierre. "They know how to make people into stars."

"Okay?" I said aloud. Then I made a face and added, "Calvay okay. Why does it sound so vulgar?"

I couldn't possibly rest. My head was still spinning. I had some free time and I was in New York. From the twentieth floor I took the elevator to the lobby, a fast efficient ride in contrast to our poor, sad French elevators that start with the pull of a cord. My stomach jumped with the speed of our descent. The mirrors in the hall reflected a bouncing, happy, smiling young lady as I walked by. I was glad to be in America. Out of all the talented, beautiful actresses in France, I had been chosen. Why? Did I deserve it? Did it happen because I wanted it the most? Had I made it happen? I couldn't be sure, but here I was, walking on Fifth Avenue.

"I am in America! I am in America!" The little ballad kept sounding in my ear. Dizzy, my head turned upward, I looked at the skyscrapers. I felt I was a small giant about to grow immense.

I was no more than a few steps from the hotel entrance when I caught sight of a candy store with its window full of tempting sweets. For the last four years I had tasted candy only when I had enough ration coupons. The shop was irresistible. I walked in, and to my delight, the people running the store were French. All I needed to buy candy was money. I was told I could buy as much as I wanted of whatever I wanted. It was unbelievable. I ended up with twelve different little packages. I lost all desire to see New York. I wanted only to be alone with my sweet treasures.

Back in my hotel suite, I took off my clothes, put on a robe, and lay down on the floor of the living room in the middle of the Louis XV furniture. My twelve little boxes, each filled to the rim with every size, color, and shape of sweets, were scattered around me, beckoning. I began to taste one after the other. Years of deprivation compelled me to eat. The only problem was deciding which candy I liked best. By the time Mr. Innes picked me up I was as green as if I were still on the ship, caught in a violent storm. Innes took one look at me, one look at the candy wrappings on the floor, and went to the phone to cancel the luncheon date. I was put to bed, and the hotel doctor was called.

When I recovered, I had my first contact with the institution called American Puritanism. Since Paramount had spent a great deal of money on my wardrobe, they wanted to publicize it. A woman was sent to the hotel to coordinate pictures of the dresses for the fashion pages of *The New York Journal American*. I wanted to talk about the clothes and their styles, but the lady seemed more interested in the cost of each outfit, which I could not remember. She became irritated, pointing out that the readers of the paper would be interested in the cost. I smiled, and kept quiet.

"Mrs. Farley would know," I finally told Innes. "She paid for them."

Everyone relaxed after I began to pose for the pictures. Finally there were only evening dresses left to shoot. I put on my favorite, a matte violet jersey gathered up in a Grecian manner with a train that could double as a wrap over bare shoulders. I felt very classical in that dress, ready to appear on Broadway in a Greek tragedy. Tragedy it was. The lady from Paramount was screaming.

"Stop, stop! Don't shoot. Don't shoot!"

"Why? What's the matter?" the photographer said.

"Come here, Miss Calvay," said the hysterical woman who was running the show. Waving me into the bedroom, she closed the door behind us, marched me to the dresser, and made me lift my arms in front of the mirror.

"Look there," she said, with her head turned to one side as if she were witnessing indecent exposure.

"Yes?" I questioned.

"You have hair under your arms." She almost choked on the words.

"I have a little fluff of blonde hair," I acknowledged.

"You could have shaved, knowing you were going to have some pictures taken."

"But I've never shaved. I don't need to. You almost cannot see it."

"Well, everybody knows that the French are a little backward about cleanliness," she said with obvious condescension.

Even if my French was not understood, my voice, mannerisms, and the expression on my face made it unmistakably clear that I was outraged. My anger was making me violently sick again. When I came out of the bathroom they had all gone. The photo equipment was still there in the living room. I was resting on the bed when the same arrogant woman from Paramount returned with a package in hand. Without a word she went into the bathroom and came out with shaving soap and razor. I felt cornered, and gave in.

For years, every time I had to repeat this gesture, the removal of nearly invisible hair, I used to resent this woman.

When I later looked at the photographs that were finally completed that day, I realized that they typified what was to happen to me in the following year. I looked uncomfortable in those pictures, my hair pinned up, like a child dressed in her mother's clothes, haughty and distant. None of the real me was showing. Where was the real me?

The city of New York was spectacular. The release that came with the end of the war was felt in the United States just as it had been in France, but there was something else, something I would learn about when I reached Hollywood. It was the beginning of fear, recognition that the world was no longer so simple, that America was no longer the same place far away and disconnected from all the problems of the postwar world. But despite the contradictions that may have lurked beneath the surface, I was taken by the wonder of New York, the steel and cement canyons, the buildings that seemed to disappear into the clouds. The luxury of the large apartments on Park Avenue and around Central Park was stunning, and my dear professor at L'Ecole du Cinema would have been pleased to know that during the six days I spent in New York my eyes widened to such a degree that I lost my bad habit of squinting when I concentrated.

More and more as I stayed in New York, I felt like a piece of clay being pulled and squeezed by the publicity people from the studio. In addition to the battle of the underarms, there was a long-nosed, bespectacled, red-haired man who kept asking me why I didn't use the title of countess.

"Because Calvet is not my family name. It's Dibos. There is no Countess Calvet, or Calvay," I answered sharply, exaggerating the last syllable of each name. "Besides," I added, "I have heard that in America there is no difference of class."

That remark was received with a burst of giggles. I was perplexed. They gave up insisting that I use the title of countess. Nevertheless, what followed was the announcement in *Life* magazine that an alluring descendant of Louis XIV had been signed by Paramount, and in *Look* I was crowned the "French Love Goddess."

Each night when I was finally alone, exhausted from the continuous cycle of interviews, luncheons, radio shows, and photo sessions, I retreated to the shiny, black bathtub in my hotel suite, cradled by moist, luxurious bubbles. Letting hot water trickle over me and moving my legs gently up and down, I made waves that carressed my yearning body like the presence of a tender lover, thinking how much I missed Jean-Pierre's touch.

Barely dry, I would get into bed. The sheets were like the cool understanding wings of an angel, protecting me as I slept.

My last weekend in New York I was invited to the Long Island home of Mr. Russell Holman, the Paramount executive who had signed me in Paris. Mrs. Holman was a charming woman with two daughters. There were lots of games to be played, Ping-Pong, croquet, and gin rummy. It was a happy family. There was laughter in the kitchen. Everyone helped with the dishes. For the first time since I had arrived, my heart began to open to America with the recognition that maybe families were the same the world over.

The weekend concluded, I was about to start on a great adventure that would take me across the country to the land of palm trees and movie stars. In the rush of Grand Central Station, with eight photographers and publicity men along with Mr. Innes and Mr. Holman, I did not have time to get answers to the list of questions I had prepared. How long did the train take? Who would meet me in Hollywood? Where was I going to live? The only thing I had time to do was to pull my skirt higher and smile, keeping my eyes from blinking at all the flashbulbs. I thought someone could be driven insane by the constant explosion of flashbulbs all around. My eyes felt as if they were being attacked by a million sharp knives.

It was time for the Paramount staff to leave. I was standing on the steps of the train near a very affable black porter. Just before departure Mr. Holman stepped up close to me and asked if I was sure everything was all right. He told me how much his wife had enjoyed having me as their guest. Then he hesitated for a moment.

"Can I talk to you in the way I would talk to one of my own daughters?" he asked with great consideration.

"Yes, please do." I kissed him on the cheek.

"There's a man at the studio. . . . Don't go near his office alone, make sure you have an agent or someone with you. He's a terrible wolf."

"A wolf?" I inquired.

"A man who cannot keep his hands off women."

"Same as a Casanova," I said, matter of factly, attempting to appear sophisticated.

"Worse, much worse." His voice grew stern.

"All aboard, all aboard," the public address system boomed. Twice Mr. Holman whispered the wolf's name. Then he was gone. I was touched that he had wanted to protect me. As the train moved out of the station, I became terrified at the enormity of my undertaking, and the imponderables concealed in the shadows of my Hollywood future.

PART TWO

Hollywood—
The Magnificent Zircon

Chapter 6

Like a silver bullet leaving New York for Chicago, the Super Chief was gaining speed. The wheels passing over the rails repeated with demanding insistence, "What's his name . . . ? What's his name . . . ? What's his name . . . ?" During the ten days in New York, I had felt manipulated by publicity people. The horrible woman who forced me to shave under my arms, the bespectacled red-haired man who wanted to call me Countess "Calvay," the photographers and journalists, had all made me feel used.

Now I nervously searched for a pen. I sat down to spell the name of the wolf. I could not. The more I tried, the more the name slipped away. "What's his name . . . ? What's his name . . . ? What's his name . . . ?"

In my uneasy slumber I found myself communicating in a dream state with Colette, the French novelist who had known my mother. I heard melodious sentences about the love affair between the flowers and the bees. I was savoring the sensation that accompanied these thoughts when I was awakened by the sound of a bell. Or was it a chime?

"Last call for dinner!" The voice filtering through the locked door was insistent.

I was famished. I followed the porter to the train's dining car. I was shown to a seat across the table from two gentlemen. They introduced themselves. One was a European man, who had produced a number of important French films, and whose brother would later produce a film of mine. I never met a man quite so persistent. Over the years he has never been discouraged by my refusals.

It was pleasant to speak French with someone, which must have encouraged this man. But I was totally unprepared when he walked uninvited into my compartment, and without a word began to force himself on me. It was only when I reached for the porter's bell that he finally straightened his tie and departed. I locked my door, shaking with anger and feeling frightened and lonely.

For the rest of the trip I did not leave my compartment. I took all my meals there, and only answered the knock of the porter, who now used a special code. I felt like a prisoner. I had no French books with me, and my English was barely good enough to comprehend the captions under pictures in magazines. How would anyone ever understand me?

In Paris, people took notice when I spoke. They would say, "Yes, I can see that. I never thought of it that way." It made me feel worthwhile. Now, in America, I feared that because of my limited English vocabulary I would be unable to communicate intelligently. Isabelle, I wish you were here, I thought. You could help me express myself.

As we entered the final phase of our journey across the country the train was slowing down. A face suddenly appeared at the window, accompanied by waving arms and a body covered with beads. It was an Indian riding bareback, with war paint on his face and feathers in his hair. I thought of Gary Cooper discovering a sobbing orphan in a burning wagon. Now there were more Indians. They were brandishing hatchets. American movies had depicted the red men as crude savages, and that was all I knew.

"My God, we're being attacked."

Call it nerves, loneliness, claustrophobia, or temporary madness. Whatever it was it had me on my knees praying, wondering if I could escape being scalped by offering my body to a handsome Indian chief. Even after I realized that they were only selling souvenirs during our stop in El Paso, I still felt a sense of trepidation. It was the memory of this experience that later kept me from falling head over heels in love with Jeff Chandler. Every time I looked at him I would see him as Cochise in the film *Broken Arrow*. Whenever we got close to an embrace I saw his face become that of a painted warrior.

The Hollywood I was coming to in 1947 was something less than the famous dream factory of the 1930s. I had illusions, but even my illusions were based on an area of the industry that was quickly passing from the scene. Most of the studios were now suffering economically, and the industry was going through a painful transition, with government attacks on their monopoly of film distribution, the threat of television on the horizon, higher production costs, and restrictions on the export of films to European markets. All of this tended to bring out panic in the industry. At its worst, this took the form of accusations of un-Americanism against some of the most brilliant people in Hollywood. To me it was all too familiar. I had lived with the Gestapo in France, and I was well aware of how destructive an atmosphere of suspicion and innuendo could become. Little else in my experience, however, prepared me for what I would encounter.

I had been told in New York what to wear when I stepped down from the train in Hollwyood. I was to look very proper and European in a hat, suit, and gloves. But I was not prepared when my destination turned out to be Pasadena rather than Hollywood, and thought that some mistake had been made. But when I looked out of the train and saw the usual small army of photographers waiting expectantly I put on my hat, crossed myself, and walked bravely out to face my new life.

The Pasadena station looked as if it belonged to a small village. There were about eight palm trees and a quaint red tile roof. The Paramount representatives were very friendly, and there was none of the mad rush of New York. I sat on top of my trunk, and was told to wave good-by. I was soon rushed to a car and driven directly to Paramount studios where a new battery of newsreel cameras recorded my official introduction to Ray Milland and the studio's other big stars, Bob Hope, Bing Crosby, Alan Ladd, Robert Preston, Marlene Dietrich, and many others. Betty Hutton was bicycling from her dressing room to the set where she was shooting *The Perils of Pauline*. Hope and Crosby were in the middle of *Road to Rio*. My spine straightened, my eyebrows lifted slightly, and my hand moved out to all in a gesture of recognition. I was in control. I felt a strange sense of equality. I was among my peers. The cameramen wanted me to go back to the gate so they could film Bob Hope welcoming me as Paramount's new star.

Once more we were driving. This time I was taken to a house next to the Beverly Hills hotel. The house belonged to Paramount, and was serviced by the hotel staff; all the New York executives stayed there when they visited Hollywood. It had ten bedrooms, and I was left with all of my luggage in one of them. I was informed that I would be picked up at one o'clock for a luncheon meeting with an important studio representative, the casting director, William Meiklejohn.

Alone in the room I looked around, jumped on the bed, hugged a pillow against my body, and peeked into a huge bathroom. Once again I found the precious commodity, hot water, in abundance. I prepared my bath, trying to recall all the people I had been introduced to.

When I was ready for lunch, I was met by three publicity men, one of whom spoke French. Since we were a little early we drove to Sunset Boulevard where I was shown the famous nightclubs Ciro's and Mocambo's. Halfway between exhilaration and the anesthesia of culture shock, I was feeling very light and gay. The gentleman who spoke French with a heavy accent was carrying on about how much he loved French people. The gleam in his eye was unmistakable. It was the same look men had when they looked at the famous naughty postcards offered for sale in Montmartre. Very soon, I would come to recognize that look much too often.

I was already encountering the stereotyped notions American men had about French women. Their eyebrows would go up and they would leer sideways as they greeted me. American GIs, soldiers whose experience with French women was usually limited to girls of questionable repute, had been partly responsible for this reaction. But such impressions were entirely false. Most French women were raised with an emphasis on being good wives and mothers, and it was absurd to conclude that they were in any way promiscuous. Immediately I realized that in the minds of many American men, however, French women were decidedly oversexed, and that I was a prime example of French womanhood.

After our Sunset tour we went directly to Romanoff's restaurant where we found the "very important man from Paramount" waiting for us. His stature was imposing and yet incongruous. He looked more like an athletic coach than a man who dealt in the art of casting motion pictures. Very pleasantly he pointed out all the important studio executives in the restaurant. I was overcome but tried to hide my awe. In between swallowing oysters I managed some monosyllabic comments, mostly a succession of ahs, ohs, hmms, and ouis.

Lunch over, I was taken back to the house and left to do what I wished. What was I to do with this free time? I knew no one. I had no car. I couldn't speak the language beyond a minimal level, and I felt completely lost. After I had unpacked my suitcases I reread love letters I had brought with me from Jean-Pierre and Gilbert Lafitte. I listened for signs of life in the next room. I was bored and lonely. When I heard the phone ring in the hall I opened my door. Coming out of the room next to mine was Murvyn Vye, a bearded actor I had met on the set of the film *Golden Earrings*, where he was starring with Marlene Dietrich and Ray Milland. I had seen him only a few hours ago, but it seemed like a lifetime. I could have kissed him, I was so happy just to see a face I knew. He turned to me and said the phone was for him. His tone conveyed his demand for privacy.

I went back into my room and proceeded to put on a low-cut dress with every intention of going out in the hall for the next call so he could see me at my best. The phone rang again. I opened the door. Once more Murvyn was answering. He handed me the receiver, and with his famous deep voice caressed me with the words, "For you, Mademoiselle Calvet." The dress was working, because he stood there looking at me. I was under his spell. I couldn't understand a word of what was said to me until I finally turned my back on him.

I was susceptible when a man looked at me the way Vye was looking at me then, a look of total interest in the "whole" me. There was danger in my weakness, but that danger held an attraction for me. I handed the phone to Murvyn, who translated. I was lucky, he said, because Mr. Bill Meiklejohn had been very impressed with me at lunch, and wanted to take me out to dinner.

We returned to Romanoff's, which was again full of famous people. Gary Cooper asked to be introduced. He lifted my hands to his lips. I felt faint. His eyes looked directly into mine and I felt his hot breath on my skin before he let go. I wanted to giggle—it was a dream come true. "Maybe we will work together one day soon," he said before he left. What did he mean? I wondered why he had hesitated before he said "work."

"Is he married?" I asked.

"Yes, very much so."

The answer disappointed me, but soon my attention was drawn to another man sitting a few tables away. The man with the moustache was Darryl Zanuck. Joe Pasternak was there with his young wife and her young companion.

"A very French arrangement, n'est ce pas?" Meiklejohn said, his eyebrows moving up and down like Groucho's.

"What do you mean?" I questioned.

"They have an arrangement in their marriage. He has his freedom and she has a younger lover."

Sol Siegel was deep in intimate conversation with the dashing Howard Hughes. With the help of an interpreter, I had a chance to express myself, that is until I almost choked on a piece of bread when my great hero, Robert Taylor, was shown to a nearby table. He was seated with his wife, Barbara Stanwyck, just across from us. He looked at me and grinned his recognition. I became very gay and voluble, constantly watching, hoping he would come over. But he was involved in talking with Barbara, and never again looked in my direction.

When dinner was over, Meiklejohn decided that we would go and see the show at the Mocambo. We were all standing outside, waiting to get into two cars. After a very smooth shuffle I found myself alone in the big Cadillac with Meiklejohn, while the other five Paramount employees wound up in a much smaller car. After fifteen minutes of silence, I suddenly realized we were driving on a wide highway, framed by numerous trees. From my earlier tour, I recalled that there were no such roads between Romanoff's and the Mocambo Club. The car was gaining speed. The headlights made the dark road eerie.

"Is this the way to Mocabmo's?" I asked.

"No."

"Is it the way to my hotel?"

"No, not yet. I thought we'd go and have a tête-à-tête at the beach."

"It's very late. I'm very tired. Please take me home Mr . . ." I had forgotten his name.

"William Meiklejohn, but call me Bill."

"But people wait for us," I managed in imperfect English.

"Who cares? That's what they're paid for."

Meiklejohn? I thought about the name. My eyes widened in recognition. That was the name! The name I couldn't remember. The Paramount wolf!

"Please turn around and take me home," I said with cold controlled fear.

In response, his hand moved up between my legs, forcing my knees apart. With a rapid movement I twisted one of his fingers. He let out a yell, and withdrew his hand.

"Bitch!" he said under his breath.

He made a quick turn and a short while later we arrived at the Mocambo. The others were sitting around the table with funny smiles on their faces. My expression was somber, but Meiklejohn looked as if he had just licked the milk out of his bowl. I was infuriated by his smug complacency, and proceeded in my inimitable English to tell everyone that Meiklejohn had tried to kidnap me and take me to the beach. There was much embarrassed laughter, as if the whole thing had been a joke, but I got my point across. I was protecting my reputation, but I failed to see that I had humiliated Meiklejohn, making a fierce enemy out of him.

In France one would call what I had just done the coup de grâce. Meiklejohn's revenge would come just as fast as he could arrange it. He almost succeeded in blocking my career completely. For the next four days I was totally abandoned. No one from the studio called. But my mood remained rather positive. I had felt at home in the midst of the Hollywood luminaries at Romanoff's. I mailed the four letters of introduction Mrs. Farley had given me to send to her friends. I waited in vain for answers. In the meantime, the only contact I had with the outside world was listening to the love-making that followed the arguments between a Paramount executive and his wife who had the room next to mine. In desperation I knocked on Murvyn Vye's door and asked him what to do. He took me to see a certain Gogi, a well-known Russian who was the social director for the Bel Air Hotel. It was like finding an old friend, for Gogi spoke fluent French. He advised me to go to the studio and ask them what to do. It sounded like a reasonable suggestion, since they owned me, lock, stock and barrel. What neither of us knew, of course, was that my return to Paris had already been mapped out by Meiklejohn. I approached his office with trepidation and a good interpreter.

"What do you want?" Meiklejohn said without looking at me.

"I want to get situated, find a place to live, and get my car."

My contract stipulated that I received transportation from the studio.

"It's difficult. I really can't even talk to you anymore until you get an agent."

By the time I got back to the Bel Air Hotel I was feeling defeated. Gogi took me into the bar and handed me a glass of champagne, then a copy of the *Hollywood Reporter*. I was excited. I had made the paper already. There was my name in print. I was baffled and hurt as I read:

> Corinne Calvay is giving Paramount a lot of trouble. She should remember that the boats come to America, but that they also return to the places from whence they came.

It was my first experience of an unjust attack by a newspaper. It would not be the last.

The Bel Air became my new home. It was a luxurious paradise to me after wartime Paris. Lush foliage surrounded a pond with swans. There was a fountain, flowers, and a swimming pool. Many celebrities passed through the place during my stay there. Joan Crawford, Van Heflin, Tony Martin, Van and Evie Johnson, Zsa Zsa Gabor, and Murvyn Vye were among the ones I remember from my first days. Vye, who moved to the hotel about the same time I did, had the room just below mine, and I found his amorous activities nerve-racking. My fidelity to Jean-Pierre was being put to a test. I asked Gogi to move me to another room, but that proved no better, since my new suite was below the fiery Joan Crawford.

The studio reiterated their request that I get an agent. They no longer wanted to deal with me personally, but I knew no one and asked the studio for the name of someone they would find satisfactory. They gave me the choice of three, but it was soon obvious that I should sign with Famous Artists, the agency owned by Charlie Feldman, because there was an agent there named Fefe Ferry with whom I could communicate. Fefe advised me that since they had not negotiated my contract in Paris, I was in a position to ask the agency for a gift approximately equivalent in value to the percentage they would be taking out of my checks. They would then collect fees on what they would get me above what I had signed for.

"How valuable would this gift be?" I asked.

"Something worth a minimum of three thousand dollars," Fefe said.

"That would be enough to buy my own car!" I exclaimed.

"A Mercury, or something like that," Fefe said. "That is what you should do. Make it simple. Tell them you'll sign with them if they give you a car."

I was still not clear on the function of an agent.

"In Hollywood today," Fefe explained, "agents are using all sorts of inducements to get clients who can insure them an income. Boats, money, cars, and even sometimes houses."

"Mr. Feldman is ready to see you now." A secretary announced.

Charlie Feldman was a good-looking, dashing man with a certain charm and an intriguing light in his eyes. I made my demands.

"Certainly," Feldman said. "What kind of a car?"

I was not ready for that. I really had no idea what the differences were.

"A convertible," I said.

"What about a new Mercury?" Feldman suggested. "I have one ordered. A beautiful, black one, with a white top and red leather upholstery inside. It should be delivered in two weeks."

Without another moment of hesitation I signed the contract. I thought I had been pretty smart. What I didn't know was that without payment of some kind their contract with me would have been invalid. It was the first time in Hollywood that I made the mistake of believing somebody's word and I was filled with a false sense of security. A month went by and I saw no sign of the car. After a few phone calls I got my first taste of what is called the "agent's double shuffle." Mr. Feldman would always be busy in a conference, or he had just left the office. The efficient voice of his secretary would assure me that he would return my call as soon as possible. But the telephone never rang.

After demanding a copy of my contract, I asked Gogi to read it for me. We found that any mention of the date of delivery of the car was carefully omitted. I had Gogi call Feldman. Until then he had been dealing with a naïve, insecure foreigner, but now someone respected by the whole Hollywood community was speaking on my behalf. That was a different story, and soon a

black Mercury with red upholstery and a white top was delivered
to the parking lot of the Bel Air hotel. I was thrilled. It was my
first expensive possession. I felt bad about having been impatient,
suspicious, and unjust in my evaluation of Feldman.

I had been driving one of the Paramount fleet cars furnished
by Chrysler Corporation in return for Paramount's use of Chrysler cars in all productions done on the lot. The particular car I
had on loan from the studio was covered with scratches and
bumps occasioned by my inexperience as a new driver. I offered
to pay for the damage I had done to the car, but the man in
charge of the studio garage laughed when I made the suggestion.

"Don't worry about it. I have two body finishing men sitting
around here with nothing to do, just picking up their checks. This
will give them some work for a few days." Taking a closer look at
the car, he added, "By golly, you really did a good job banging
this baby around. The more I look at it, the more I think I'll keep
it just the way it is. We often need a banged-up car, and this is a
beaut."

Two specialized men on the payroll every week of the year
with nothing to do. This was just one unimportant department,
but typical of the sort of problem the studios were having in this
period, high overhead that had carried over from the days when
the unions had established themselves in the industry and the lots
were humming with big productions.

"Are you going to report the condition of this car to anybody?" I said to the man in the garage, frightened that I would
incur still more enmity at Paramount. "I don't want the front office mad at me."

"Don't worry about it, Mademoiselle. I won't say anything.
You know, your English is improving."

"Thank you. I go every day to the English coach for an hour
and a half, but I don't really know if I'm making any progress
because every day my teacher makes me read from a book and
then falls asleep. I don't know what to do. I try to raise my voice,
but the more I do the louder he snores."

"Oh, they stuck you with the appointment after lunch."

"Yes. I go there from one until two-thirty. How did you
know?"

"Everybody knows Lester Luther, your coach. He's one of the

nicest men in the world, but he has a problem with his digestion, and takes a nap every day after lunch. Nobody wants to go then."

"Thanks for telling me," I said, laughing. "I'll go and change it."

But I could not. Lester Luther was one of the best diction coaches Hollywood ever had, and every one of his other available hours was booked solid. So I read on and on. Lester had developed a sixth sense. If the word I was reading was totally unrecognizable he would grunt in his sleep. I would try to read it over and change the pronunciation until I heard a deep sigh. Under such a method, it was no wonder my progress was very slow.

I was frightened of everyone. When a man called me "darling" I would recoil into myself, thinking that he might be another "wolf." It was difficult for me to understand that those words were not employed as they would have been in Europe. In France, no one would ever think of using a tender expression of endearment toward a person of the opposite sex unless they were engaged, married, related, or in close intimacy. The barrage of terms such as "darling," "sweetheart," and "baby" had me in a full state of paranoia. I was surprised by the overwhelming success I thought I was having with men, but at the same time I was insulted by the lack of respect I felt these terms demonstrated, and dismayed by the rampant sexual desire of American men.

At times the clash of cultural values and the problems I had expressing myself clearly in English created serious, if not comic, misunderstandings. One day I was walking back from my dancing class when William Demarest approached me and invited me to join a few of the players on the Paramount lot in Bing Crosby's dressing room.

"I'd love to," I said with excitement. "I'll join you in a little while. I just want to take a douche first."

"You want to do what?" Demarest's face became as red as a beet.

"I want to take a douche. I just finished my dancing class."

It was a natural mistake. The French word for "shower" is *douche,* and of course I didn't know the word's meaning in English. I was not ready for the giggles which welcomed me when I entered Crosby's dressing room. It was embarrassing. I didn't know what was wrong, but I could guess from the expressions of the people who surrounded me that it had something to do with sex. Of course they were all laughing nervously, thinking I wanted to be sexually prepared for my encounter with Bing Crosby.

It wouldn't have been so bad if the matter had ended there, but the story spread through the lot like wildfire, and I gained the reputation of sexually forward. Now I was approached by all types of men, from the ones with neckties to those with overalls. My nerves were at the breaking point. It was a nightmare. I was alone, misunderstood, and being taken for the exact opposite of what I was. My principles stood in stark contrast to the way I was being perceived. I was an aristocratic, French, spiritual woman. I had had certain experiences in life that made me aware of most sides of human nature, and I was not a prude. But what was happening to me now was hellish.

Feeling sorry for myself, I was sobbing in my dressing room, lonely for my Parisian friends, when Bill Demarest knocked on the door and came in.

There was always a paternal warmth about the man, and he now stroked my hair gently, easing my pain.

"Why is everyone laughing at me?"

"Well," he said, "what do you expect, Corinne? Women don't usually go around talking so freely about taking a douche."

"Don't American women take showers?" I said incredulously.

"Of course."

We got it straightened out. Demarest quickly clarified the matter for the others. But the story was too good to die. For months afterward I felt embarrassed to the roots of my being every time anyone smiled at me.

I had not been driving the new car Charlie Feldman had given me for more than a week when it came to an involuntary halt on San Vincente Boulevard. It made a strange noise and just quit. Luckily it had stopped right in front of a gas station. I was not prepared for the diagnosis handed down by the mechanic.

"It'll need a new transmission, Miss," he said. He had to explain to me what that was.

"But that's impossible," I said. "The car is brand new. It couldn't be more than a month old."

I could not believe what he was telling me, so I drove off in first, the only gear still working, to the parking lot of the Famous Artists' office where Charlie Feldman sat in regal splendor. I explained what was wrong with the car to the parking lot attendant. "That looks like Mr. Feldman's old car," he said with a laugh.

"It is?"

"Well it doesn't surprise me. I don't think I know a man who is tougher on his car than Mr. Feldman. That brand new Mercury, the one he got a couple of weeks ago, will be completely ruined in three months."

Tears welled up in my eyes. I ran away from the man in the parking lot as quickly as I could. My hurt and disappointment soon turned into fury.

In the elevator on the way up to Feldman's office I breathed in deeply to gain control over the tightness in my throat and trembling body. I knew that Feldman's secretary would try and stop me, but I was not to be stopped. I walked right past her and demanded Feldman's immediate attention.

For the next half-hour I was faced by three men giving me a stream of double talk. The substance of their position was that in our verbal agreement the year of the car had not been stipulated. My complete inability to express myself properly in English, and the sense that I was losing ground in my discussion with these sharpies, drove me to revert to my native tongue. Speaking in French, through Fefe as an interpreter, I demanded an immediate release from my contract or else I would file suit against them for misrepresentation. An hour later I left with Charlie's brand new Mercury, as well as a reputation for using threats to obtain what was justly mine. I had learned that agents were not exactly the way they were usually depicted in movies. Most big agents were neither friend, adviser, or helper, but collectors of fees, whose emotions did not extend beyond the money they made off their clients' talent.

Quick to forget a painful experience, I allowed myself to enjoy driving the new car, believing it was mine, not realizing that I should have asked for the certificate of ownership.

My social life was improving. Through Gogi I had met Sir Charles and Lady Mendl (she was Elsie de Wolfe), the loved and respected English aristocrats who lived in Beverly Hills. At a memorable small dinner party at their house I found myself sitting between Cary Grant and David Niven and directly across from Greer Garson and her young husband. By the time dinner was over I had a date with David and the expectation of a call from Cary.

All eyes were on David Niven and me as we walked into the Beachcomber restaurant in Hollywood. I had been told that David had recently lost his beautiful wife, who fell to her death, slipping down the cellar stairs at their new home. David introduced me to a rum drink called a Scorpio—it tasted sweet and refreshing. I felt shy and ill at ease until I finished my second Scorpio. All at once it hit me and tearfully I told him that I knew how he must feel about losing his wife and how lonely he must be and how lonely I was. Over the eggrolls we were both in tears, lost in the past. When I got home I felt good; I thought that at last I had met someone that I could be close to. In retrospect, I can understand why I never heard from David after that evening—he wanted to forget his sorrow, not to wallow in it with someone he had hoped could help him.

My disappointment was short-lived, as I was busy preparing to test for the film *Sealed Verdict,* the Ray Milland vehicle for which I was originally brought from Paris. The scene was a long monologue. The words were difficult and complicated. I knew the general meaning of what I was saying, but I did not know what the words really meant taken one by one. I was petrified that morning when they brought me breakfast in the make-up department. How considerate of them, I thought. It was six A.M., and I didn't know that it was a union rule that the studio must furnish food if you were called in five hours prior to the lunch break. After I ate I was placed in the hands of a woman named Nellie, who was head of the hairdressing department. Nellie was a close friend of Marlene Dietrich, and she was not overjoyed to see another European actress under contract to the studio. Because of her devotion to Dietrich, she wanted Marlene to get every part available for a foreigner. Against my wishes she decided to set my hair so it would be pulled up and combed out into a million curls on top of my head. I thought I looked ridiculous. Next, I was put into the hands of a make-up man who proceeded to pluck out most of my eyebrows. By the time I was ready to put on the costume they had laid out for me, none of my own personality was left. My lips had been painted way above their natural line. I was given a black, sexy, dress showing one naked shoulder, and a pair of long earrings that made a jingling sound each time I moved my head. I was a sight. I looked as if I belonged in a dog act. But I kept telling myself over and over that they knew what they were doing. I have never seen the results of that test, but from what I have been told it has been kept as one of the classic humorous and ridiculous performances of all time.

The result of this fiasco was immediate. Feldman asked me to come into his office.

"Paramount thinks it has made a mistake in bringing you over from France. They've decided that you do not have what it takes to be a Hollywood star. Your English is still atrocious, despite the coaching the studio has been nice enough to give you."

I said nothing, and he continued.

"They're offering to give you half the money due in your contract, and pay all of your expenses back to France."

Back to France? To return a failure? It was unthinkable. The idea started my adrenalin going, and I decided to prove Paramount wrong.

"You can tell them for me," I said very softly, "that I have no intention of going back, and since this is the way they feel I expect them to mail my check every week until they finish paying me every dollar of my contract."

I stormed out of Feldman's office and drove back to the hotel, where a telephone message said that Cary Grant had called! I of course accepted his dinner invitation.

Cary's house was adjacent to the Bel Air hotel. I could walk over there through the hotel gardens. My heart was beating fast. His house displayed the irreproachable Grant taste. And his charm was even more enveloping in person than it was on the screen. At that first dinner we were six; at the second we were four; and from then on it was tête-à-tête.

I was dizzy with happiness, sharing my evenings with a sophisticated, educated, world-renowned star, a gentleman who showed genuine interest in me.

One night when I arrived, the butler showed me into the study that was also a projection room. Cary was watching *Rhapsody in Blue,* starring Robert Alda (the reviews had compared the newcomer Alda to a younger Cary Grant). A bottle of champagne later, we sat down to a small table that had been set up in the study. The film had made me lonely for France and I confided to Cary my confusion and my dilemma.

"What's happened is good," he started in. "I know it's diffi-cult for you to see it this way just now. What do you want to do? Go back to France?"

"No," I replied without hesitation. "I couldn't face it."

"All right then. What do you think you need to do?"

"I don't know."

"The first thing is to learn to speak English correctly. Ob-viously you're not making progress at the studio. I'm going to make a call and arrange for you to meet a wonderful English woman, Mrs. Gertrude Fogler. She works at MGM and in my opinion she is the best diction coach in town. And she doesn't have any problems with her digestion. She's a vegetarian. You have six months in front of you. Concentrate on your pronuncia-tion and your vocabulary. Maybe what you should do each night is to open the dictionary at random and learn the meaning of a few words before you go to sleep. You'll be surprised how fast you'll gain mastery over the English language."

"I love you, Cary," I blurted out. "You're so sweet to me. Yes, that's what I should do, and that's what I'm going to do."

I walked over to him with stars in my eyes. His kiss was ten-der. We sat down to dinner. The candles were flickering, teasing, and glowing in his pupils. I had seen a scene just like the one I was living in a movie with Katharine Hepburn and Spencer Tracy. And now I was in the same position with Cary Grant. Was I falling in love? Then came the moment when the foreplay was in need of a follow-up. But there was none. It was a new sensation for me, meeting a man who apparently did not desire me. We still had to go to Fefe's birthday. It was strange arriving with Cary on one of his rare public appearances. It was even stranger having everyone look at me thinking that Cary and I were lovers. But I could not lie when Louella Parsons came up to me and asked if I was Cary's new love.

"No," I said. "But I wish with all my heart that it could be."

We had bought Fefe a present at Tiffany's, a beautiful gold chain, with of all things, a gold toothpick at the end. To my sur-prise, gold toothpicks in 1947 were as popular as Tiffany roach holders became in the 1960s.

Returning, Cary parked his Rolls in the driveway of his house.

"I'll walk you back to the hotel through the garden," he suggested. His voice was so tender that I trembled when he linked his arm in mine. The summer rain had stopped, the earth grateful for the unexpected moisture. Cary tenderly kissed me good-by. Our "romance" was over.

From Louella Parsons' gossip about us, I became an object of attention. I became part of the "in group" at the Bel Air hotel. I was kept busy with lunches around the pool, cocktail parties, dinners, and nightclubbing and so had no time to feel lonely. Every day there was new gossip.

"Did you hear that last night Zsa Zsa Gabor was walking around the hotel in a very transparent nightgown knocking on doors and distributing her jewelry until Gogi called Conrad Hilton, whom she is divorcing?" The rumor had it that they took her to a hospital, but she was back a few days later looking as gorgeous as ever.

"And Howard Hughes was seen walking by Tony Martin's bungalow, attempting to listen. Cyd is falling hard for Tony, and Howard is offering her marriage. Did you hear the fracas that Joan Crawford created when she ran after her lover? Hitting him with her umbrella?"

The letters still arrived on schedule from Paris. Everyone was complaining of my silence. I didn't want to admit my setback, and I was faced with the impossible task of explaining all of Hollywood's unconventional behavior patterns to my ideologically rigid family.

About this time, Anita Colby, a top fashion model turned columnist, introduced me to Clark Gable in her apartment. Clark, in the late forties, was the uncontested king of Hollywood's solid citizens. Through his genuine despair at Carole Lombard's untimely death he had vastly multiplied the dedication of his fans. He was a man's man, quiet, charming, accepting the fact that Anita wanted to wait on him as he felt a woman should. He was talking about his hunting expeditions, and the deer he had killed. His description of how the animals were cornered made me want to whimper, as if I could feel the fear of the innocent, wide-eyed, confused creatures that had no preconceived idea of man as an enemy. I excused myself and left. Hunters and killers were in no way compatible with me.

There was another king in Hollywood—the King of the Bad Boys, the dashing Errol Flynn, prey for paternity suits, rape charges, and various other legal actions. His cronies had included John Barrymore, Bruce Cabot, Freddie McAvoy, all practical jokers, well known for their games and pranks.

I had been introduced to Flynn next to the swimming pool at the Beverly Hills hotel. The atmosphere was quite romantic, pink towels and tablecloths, lush, green foliage, and the man himself, his kind attentive eyes following me closely, the suntan and smell of coconut oil, his faultless French. He was a prince, strikingly handsome and almost old enough to be my young father. I was pretty much swept off my feet.

"Do you have a lover waiting for you in France?" he inquired.

"Yes. His name is Jean-Pierre."

"Tell me about him." Flynn's eyes were caressing my body.

I became animated and enthusiastic as I talked about Jean-Pierre, though his letters, sometimes three or four of them arriving in a single delivery, were now going unread until much later. I was experiencing a new world, while he was writing about an old one.

"Did you make love to him?" Flynn inquired presumptuously.

"Oh yes. He's the one who made me a real woman." I laughed self-consciously.

"How?" He smiled encouragingly.

"Well, you know. . . . I had read about how a woman is screaming and twisting when she's having a good time, and how it makes the man feel proud. I never felt anything. Even when I was with a man for the first time I felt no pain. I think I lost my virginity on the saddle of my bicycle one day when I fell down."

"Really?"

"Well, I don't quite know. I was wearing a loose dress and when I got home I had blood all over myself."

"Hmm." Flynn was nodding his head.

"Anyway, here I was with Jean-Pierre. I had met him in our acting class, and he would give me his chocolate rations every week." I proceeded to give Flynn a fairly detailed account of my love-making with Jean-Pierre. Finally he interrupted after listening with considerable fascination.

"I have to get home. A few friends of mine are coming for dinner. Why don't you go and change and come with us when we leave here?"

At the end of an elegant dinner Flynn said to his guests:

"Time to retire to the study. But not you," he whispered to me. He moved his chair closer to mine and kissed my hand, moving his lips into the niche of my elbow. He looked up, and must have seen an expression of fear on my face, fear of losing a friend I could talk to. If I let him make love to me I could never speak of Jean-Pierre again. Reacting to my fear he pulled back.

"Tell me more about your boyfriend."

"He's my fiancé," I said. "I'm hoping to bring him here as soon as I can. In the meantime he's learning how to speak English."

"Little dove, you're beautiful and sweet and, I'm afraid, faithful. If you do decide you want a lover here let me be the one."

"I . . ." I started to speak, but he was already standing.

"Let's go and join the others."

Since he respected my faithfulness, I suddenly wanted him to take me in his arms and kiss me, but I held back letting him know how I felt. So he kept his distance, and made sure no one else approached me.

Having a big star like Flynn for a friend and protector had its advantages and disadvantages, as I soon found out. He visited me frequently at the Bel Air hotel, but never came alone. He was always surrounded by a group of pals. The whole crowd adopted me as a kind of mascot, and we were on a constant merry-go-round, from restaurant to nightclub to luxurious hilltop houses. My mistakes in English were a constant source of amusement to them, but I did not feel that they were laughing at me, rather that I was making them laugh. As the evening wore on this laughter would get louder and louder, since they all drank heavily. I was in awe of the attention Errol would get when entering a public place. He had starred in so many period pictures that his public, the waiters, the maître d', the waitresses, cigarette girls and onlookers all treated him with the deference accorded to royalty.

Rarely did Flynn and his buddies take a girl anywhere. Instead, they engaged in the game of finding what they called "delicate morsels," according to their moods. Most of the time I was surrounded by four or five men.

One evening Bruce Cabot got inebriated and imposed his advances upon me. This big and powerful man had me cornered in a bedroom. I begged him to let me go. Flynn heard me and came to the rescue of a damsel in distress. He and Cabot almost came to blows, and Flynn made it very clear I was off limits for anyone in the group.

"She's our little sister. We're going to show her the big time, but we're also here to protect her from dirty minds like yours," Flynn told Cabot.

Flynn was gay, amusing, charming, and courteous. There had been tremendous amounts of gossip about him, but I never saw him being anything but a complete gentleman at all times.

One of the games Flynn's crowd played with me was to teach me American slang. They would make me repeat odd words without knowing the meaning of what I was saying. It seemed innocent enough, and they were vastly amused.

One Friday night we were all sitting at a ringside table in Mocambo's. The place was studded with celebrities. Jack Warner, the head of Warner Brothers Studio, who held Errol's contract, was sitting a few yards away. Jack was a very powerful man in the industry, and Errol's staunch enemy.

"Here's your chance, Corinne," Errol told me, "We'll teach you what to say and you can walk over and introduce yourself."

They coached me until I was ready.

"What am I going to be saying?" I asked.

"You're just telling him how important you think he is," Cabot said.

"O.K., here I go."

I approached Mr. Warner confidently and addressed him in perfect English.

"My name is Corinne Calvet. I think you're a son of a bitch, I think you stink, and that your pictures are really crap."

I delivered all this with a beautiful smile on my face. Warner's expression surprised me. I was waiting for Warner's reply when Errol came up, took my arm, and walked me back to our table.

"Good evening, Jack," he threw over his shoulder.

The laughter that welcomed us back to the table, in combination with Warner's expression, made me immediately suspicious.

"What's so funny?" I asked.

"His face when you told him," they snickered.

"Yes, why did he have that expression?"

"I bet no one ever talked to him that way before," Cabot ventured.

"What way? What did you make me say?"

"You told him what Errol never had the guts to tell him himself," Cabot went on, looking mockingly at Flynn.

Warner had summoned the maître d' to his table and they were both looking in my direction. I knew that I must have said something terrible, and ran off into the ladies' room. I was still shaking when I came out. The maître d', who was European, stopped me.

"Miss Calvet, did you really say those terribly insulting things to Mr. Warner?"

"I only said what they told me to say. What was it?"

Hesitantly, he told me. I felt myself blush.

"I can't go back in there. Tell them I went home."

The maître d' called a taxi.

I'm through. I've had it, I thought to myself. Paramount doesn't want me, and now I've alienated another big studio, Warner Brothers. I'll never work there either. Why did they make me do such a thing? I was sobbing when the phone rang. It was Gogi.

"I was passing through the hall and heard you crying. Are you all right?"

"No, I'm not. Oh please Gogi, help me."

"I'll be right over."

Gogi came and quieted me down.

"They didn't realize what they were doing to you," he said. "Maybe it's none of my business, but don't you think that group is a little too rough and wild for you?"

"I never want to see them again."

"I think you'll be better off. Why don't you try to make friends with some of the actresses at Paramount?"

"I've tried," I said. "But they're all so distant. Maybe I don't know how to make friends. I'm so lonely, Gogi. It's been almost seven months since I've seen my boyfriend. I need to be loved. I need a man's arms around me."

"That shouldn't be difficult. You can have anyone you want. You're aware of the effect you have on men."

"But I'm lonely for someone I can talk to in my own language, like I do when I'm with you."

"What happened to Cary Grant?"

"Nothing. It didn't work out." I started to cry.

"Come on now. Get into your night clothes, and get into bed. I'll order you some hot chocolate. You should go to sleep, Corinne."

My search for success, romance and understanding in Hollywood had failed. It was then, when I was totally discouraged, that I met Rory Calhoun. I was ready to fall in love but the fears, pain and disappointment that ensued were more than I could bear. My last illusion about the movie capital perished when my relationship with Rory ended. Little did I know that Rock Hudson had come between us. Henry Willson had given Rory an ultimatum: "Break up with Corinne or I'll take the young man that delivers her mail and make him a big star." (But he did anyway, starting by changing his name from Roy Fitzgerald to Rock Hudson.) I had been betrayed. I was emotionally exhausted when I decided to go back.

In one of his letters Gilbert had suggested that I bring back a luxurious American car, like a Buick or a Cadillac. He explained that after I enjoyed it for awhile myself I could sell it in France for an extravagant profit, since no American cars were being imported. I ordered a magnificent Buick Roadmaster. Arrangements were made for it to be delivered in New York so I could take it with me on the boat.

It was a beautiful, shining day. A part of me felt sad that I was leaving such a wonderful climate behind, but I found myself caught up in the excitement of returning to France and my own contemporaries. Gilbert had some picture deals lined up for me, and Jean-Pierre's letters continued to arrive with a message of solid, immovable love. The year in America had been an incredible, nightmarish experiment.

I was on my way to Paramount to pick up my last paycheck. With the top down on the Mercury, still registered to Charlie Feldman, I was driving on Sunset Boulevard. Traffic was moving at a high rate of speed, and my attention was concentrated on a series of curves that adorned the famous boulevard near the entrance to Bel Air. Suddenly the car in front of me screeched to a stop without warning. To my right was a convertible full of gay young students returning from UCLA. There must have been nine or ten of them piled up on top of each other. The brakes were out of adjustment on the Mercury, and the car pulled to the right whenever I stopped. If I brake, I thought instantaneously,

I'll run into the kids. They'll all get hurt. Lifting myself up off the seat, bracing myself with my hands against the steering wheel, I thought I would take the blow in my stomach, rather than in my chest. I crashed into the stopped car. My neck was jolted, and my head fell forward against the wheel.

I was bleeding. I heard people screaming. Someone pulled me out of the car and I was placed on the grass. I wanted to feel my bleeding face with my hands.

"No," someone said. "For Chrissake don't let her. Hold her hands down."

I could just make out a massive tree overhead protecting my motionless body from the sun's rays. I was in two places at once, and felt no pain. One of me was standing detached and curious. The other was on the ground, injured, but still alive. In the crowd around me I heard French being spoken. I opened my eyes. I was going to be all right. There in the crowd I saw the French actor Louis Jourdan standing with two women, watching me.

"Aidez moi. Aidez moi." I whispered to them.

"Allons, viens. Allons nous en, on ne veut pas être responsable d'elle," said one of the female voices. She told the others that they should not stay because they should not get involved.

At that point an hysterical woman came and stood over me. She had on a funny hat full of flowers and plastic fruit. The hat had been knocked forward. I realized that she was the driver of the car I had hit. She was screaming at me, accusing me of ruining her automobile. I wanted to get up and hit her, but somebody was holding me down. I heard sirens, piercing my ears like knitting needles. It was the last thing I remembered as I was being strapped onto a stretcher.

"Give her oxygen." I could barely make out the voice.

I woke up as I was being wheeled into an operating room.

"Doctor?" I said to a man walking near me.

"What's your name, Miss?"

"Colette?. . . . Sarah?. . . . Joan?. . . . George?. . . . I don't know," I said desperately. I started to cry.

"Don't cry," the man said. "Everything is going to be all right. We're going to fix you up."

"Doctor, my face. How bad is it?"

"Not bad, but it needs quite a few stitches."

"My face," I said. "Doctor, my face is very important. I don't know why, but please save my face."

I was engulfed by a violet cloud. My eyes closed, my body went limp. I followed the swirling spiral of bluish smoke, and entered the world of red and pink bubbles with orange hues filtering through. Abandoning resistance, I was bathed in white light.

When I woke up in a ward I started to scream. A nurse came running. My hands went to my face. I could not feel any skin. My face was covered with bandages.

"Let me have the mirror," I said.

"Now be quiet, please. We don't have one."

"Where am I?"

A doctor came in.

"Move her into an empty room for the time being," he said to the nurse.

Everyone was moving around and behaving strangely. I didn't belong. I felt caught in the middle of an unknown situation peopled by alien beings. Once I was in a private room the questioning started.

"What's your name? Where do you live? Who should we notify about your accident?"

The questions were impossible to answer. I simply didn't know. There was a vacuum in my mind, a pleasant vacuum. I was still groggy from the anesthetic, and could only mutter.

"I don't know. Leave me alone."

But they wouldn't leave me alone.

"You don't have a wedding ring on your finger. Are you married?"

"No, I don't think so." After a moment I cried out. The pain in my head had the sharpness of photographer's flashbulbs.

"Are you engaged? Where's your father?"

I didn't know, and I would not answer. I was busy looking inside myself at the feeling of pain that had now moved from my head through my throat down to my heart. It was something like black gel, a jellyfish. It was alive, and it had claws, claws like those of a bird, but it did not really have any special form. It was like an amoeba, changing, moving, gripping itself to the inside of my stomach and reaching for my heart. And each time it gripped the pain would shoot out like a milion sparks into every other part of my body. I was inside myself looking out. I was a witness to my own pain, curious and detached. I woke up alone.

"Rory," I cried out. "Rory, where are you?"

I called the nurse.

"Call Rory, please."

"Rory? Rory who? What's the number?"

"I don't know. I don't know. Give me my purse."

"We didn't find a purse with you."

"But I had my purse. I'm sure I had my purse."

For forty-eight hours I was in the throes of amnesia. The registration for the car had given the address of Charlie Feldman's office, but no one was there during the weekend. My consciousness oscillated between the reality of the moment and the illusions of my memory. Scenes passed before me. Parts of my relationship with Rory were like pieces of celluloid on an editor's reel.

On Monday, a representative of Feldman's office came to the hospital. After he left, the doctor came in and reminded me who I was. It all came back slowly. It was not long before the insurance man came to ask me questions about the accident. He gave me some papers to sign. I was still doped and dazed. As he was leaving I asked:

"Why did the woman stop?"

"She was lighting a cigarette. The match fell on her lap, and she was afraid it would catch fire."

Unaware, I signed a paper absolving the woman of all responsibility for the accident. I later found out that she was a big interior decorator in Beverly Hills, and the mother of Loretta Young.

The accident was reported in the papers. Murvyn and Gogi came to see me. Even Rory came, once alone, and once with Henry Willson. I was told by the doctor to cancel my immediate plans for returning to France. I could not move my jaw. It was broken. I was to be under the doctor's care for the next few months. I could consume only liquids. I felt sorry for myself. When I was told that I could leave the hospital I refused. I was too weak to walk. What was I going to do alone in my Westwood apartment? There was no one to take care of me there, and I didn't want to go and face the world. Here in the hospital I was safe.

Errol Flynn sent magnificent roses from Acapulco. Charlie Feldman sent a note: "Don't worry about the car, get well soon." Why did he say get well soon? What for? I didn't even know whether or not my face was going to be disfigured.

Murvyn had brought me some of my things from my apartment, and one evening I was busy taking a peek at my face by lifting some of the bandages. Suddenly I felt a hand on my shoulder. It was dark outside the hospital window.

"Come now . . . everything will be all right."

A stranger was standing by my bed, framed by the hallway lights.

"Are you a doctor?" It was still difficult for me to speak.

"No. I'm visiting my mother in the next room. You shouldn't touch your bandages."

As he turned on the nightlight I was bathed in his broad smile. He bent down gently to wipe my eyes. His hand smelled of lemon. I inhaled deeply. The hair of his forearms was like a lining of silk over his muscles. His skin was cool. Instead of resisting the touch I grabbed his hand.

"Who are you?"

"My name is John Bromfield. The nurse was telling us about your accident, and that you didn't have many visitors. So I thought . . . maybe I could visit you and offer my friendship." His eyes were sincere, large and blue green, like the ocean. He was a devoted son. He visited his mother twice a day.

He always stopped by my room, and when it was time for him to come my heart would begin to beat faster in anticipation. I found myself getting ready for his visits. I would put on perfume, and a clean nightgown. The nurse, seeing the change in me, became my accomplice, and would come and tell me when he had arrived to see his mother so I could anticipate for his visit. Closing my eyes, I would see his broad shoulders under a suede jacket that was soft as the innocence of a baby fawn. He was tall when he bent over me to rearrange my pillows. His square, solid, football neck supported his tanned face. I got great pleasure out of letting my eyes travel over his features. His chin was pocked by a dimple placed slightly to the left, a trait that gave humor to his strength. Through his almost translucent, golden skin I could see the perfect cartilage of his aquiline nose with vibrant nostrils. His ears lay close to his head, the faultless complement to his square jaw. His short hair fell low on his broad forehead, and his eyes made me feel vulnerable. They were almond shaped and immense, framed by long, black lashes and shiny dark brown eyebrows.

One day he was late.

"I have to take my mother home," he said from the door.

"Oh . . . I'm glad she's recovered," I said. I was suddenly very sad that he would no longer have a reason for coming to see me.

"Thank you. Good-by," he muttered as he left.

"Well, that's that. It would have been too good to be true," I said to the nurse.

But I was wrong. The next day he appeared at the regular time.

"Did you think I wasn't coming back?"

"I didn't think you'd have a reason," I said defensively.

"Well, that's silly. If I didn't come back, how would I ever find out whose face belongs to those magnificent blue eyes."

Worried I said, "They want me to go home. The hospital needs the room."

"It'll be all right. I'll take care of you," he said impulsively.

John took me to my apartment, cooked for me, and left only when I went to sleep. A fresh flower was on my breakfast tray each morning when I awoke. When the bandages were finally removed it was clear from the look in his eyes and the smile on his face that the accident had not altered my face.

Chapter 7

In the hospital I had reflected on the timing of my accident. It seemed to have been ordained to bar my flight. I had wanted to run away. I had wanted to quit. My relationship with Rory had crushed me. It was not long after my accident that he married and became the father of four daughters. I had not been able to find my niche in Hollywood. I had acquaintances, but no real friends. And I still yearned for the familiar, the habits and patterns of my Parisian life.

I also realized that my creative capacities had gone unused for a year, and most of what I was doing lacked any intellectual content. I had been worn thin by the adaptation I had been making to a new language, new surroundings, and an entirely new set of social elements. Since I had not been allowed to work, the source of my enjoyment in life, the lure of a possible resumption of my career in France had been attractive. I had not received the recognition and respect I expected when I came to America. Hollywood morality had clashed violently with my Catholic upbringing, and it was particularly difficult to relate to anyone when I could not command the subtleties of the language and I did not understand the behavior of the people.

Even the churches were disappointing. Their architecture made these buildings appear more like well-lit union halls than houses of God meant for meditation. I yearned for a chance to kneel in a cathedral with massive pillars and arched ceilings, whose dark niches illuminated by stained glass were more conducive to one's spiritual uplifting.

When the plastic surgeon told me that I had to stay in America for a few more months, I knew that the future was going to unfold for me, and that I was no longer in control. I was just a player. The affair with Rory had cost me my enthusiasm and determination to create my future. I told myself, not my will, God, but Thine.

John Bromfield had been a tuna fisherman when the agent Helen Ainsworth discovered him repairing nets on the Santa Monica pier. A former All-American left end at Saint Mary's College near San Francisco, he had just come back from doing his first film in Alaska, where he played a fisherman harpooning whales. Helen subsequently introduced him to Henry Willson. After a few evenings on the town, Henry asked John to join the same David Selznick acting class attended by Rory Calhoun. John had married a car hop of the famous Dolores Drive-in on Wilshire, but the marriage had been short-lived. I later learned that it had been strongly opposed by John's possessive mother. I was ignorant of all this, and found myself extremely grateful for John's doting attention. By now all my stitches were out, and I considered that we were living together, even though he did not sleep with me at night.

John proudly introduced me to Helen Ainsworth, who was to be responsible for my success in Hollywood. A deeply spiritual person, Helen was a Christian Scientist with a heart of gold and an unshakable and sincere devotion to her "children," as she referred to her clients. During the first week after I signed with her she obtained an MGM contract for me, and it was decided to return to the original spelling of my name. Once again I was Corinne Calvet.

It was a strange contract. It started with a three-month period during which the studio would shoot a test of me directed by one of their top directors. At the end of three months they had an option to pick me up for the following seven years, while I had the right not to accept their offer unless the studio specified by name two pictures in which I was to star during the first year.

There was an imposing woman in the talent department of MGM named Lillian Burns. She helped me choose the scene for the test, and wanted me to play a young, dramatic virgin. I resisted the idea because my friends Diana Lynn and Mona Freeman were always complaining about how monotonous and restricting it was to be typecast as inexperienced young women. They were afraid that as they grew older they would have no acting future. So I announced my desire to play some sort of vixen. Lillian Burns came up with the scene in which Lana Turner had gained recognition as a movie siren.

Lana and I had met at the home of director Anatole Litvak in Malibu, where Lana was living with Tyrone Power. Given my fascination with male beauty, I was completely awed by Power's looks, the melodious smoothness of his speech, and the continuous flow of his movements, as if life for him was a ballet. At dinner Ty asked me to sit by him, instigating Lana's jealousy. After dinner was over, Ty had me in his spell as he whispered provocatively:

"It's very warm in here, isn't it? Would you like to take a walk with me on the terrace?"

Before I could answer, Lana broke in between us.

"Anyone for hot coffee?" she asked, touching the silver pot to my bare shoulder. Had she willfully burned me? I had no intention of trying to take Ty away from her, and she had sufficiently frightened me that I tried not to be alone with him the rest of the evening. But he was insistent so I left early.

The day of the screen test I got up at 5 A.M. and was due at the MGM studio department at 6:45. Since I was to be in front of the cameras taking my first positive step toward success in America, I wanted to go to confession in an effort to feel clear of any past "sins." I rang the bell at the side entrance of the church. After a while, a very young priest came to the door. My request surprised him. Soon I had finished my confession, ending by saying that I was living with John. There was a long silence. Then the priest told me that I had to tell John I could no longer live with him, and that I must also promise God I would no longer have sex with John until we were married.

"That's impossible," I said.

"I cannot give you absolution unless you do."

I was getting angry.

"If I could break up with John that easily, then I obviously can't be in love with him. And if I'm not in love with him, then going to bed with him would be a sin," I told the priest.

"Pray, my daughter, for forgiveness." He was mumbling something in Latin.

"Do you mean to tell me that if I promised, and then was weak enough to break my promise, you'd forgive my sins?"

"It is your intention right now that counts."

"My intention right now is to go on with my future and my life, without the blessing of the church."

I crossed myself and left, leaving behind many moralistic rules that had been part of my behavior.

Vincente Minnelli had been chosen as my director, and it was the most rewarding day I had spent in Hollywood, the kind I had dreamed about. I knew I was in good hands, and I knew I was more than good. Minnelli, who was married to Judy Garland at that time, brought their daughter Liza, then a toddler, to the set accompanied by her nurse. We all went to lunch together, and Liza and I found a great deal to talk about. In my dressing room I had a toy bear that John had brought me as a mascot for the test. Donald Duck was also presiding on my table. Liza understood why I would have such friends.

"What about you? Do you have any companions like that?" I asked.

"No." she said. "But I have all kinds of dolls, lots of them."

"Don't you have a duck, a bear, or a sheep?"

"No," she answered, her forehead drawing into a frown.

I bent down to kiss her. It was time for me to go back to the set. A few days later I went to Uncle Bernie's in Beverly Hills, and in this beautiful toy shop I found what my heart knew would fill Liza's life with the kind of companionship I enjoyed from my animals. The store delivered my gift to the Minnelli home, accompanied by a note asking her to thank her daddy for directing me with such sensitivity.

Years later I saw Liza on a television talk show with Gina Lollobrigida. Liza turned to Gina and related the story of how she had received the toy animal, and how sweet and kind Gina had been to her as a little girl. The expression of complete incredulity that swept over Gina's face was unmistakable; she said nothing in denial. Even if I did not get credit for the gesture, I had the satisfaction of knowing that it had been appreciated and remembered.

The test was a success. I was the talk of the lot. But MGM was going through some head office changes. The head of the Paramount publicity department in New York, Dore Schary, had just been offered the job as head of production at MGM. Schary was the man who had changed my name from Calvet to Calvay, and

I'm sure he remembered my unhappy reaction. Since he would not assume his new position for three months, no one wanted to make any interim decisions. As a result, I was told that my test was great but they were not going to pick up my option.

Helen immediately asked MGM if she could show the test to another producer. The answer was negative. The test had been held back, and was not shown. That meant that the combined efforts of Minnelli, the cameraman, myself, and the whole crew were in vain. Helen was not easily deterred. She contacted a film cutter friend at MGM who gave her a print of my test to be kept in her safe until needed, and needed it was. Hal Wallis had announced that he was starting production on a star-studded film, *Rope of Sand,* an epic concerned with greed and rapacity in the diamond mines of South Africa. Burt Lancaster, Claude Rains, Paul Henreid, Sam Jaffe, and Peter Lorre had already been cast. A number of foreign stars were under consideration for the female lead.

Helen had established good relations with Hal Wallis when she presented John Bromfield as another handsome Burt Lancaster type. Wallis signed John to a contract after seeing the test John had done for the lead in *Samson and Delilah,* directed by the great Cecil B. De Mille. Of course Wallis had his own reasons for wanting John under contract, and had outsmarted Helen in this transaction, which was ultimately to do John great harm. As soon as Wallis signed John, De Mille lost interest. The genius who had built Paramount was not about to use his resources to build up a young star who was under contract to someone else. Helen had thought that since Wallis's productions were using the same lot, release, and studio facilities, an arrangement could easily have been made for sharing John Bromfield's contract. Did Wallis want to eliminate Bromfield as a rival to Lancaster, in whom he had invested a great deal of money? It definitely would have been to Wallis's disadvantage to have another star of similar character appear so suddenly on the horizon. Bromfield as Samson, with the resources of De Mille behind him, could have been a threat to Lancaster's future. Anyway, with a two-hundred-and-fifty-dollar-a-week contract Wallis eliminated that possibility. John lost the part of Samson to Victor Mature.

When Wallis saw my test, he wanted me for *Rope of Sand.* But we had to wait three more weeks before I was totally free of my

MGM contract. I applied to the Department of Immigration for a six month extension on my visitor's visa, noting that I had been unable to work for the three months it took for my face to heal from the accident. To everyone's surprise the extension was denied. Wallis had already announced that I would be the female star in *Rope of Sand,* and after pulling a lot of strings we discovered that someone had written a letter to Washington questioning my association with the political existentialist element in France, and expressing doubt about my worth as an American citizen. It was not surprising for several reasons. Recently ten of the leading film-makers in the industry had been convicted of contempt of Congress because of their testimony before the House Un-American Activities Committee. They were given the maximum sentence and blacklisted by the industry; after their release from prison, some were forced to go abroad, while others managed to obtain work in Hollywood under false names. In such an atmosphere rumors, gossip, or a letter such as the one sent about me could be very damaging. I tried to establish in my mind who had done such a thing, and began to realize that I had put Paramount Studios in a very embarrassing position. Wallis, an independent producer at Paramount, proposed to make a star out of someone the studio had declared to have no future in Hollywood. I had originally been signed by New York Paramount, and discarded by Hollywood Paramount. The Department of Immigration told me that I had to return to France for six months, and then I could again apply for entry into the United States after clearing myself of all questionable associations. That would mean the loss of the picture. Everyone suggested that I marry an American and obtain an automatic visa. The obvious solution was to marry John Bromfield, but John had been very definite. No marriage for him. Even my refusal to see him again had brought no change in his attitude.

As a possible solution, Helen introduced me to a homosexual lawyer who had political ambitions and wanted to use a widely publicized marriage to dispel gossip about his sexual preferences. I admired the man for his intelligence. He was a charming host, elegant and dignified, who suggested that I could have boyfriends, since he had his. It would be a classic marriage of convenience. I yearned for someone to make the decision for me, as I could not in my heart take the responsibility for deliberate deceit.

Still, I had to do something. It had been suggested that it was possible to marry someone for only a few months, give them a thousand-dollar fee, and then get a divorce. The marriage would not be consummated. It was illegal, but if my husband and I received mail at the same address, nothing could be proven, or so claimed the sleazy attorney who offered this solution. The whole thing was inconceivable. Marriage to me was a commitment. I couldn't make up my mind. I believed that if I was meant to remain in Hollywood and do Wallis's film the right opportunity would appear, and a part of me knew that whatever happened it would be perfect for me. I must not interfere with my destiny and the lessons I was going to learn.

My mind was in turmoil. I was wrestling with the problem when John Bromfield burst in with his proposal of marriage.

"Corinne," he said excitedly. "I don't want you to have to go back to France. I need you. I love you. Pack some clothes. Let's go to Las Vegas and get married."

"What are you saying?" I was shocked at his reversal.

"I'm asking you to marry me."

"Can't you be a little more romantic about it?" I said softly, still reacting to the surprise. "Aren't you nervous about your mother's threat?" His mother had threatened to kill herself if her son married a foreigner.

"Leave my mother out of it."

"How can I? She's going to be my mother-in-law. Have you talked to her?"

I waited, but he said nothing.

"I'm sure she was exaggerating," I offered.

"I'm not calling her until it's done," he said with considerable agitation.

"Are you sure it's what you want?"

"Yes. I'll go pack a suitcase. We'll drive all night and be there in the morning."

"Darling, I'm so happy." At last I accepted the fact that it was really going to happen. I needed to find someone to protect me. It was going to be John. So why did I feel uneasy?

What made John reverse his position, and why was he in such a hurry? He is taking over, unafraid of his mother's threats, I thought. He is going to override his mother in a way that none of my previous lovers have been able to do. First there was André, whose mother did not want to share her son with another woman, and then Jean-Pierre, whose mother saw me as unsuitable for her son because I wasn't a Communist. My uneasiness turned into trepidation.

I looked through my closet. There was a blue suit I had worn only a few times before the accident. John had never seen it. It would have to do. I found a hat to match, and was ready when John returned.

As we started the long drive I began to repeat gently to myself, "I love him, I love John, no one else is as sweet as he is, he's handsome, he loves me. I'm grateful to him, God bless him, I love him, I love John, no one else. . . ." I kept the refrain going as long as I could. By the time we got to Barstow, the halfway point between Los Angeles and Las Vegas, we were too tired to drive further. John took a room in a motel. He became irritated with me when a strange shyness overtook me. I did not want him to see me undress the night before our wedding. Even if I was only going to be chaste for one day, I wanted to feel that I was giving myself to him on our wedding night. I wanted him to take two rooms. Sleeping with him now would be bad luck.

"That's crazy, Corinne."

"I won't have it any other way." I was insistent.

By the time we arrived in Vegas the next morning I had tried unsuccessfully to repeat my refrain. To no avail. It was not working. John now refused to be married in a Catholic church, and I would not allow our union to be sealed in one of the artificial, tinsel chapels of Las Vegas. We decided that we would go to the small town of Boulder City and find a protestant minister.

In the Nevada heat, the land undulated with mirages. The sun beat down mercilessly on our speeding car. Telephone wires wailed like tea kettles.

"Don't do it . . . don't do it . . . don't do it . . . don't do it." The sound was overpowering.

"Did you say something, John?" I asked.

"No," he answered, his forehead dripping.

I squinted. In the distance, wavering in the heat, was a gray stone mass. A small figure dressed in a laboratory apron stood in front of what now looked like a replica of the Pasteur hospital in Paris.

"John, please stop the car."

He complied, and I got out. Running toward the mirage I did not feel my feet touching the ground. A gust of wind swirled around like the hot breath of a dragon about to engulf me. I felt faint. I recognized Madame Curie as the apparition faded away. I collapsed to the ground. The sizzling sand felt like burning coals through the cloth of my light blue gabardine suit. Dazed, I returned to the car.

"Did you have to go to the bathroom?" John asked.

I shook my head.

Driving in silence I was lost in thought. What was the meaning of Madame Curie's appearance? I need this marriage, I told myself. John is the kindest man I've met in America, and I yearn to have a family.

"Yes," I heard a voice in my head say sarcastically. It was Madame Curie. "His parents are a mother who hates you, and a weak, broken-hearted father. You know she's a hypochondriac, controlling both her son and her husband with her imaginary malaises."

"It's still better than being married to a homosexual lawyer," I protested, continuing the inner dialogue.

"At least your heart wouldn't be involved in that."

The minister's wife served as our witness. Putting aside my romantic ideas about a big wedding, we said the words that made me Mrs. John Bromfield.

After dinner at the minister's house we drove to a motel at the edge of Boulder Lake. The room reserved for us there had no room service, was depressing, and smelled rancid. Without a word we went back to the car and drove to Las Vegas. I lay with my head cuddled on my husband's shoulder, and abandoned myself to the happiness swelling in my chest. I was married to a handsome young actor. I was about to star in a film in which I was to be the only female surrounded by five of the top box office stars.

We checked in at the Flamingo, and the staff of the hotel found out that we were honeymooners. Two bottles of champagne had been placed in our room, along with fifty silver dollars.

"Look," John said, pointing to the money on the table, "let's go try our luck."

In the dining room, we were soon recognized. Danny Thomas sang a wedding song for us while John was being very attentive and tender. Photographers had a field day. We had been up early, however, and I wanted to go to bed. But the silver dollars were burning holes in John's pockets. He began to gamble. After he lost the money the casino had given us, he went for some more. I was bored and crushed at the prospect of spending the first night of my honeymoon at the roulette table. Finally back in our room, I complained. We argued, then made up; by then the dawn had come. We fell asleep in each other's arms without completing the marital rites.

When we arrived back in Los Angeles we were surrounded by friends and well-wishers. Hal Wallis joined the festive mood by sending me my contract as a wedding present. John's mother had not committed suicide when she learned of our marriage, and John's father turned out to be surprisingly supportive and friendly, always ready to explain and take my side.

The shooting for *Rope of Sand* began on location in the Nevada desert. The sand dunes were so wide, tall, and virginal that it was easy to imagine that we were indeed in Africa. John had a small part as one of the guards of a diamond mine, and we were happy to be on location together. John was a loving, devoted husband, and for the first time I felt really secure.

When we returned to Los Angeles, John was immediately sent out to another location. This time Wallis cast him in a larger part, in a film called *The Furies*, starring Barbara Stanwyck and Walter Huston. John was to play the emasculated son of Walter Huston, a father who had been so disappointed in his son's lack of manly qualities that he had raised his daughter as a tomboy. I was surprised by Hal Wallis's choice of John for the role, because the script described the character as a young Leslie Howard type. Nevertheless, with tears in my eyes and joy in my heart, I said good-by to John one morning. He was going to be away ten days. Since they were shooting scenes in *Rope of Sand* in which I did not appear, I asked to be allowed to go on location with John. But I was told by the production staff that I must be available to report for my film on short notice in case the schedule changed.

That afternoon after I phoned John in Arizona I looked around the apartment and began making plans to redecorate. I took an extended bubble bath to contemplate the changes I wanted to make in the decor. I decided I would make the place more masculine to accommodate John's presence. Dressed in a hostess gown, I lit candles and danced alone to soft music filtering through the radio.

I was having fun imagining how different areas in the room would look. I tried positions, searching for the right light and pose to be the most desirable wife in the world. The doorbell rang as I lay with my hair spread out on the soft rug.

"Who is it?"

"Your boss, Hal Wallis."

Wallis? At this hour? It was 8 P.M. My God. Had something happened to John? That's silly. The tone in Wallis's voice does not sound like bad news. Am I decent? Better close a few more buttons on my outfit. I opened the door.

"May I come in?" Wallis said, pushing past me. "Very nice. Very nice indeed. Expecting someone?" His eyes were taking in my gown.

"No, no." I said.

"You mean you look like this even when you're alone and not expecting anyone?"

"Well, no. Not really. It's just that I was trying some positions."

"Trying what?" he exclaimed, taking off his coat.

"I'm going to change the apartment around to please John. I was looking for positions that would be nice for cozy evenings."

"Show me one," Wallis said with a quizzical half-smile.

"Well," I hesitated.

"Come on, show me."

"Okay, you sit here as John would. Put your feet up there." I pointed to an ottoman. "Now I'll sit right here." I was sitting on the floor, my hair flowing smoothly on the sofa, my head tilted, looking up at him.

"That is a beautiful position," he said. "Show me another one."

"Earlier, I was working on the one I would take when I want to tell John that dinner is served." I was leaning against the dining room door frame. Looking mischievous, I pointed to another chair.

"John will be sitting over there." Then I cleared my voice and said in a deep sexy tone, "Dinner is served. Do you like that?" I asked Wallis.

"Do I like it?" His voice was choked. He was suddenly next to me, pushing me against the wall. I was totally unprepared for his passionate attack. His hand reached inside my negligee for my breast.

"Stop," I protested. "What are you doing?"

"What comes naturally."

"But Mr. Wallis, please, you don't understand. John and I, we love each other."

"Oh come on, Corinne. It was nothing but a marriage of convenience for you both."

"It was not," I protested defiantly.

"You have a short memory," he said crisply. "You needed a visa. I told him that if the marriage took place at once I would not lose my star, and my star would fare better with a husband under contract. I convinced him that it was to everyone's advantage that the marriage take place."

"You did what?" A wave of shame swept over me.

"Get out of here." I spat the words at Wallis.

Wallis moved toward me. I ran past him and locked myself in the bathroom. Panting, I waited until I heard the front door close. He left without saying a word. I wanted to scream. I hurled my body to the floor and banged the linoleum with my clenched fists. I sat with my head leaning against the cold toilet bowl.

"Jean-Pierre, why did you let me go?" "I hate all men. I hate them. I hate them."

From Arizona I received a love letter from John. In six days he would be back. I decided to wait to tell him in person what Wallis had said, but the venom was eating at my insides. Then the studio called to tell me that John was returning that evening and was going to be replaced, since the director had decided that he was wrong for the part. John was going to come back depressed. Was it Wallis's revenge for my rejection of him? And why was I feeling guilty? I decided to keep silent.

John came back confused and broken.

"The only thing I have is your love," he said sadly.

He was waiting for me each day when I came home from the studio, and would bring a chilled martini to me in the bathtub while I was removing my make-up. Lighted candles were on the table and dinner was ready when I emerged, refreshed and totally indulged by my doting husband. I decided to forgive John in silence, but my hurt and disappointment had to find some channel for expression. I chose Hal Wallis, and began to build in myself an equally silent hatred for the man who had so heartlessly shattered my romantic illusions.

Early one morning on the set of *Rope of Sand* we began shooting a scene in which Burt Lancaster and I had to share an intimate moment. It was in his hotel bedroom, decorated with the typical furnishings of an English tropical colony, bamboo screens, and a slow-moving ceiling fan. Up to this point we had been shooting exteriors that included lots of action. This scene was the first that would really test my talent as an actress. I had rehearsed the scene with John, but I was nervous. I knew the camera would be very close.

Lancaster was lying on the bed, heavily bandaged. In the script he had been whipped by the police chief, Paul Henreid. I was to nurse him, changing his bandages while we exchanged some important dialogue that would further the development of the plot. We rehearsed a few times and it went well.

"Okay, Burt, take your shirt off," William Dieterle, the director, ordered. "We're ready to shoot."

We were back in position for the start of the scene. I began to perspire. I felt nauseous. Suddenly the food I had eaten that day started to churn in my stomach. I had to kneel beside Burt and lay one side of my face on his bare back. We went through the scene once. I tried to ignore what was happening to me, thinking it was pure nervousness at playing such an important part in a big movie with a big star like Burt. But to my everlasting humiliation, in the middle of the second take, my stomach turned and I threw up, all over Burt Lancaster! I was mortified. I wanted to die right there.

"Oh, I'm sorry," I whimpered.

I ran off quickly to the bathroom outside the set. What am I going to do? I thought. I can't go back and face everybody.

"Miss Calvet? Are you in there?" It was a woman's voice.

"Yes," I answered.

"Are you all right? What happened?"

"The heat, the excitement, and the food I ate today, maybe it gave me food poisoning?"

"Come," she said. "Don't stay in there. Let's walk back to your dressing room. You can lie down there for awhile." After the woman left, I lay on a very uncomfortable sofa in the portable dressing room, and it was not long before the assistant director came in with the studio doctor.

"Doctor, please report on the set whatever you find," the assistant director said before leaving. Then as an afterthought he whispered, "Don't worry, Miss Calvet, they're shooting around you for the time being."

The doctor's questions were all slanted in one direction. "How long have you been married? When was the last time you had a period? Are your breasts sensitive? What kind of precautions do you take with your husband?"

"What are you trying to say, doctor? I'm not pregnant. Didn't they tell you? I threw up because of the heat and some bad food."

"Let me have your arm. I want to take some blood," the doctor announced, ignoring what I had said.

"Why?"

"For a pregnancy test."

I moved away from him.

"Mr. Wallis has a lot of money invested in this film. He wants to be sure you'll be in shape to finish it."

"I have very small veins, doctor. It's almost impossible to draw blood. Isn't there another way to reassure him?"

"It's the best way."

When he was finished I was told I could go home.

"I don't have to. I feel much better now. I want to go back to work."

"They're busy shooting another scene. They won't need you. You're dismissed for the day."

Dismissed? What did that mean? It did not mean missing, since they were sending me away. I did not understand the meaning of the prefix "dis." But it must have meant something serious, I concluded, because I didn't hear from them again for three days.

John was in the driveway watering the jasmine blossoms when I drove up.

"Oh baby," I whispered, "pick me up and carry me around for awhile. I'm so embarrassed."

"Calm down. What happened?" John lifted me in his arms.

"We were rehearsing a scene in which I was changing Burt Lancaster's bandages. He was lying down and I was bending over him." I quickly reviewed the events for John. "I threw up all over him . . . the camera was still rolling. Everyone was stunned. I ran off the set and hid in the bathroom." I was both crying and laughing. John laid me down on the bed.

"Do you want some tea?"

"No, but please don't leave me. They sent for the doctor to take some blood for a pregnancy test."

"You did wear your diaphragm every time, didn't you?"

"Yes. You wanted me to," I said, frowning.

"I hope you put it in right." John's voice was stern. "It would be disastrous if you were pregnant. No more career. No *Rope of Sand.*"

"I'm not pregnant," my voice rose defensively.

"Let's not discuss it. As long as we don't have to face the expense of an abortion. Why don't you close your eyes and sleep for awhile? I'll go and finish watering."

Expense of an abortion? What about the suffering? Left alone I became frightened. Would they replace me if I turned out to be pregnant? What if the diaphragm didn't work? Oh God, I couldn't go through with another abortion. Thinking about it caused a shot of pain to move through my ovaries. I reached for a sleeping pill. The pain I felt was the shame I had experienced when André took me to the doctor for an "examination."

I was not pregnant. No one ever mentioned the incident again. When we got around to shooting the scene that had embarrassed me, Burt Lancaster was very kind to me, and it was in earnest that I put my cheek on his skin and willed love and devotion to appear on my face. He was an imposing man. It was hard to talk to him between scenes. He was very reserved. I knew I had to make contact with him somehow. The incident itself, and the three days' vacation, had shaken me. The director's approach had made matters worse. I had a bad case of what actors call the inside shakes.

Dieterle was an autocrat. Fully enjoying his powerful position, he ran the movie set more like the Führer's headquarters than a Hollywood production company. He had always been known for wearing white gloves, and was never seen without them. There were many rumors about this quirk. Some said he had a contagious skin disease, others that he had a phobia about germs, still others that maybe he was just a complete snob, and that there was nothing wrong with him. Since no one had ever seen him eat lunch, nobody knew whether he ate with his gloves on or off. He was a great believer in astrology, and planned the starting date of his films with the aid of his astrologer. As a director, he was uncommunicative. I confided in Burt that I could not understand Dieterle's heavily accented English. Whenever I asked him to repeat he would scream at me.

"You heard him, Mr. Lancaster," I said to my co-star. "When he says 'vye dit dey gif me such a stupit actress to verk vit?' at the top of his lungs, you've got to help me. What should I do?"

"The first thing is to call me Burt."

"Burt," I smiled. "Would you be kind enough to direct me?"

The success that came to me in that picture can be attributed to Burt Lancaster's guidance. He gave me confidence. I was good and I knew it. There were nothing but smiles around me on the set when I finished a scene.

The film was completed without further difficulty. I was getting over the annoyance of having people pat my face every five minutes with a powder puff, but I couldn't adjust to the one thing that made my skin crawl, the habit the hairdressers have of sneaking up in back of you and without notice sticking a brush or comb in your hair and pulling on it. Most of the time, I feel, they just do it to look busy. I have never been able to overcome the adverse reaction I have whenever a stranger touches my hair. I've always felt it to be an unwarranted intimacy. I have rarely been a client in a beauty salon, and by the time *Rope of Sand* was finished I had become expert at using an old-fashioned curling iron.

The publicity department had been busy setting up interviews for me, and most of my lunches were spent with newspaper people asking a lot of questions. Wallis was "beating the big drum for me," as they say in the trade. Were people really interested in what I had to say? It was hard for me to believe it. But it made me feel beautiful, smart and loved, that is until I started to read how my words had been twisted to misrepresent me in print. "As long as they spell your name right," was an old Hollywood adage. Still, I was hurt by their misinterpretation of what I had tried to communicate, though I was riding the crest of success, and everything was going smoothly except for the nightmares. Ever since Hal Wallis's visit to my apartment, hate, like a venomous snake, had lain coiled in my guts. I could not understand the motives for his callous disclosure, and vengeance was the subject of my recurring dreams. I would wake up shaking, in a cold sweat over the many ways in which I envisioned eliminating him, like sending him a present that exploded when he pulled the string on the package, or finding someone to tamper with his car so that he drove it over a cliff. Sometimes I played a seduction scene with him while I put arsenic in his drink. It was dreadful. John would wake up and try to quiet me down. I couldn't tell him what it was all about, so I let him believe that I was having nightmares about the war. Then the migraines started. Aspirin gave me no relief. Nevertheless I continued to avoid questioning John about Wallis's allegations. I was afraid that if John knew that I knew, he would leave me, and I wanted to hang on to my marriage. The many months I had spent alone without male companionship, the prey of men's desires, had frightened me. The ring on my finger gave me the illusion of safety; I could not face being alone again.

I also wanted us to own a home but it was impossible, John and I were not making enough money to save for a down payment. I confided in Helen Ainsworth, and she went to Wallis about our need for a house. She returned triumphant.

"Wallis will advance you the money for a down payment. You can repay him every week out of your salary. He said he won't even charge you interest."

The nightmares full of hate were dispelled for awhile, and replaced by visions of the dream house John and I were sure to find. It never occurred to me that Wallis was tightening his hold. Going in debt to him would prevent me from turning down scripts I didn't want to do, since we would not be able to survive a suspension.

We had looked at a few unsatisfactory places when one afternoon while driving in Beverly Glen Canyon we saw a sign on a little house that looked as if it might have been inhabited by Snow White. The next morning our real estate agent rang its doorbell. We entered. I was overtaken by a feeling of reverence. It was larger than it appeared from the outside. It was perfect, two bedrooms, a small pool, a beautiful hill in back, and a double sunken living room with a huge fireplace. It was all paneled in pine.

"Would you like a drink?" the owner asked.

She reeked of the smell of Scotch. We declined.

"It's a very special house. I don't want to sell it to anyone who doesn't fall in love with it. You'll have to come back in the evening. It will look different, even more beautiful."

The early morning liquor was making her chatter loudly as she showed us through the house.

"Come and see the outside, and the little maid's room next to the garage."

While John was talking to the two ladies in the garden, I walked back into the living room. It was quiet and peaceful. I could hear a faint, high whistle. I concentrated all my energies on my sense of hearing, and suddenly I could hear a voice whispering. It was muffled. At first it was difficult to distinguish the words, but they were repeated over and over again. It was as if the vowels were resonating through a tunnel, and the consonants assumed a whistling sound.

A few seconds later the words became clearer.

"Buy the house. Buy the house. We need you. Buy the house."

A chill was running up and down my spine. I was filled with an uncanny pleasure. I was needed. I had never experienced anything quite like this before. When the others returned I was in a daze, with a smile on my face.

John turned to me in the car as we drove away.

"Do you like it?"

"We have to have it."

"But they want more than the studio said they would lend us."

"So we'll go and get another loan at a bank."

"Well, if you want the house I guess it's yours. You always get what you want, little monkey, don't you?"

I was silent.

"You wanted me, and you got me."

"Do I really have you, John?" Wallis's cruel disclosure again crossed my mind.

"You got me, hook, line and sinker. Come on, let's go surf fishing tonight."

Fishing had become our most usual pastime. John would drag me out of bed at five in the morning on days when I didn't have to go to the studio. We'd find ourselves in a greasy coffee shop on the pier. John would talk to all his fishing buddies, and then it would be time to get on the boat, where my stomach would be put to the test. I didn't really enjoy fishing, but as a wife I wanted to do what my husband wanted. Sacrificing the pleasure of my warm bed to be a companion to my husband seemed a small price to pay.

Before the New Year began we were ready to move into the Beverly Glen house. John carried me over the threshold. The studio made all the financial arrangements. I had gone to pose for pictures for a furniture manufacturer who, in return for the advertisement, provided me with our choice of sofas, chairs, tables, and a dining room set. I obtained the carpet in the same manner. It may be that I have to take the blame for being the first woman to lie in a negligee on a deep pile carpet. In return, our house was carpeted from wall to wall in a light beige, fluffy, bouncy carpet.

For our bed we ordered a seven-by-seven-foot extravaganza. King-sized beds were not yet popular, and this one was our prize possession. I made a leopard velveteen bedspread and hung red drapes, which were reflected in the mirrored walls. Every day I would lie back, surrounded by my stuffed animals. Holding Donald, my toy duck, I would review my blessings.

We had a car, a house, and a mortgage. We had friends. But there was something missing. John had made it clear that he did not want children, not yet. Black cocker, spaniels were in vogue that year, and so we got one. Skippy, our sweet black cocker appeared in all the photographs in the movie magazines.

We settled down to be an ordinary American couple. The maid who had cleaned the apartment in Westwood became our full-time domestic. I refused to allow anything to bother me. I constantly walked around the house offering silent thanks to the voice that had told me that I was to live in this house. We were a handsome young couple. The press loved us, and we loved the press.

Our first New Year's Eve together, John had accepted an invitation for us to go to Venice and celebrate with his commercial fishing buddies. The small duplex in which the party was being given was decorated with lots of garlands and letters that spelled out "Merry Christmas" and "Happy New Year." The bathtub in the minuscule bathroom was filled to the brim with beer bottles in melting ice.

"So you're in the movies," said a bosomy blonde in a black

satin skirt that showed her legs, the fat bulging out through her mesh stockings.

I attempted a smile, and nodded my head silently.

"Hey, do you know Burt Lancaster?" She didn't wait for my answer. "Well, I tell you honey, I love my guy, but if Burt whistled for me I'd be ready to jump on his bones." She accentuated her statement with a tap on the silly, shiny hat perched on her head.

"Whistle? That's Humphrey Bogart," I heard myself say.

"Bogart's not bad, honey, but that Lancaster, I tell you."

"What does jump on his bones mean?" I was frowning.

"It means going to bed and going around the world. Hey Alex," she screamed to a man across the room. "Come over here."

A big man with huge biceps and a Christmas ball hanging from his ear on a thread swayed toward us. He pinched the cheek of a woman as he passed.

"Beautiful, you look beautiful, babe," he said, speaking to the bosomy blonde.

"You don't look too bad yourself. Hey, I always knew you had more than two balls." Her laughter was raucous.

"Alex," she said. "I want you to meet Corinne. She's John's new wife. She's in the movies, and guess what? She's going to introduce me to Burt Lancaster."

"John didn't do too bad this time," Alex said, looking me up and down, appreciating the merchandise. "I wish you would introduce her to that trapeze artist so I could dump her on him," he said to me. "I'd have myself the time of my life with a few numbers I have in reserve."

"Oh yeah?" the blonde said, removing the Christmas ball from his ear, dropping it to the floor, and stamping on it until it was reduced to a powder.

"And that's what I'll do to yours."

Slapping her loudly on her generous behind, he pushed her toward the bathroom.

"They're making boilermakers. C'mon sweetie, let's get good and stinko tonight."

I was left alone feeling totally lost. A very tall man with a gaunt face, wrinkled from exposure to the sea, walked languidly over to me.

"Hi," he said. "My name's Joe."

"Where is John? I can't see him."

"He's probably outside, telling fish stories." His smile revealed a huge set of teeth. Two of the upper ones were missing, and a lower was broken in two.

Stupefied and fascinated by the broken tooth, which seemed to be moving closer to my face as if to bite me, I put my hand on his shoulder to arrest his forward movement.

"That broken tooth, doesn't it hurt you?"

"Sometimes," he said. "But it's nothing that a little brandy gargle won't cure."

"I must find John, I don't feel well," I said softly.

"All right, lady. Stand behind me, put your hands around my waist, and let's go. Like the prow of a boat I'll guide you through this sea of humanity."

John was outside near a large barrel that had gathered rain water. He was holding up a girl who was giggling while she washed her foot.

"Marylise stepped in some dog doo doo while she was trying to catch me," John was laughing.

"Why was she trying to catch you?" I asked.

"Because the son of a bitch had a big, hot date with me, and he never showed up, never returned my calls," she said, removing her foot from the barrel and letting John put her down.

I watched as she reached for an empty glass, filled it with water from the same barrel, and threw it in my husband's face. John was laughing, wiping himself with his shirt sleeves.

"I deserved that, Marylise. Now let me introduce you to my wife, the reason I never called."

"Oh," said Marylise, nodding her head. "I see. Well I can't blame you John. She is a beauty, and I hear she talks with a French accent. *Voulez-vous coucher avec moi?*" she said with a big smile.

"You like women too?" I grinned. "John, I must speak to you. Excuse us." I took his arm, and walked him a few steps into the yard."

"We must leave," I said. "I feel sick. I can't stand this place another minute."

"No," John stated firmly. "I haven't seen my friends in months. We must stay."

"John, you don't understand. These people frighten me. I feel like I'm living in a nightmare."

"That's not a very nice way to talk about my friends."

"John, please," I pleaded.

"Wait here," he said. "I know what will fix you up."

He came back with a large glass of whisky.

"Drink it."

"No."

"All the way. It's New Year's Eve."

Giving in, I complied.

"John, what time is it?"

"Eleven."

"If we left now we could be together in our house to welcome the New Year."

"No, it's too much fun here, you'll see. They really make a racket, with horns and everything. It's very American."

"Could we leave right after midnight?" I asked weakly.

"Okay, if you're going to be a spoilsport."

The bourbon was warming my guts.

"Let's go back inside." John pushed me ahead of him.

I found a safe place in a corner, and watched incredulously from a position of relative security.

"It's almost midnight," a booming voice finally announced. "6-5-4-3-2-1. . . . Happy New Year!"

Everyone had grabbed noisemakers, and the cacophony poured into my ears like water out of a cracked dam. I heard myself scream, "Enough, enough!" My eyes searched for John. He was nowhere in sight.

The whole house suddenly went black. There was total silence. A man grabbed me and planted a wet kiss on my face. Holding my head strongly in his hand, he forced his tongue into my mouth. Stupefied, I stood frozen when he let me go. Someone else grabbed me, and my indignation mounted as the same affront was perpetrated. The third mouth to violate my privacy was different. It was that of a woman.

"Sorry, honey, my mistake."

I dropped to the floor as my eyes became accustomed to the darkness. I crawled between legs to the safety of the yard. I wiped my face and spat out my disgust. Trembling with rage, I walked to our car and waited there. When the lights came on again in the house I hid behind a tree. Alienated, I waited. John came out, looking for me. I called to him.

"Over here," I said. "Open the car door; we must go home."

"Okay, I'll be right back. I just have to go and say good-by."

I fell asleep, and woke up as John braked to miss a car. We were silent the rest of the way. It was the last time I ever went with John to visit his Venice friends.

When we got home I locked myself in the bathroom. I was contemplating the gulf in education, taste, sensibility, and values that separated me from my husband when I heard him call out.

"Let's celebrate the New Year in bed. C'mon, for Chrissake hurry up. Oooh, la la," he slurred.

I stayed longer in the bathroom, hoping he would fall asleep. But, beer in hand, he was watching television, waiting for me.

"John, no, don't touch me."

"I'm sorry, little monkey. My friends are a little rough, I must admit. Let's make it, so you can forget the whole thing."

"No John. I don't want to forget."

Chapter 8

Rope of Sand opened at the Paramount theater in New York. The reviews were everything Hal Wallis could have hoped for. He had discovered another star.

In the darkness of the movie theater the audiences fell in love with the radiance illuminating the screen. Hollywood's French import was the perfect image for postwar fantasies. For ex-GIs I was the girl they might have met in France. For women I was the figure of mystery and intrigue they all aspired to be. Men saw my vital energy as barely concealed sexuality. To women the appeal was fragile innocence. To me it was the beginning of my public existence in America, an existence that brought stardom, excitement, trauma, indignity, some humor, and pain. Fan mail poured in from both sexes. To the studio executives it was a sure sign of success.

The great minds in charge of my future decided to send me on the road to publicize the picture. It was the fastest way to establish a public following. Nothing could ever replace direct contact with the newspapermen, radio stations, film distributors and fans the star met in each city while appearing at the opening of a film. I was summoned to Wallis's office. I found a pianist waiting for me.

"Can you sing, Corinne?" Wallis inquired.

"No, not really."

He was not deterred. "Well, let's hear you anyway."

I only knew two songs. One was a French children's song about a woman who had lost her cat, and the other was "How Deep Is the Ocean," a song associated with Frank Sinatra. I ran through these two numbers as best I could, wondering why it was necessary to go through this embarrassment. I could not believe the response. The men in Wallis's office loved me. They must have been kidding. I thought I sounded horrible and out of tune.

I was given four songs to learn and a pianist who rehearsed with me twice. John then accompanied me to New York where I was to appear with the film at the Paramount theater on Broadway. I would be onstage with the twenty-five piece orchestra of Tex Beneke. Two weeks prior to my arrival the film had opened with Vic Damone headlining the stage show. Vic was present when I began to rehearse at ten in the morning. The musicians did not look too happy about the hour, and I stood on the immense stage of the Paramount with little enthusiasm of my own. The empty house looked like the dark, open mouth of a giant monster. Lighted exit signs were the edges of the beast's teeth. My toes started to shake. I couldn't control my nerves. My anxiety was overpowering. The shakes rapidly gained ground, moving up my legs, reaching my knees. I gathered all of my energies and sent them downward in my body to block the advance of the tremors, but my feet continued to pulsate at a rapid rhythm. Beneke introduced me to the orchestra. They grumbled something in return, making no effort to hide their annoyance.

"Let's start with 'I'm Always True to You Darling in My Fashion.'" Beneke suggested.

They started to play. Not even recognizing the tune, I was dumbfounded, my mouth open, listening intently. I thought that perhaps the arrangement had an unusually long introduction, but for the life of me I could not hear the melody the pianist had played when I learned it. Beneke stopped.

"Where do I start?" I asked innocently.

His eyes opened wide, but he recovered quickly.

"I'll signal you. Ready?"

I nodded. The orchestra started again. He gestured for me to start.

"There's a man in Abilene. . . ." I began.

"Stop!" Beneke's hand went up. "Miss Calvet, this arrangement is written in C."

Now it was my turn to be baffled. I had no idea what he meant.

"Hit it Peter, please."

The piano played the melody. Now I could hear the tune, but I couldn't understand why it sounded so weird.

"C," Beneke encouraged.

The pianist repeatedly hit a note. I was trying, searching to hit the same tone, but to no avail.

"Well," said Beneke, shrugging his shoulders "Let's try anyway."

I sang, and rapidly advanced to the chorus. The orchestra was so loud that I could not hear myself. It was strange to be making bodily motions, knowing what I was saying as I felt the tension in my vocal chords, but unable to hear the sound of my own voice. I felt like a puppet.

Suddenly things changed. I was singing alone. The orchestra had stopped.

"Miss Calvet. Could you follow the beat?" Beneke asked hopefully.

"The beat? What's that?"

With an expression of complete disbelief on his face, his eyes bulging out, Beneke walked off the stage. The musicians put down their instruments. I walked over to John.

"What's wrong?" I asked.

"Nothing that can't be fixed," my husband replied reassuringly.

"I don't want to sing. I can't sing. Tell them."

I was crying. Vic Damone, who had witnessed all this in silence, came over and introduced himself.

"Look, the orchestra is taking a break. I listened to you. I think you can sing. Why don't we go over your song now?" Vic's voice was warm and encouraging.

"Vic," said the pianist. "This arrangement is in C, and Miss Calvet sings in B flat. Look at the name scratched out on the top of the page. It was done for Betty Hutton originally."

I was in the dark about all that, but John and Vic exchanged knowing glances.

"What is it?" I asked.

"Betty Hutton's arrangements are not in your key." John put his arm around my shoulder.

"Well, it can be changed." Vic was nodding to the pianist.

By now it was eleven-thirty. The first show began in an hour. The stage had to be cleared and I had to dress and put on my make-up. With Vic's pianist we just had time to run through the four songs in my own key. Everyone was smiling. In the correct key I was a pleasant surprise to the sensitive ears of the other musicians.

"She is going to be all right," I heard someone say.

The theater was almost full. What were all these people doing at a movie so early in the morning, I wondered. "We don't usually have this kind of crowd," Vic whispered. He was standing close to me, looking through another split in the drapes. I pulled back and looked at Vic. That sweet little boy look he had had earlier was replaced by perfect elegance. He was magnificent in his fitted tuxedo.

"All these people are here because of you," Vic said with warm admiration.

"That's terrible. They're going to be so disappointed."

"Don't be silly," he said. "They'll love you. How can they help it?" I could not resist. I went to him and kissed him gently on the cheek.

"Thank you, Vic. Thank you for everything."

It was time for him to go onstage. I watched as he strode with confidence to the microphone and turned toward Tex Beneke when he was ready to begin, accepting the applause graciously. How secure and distinguished he was. I would copy his behavior when it was my turn to sing.

One, two, three, four, five, six numbers. They all seemed to flow effortlessly from him. How can I follow such an artist, I thought. It's ridiculous. I missed John. He had gone into the audience to watch the end of the stage show. Oh my God, I thought in a panic, I need to go to the bathroom, and I don't think I have time. I was right. I didn't have time. Vic was taking his last bow. The lights went dark and the announcer was preparing the audience for my appearance.

"The most important gift France has given America since the Statue of Liberty." His voice sounded like God speaking in a cavern. "The new sensational sex goddess discovered by Hollywood, the star of our picture, *Rope of Sand*, ladies and gentlemen, Miss Corinne Calvet."

I was frozen. I couldn't move. Vic was standing by my side. He bent over and kissed me on the forehead.

"God is with you," he said.

He couldn't have chosen better words. "That's what I needed to hear. Thank you." I love you Vic, I thought. Okay, simple. I'm an actress, and I'm playing the part of a famous Hollywood star, or a queen, like Queen Elizabeth, making an appearance in front of her subjects. The applause that had almost died down while I delayed my appearance came again in a burst close to frenzy. I was standing in the middle of the stage with only a microphone on a stand to protect me from all the eyes focused on me.

The music began, still in the wrong key. Again I could not hear where I was supposed to start. But show business is show business, and you must go on. So I started at random. Suddenly the music became deafening. I turned around in surprise. All of the horns which had been muted were now freed and blasting at full intensity. I turned back to finish the song. I must have been putting on quite an exhibition, gesticulating out there in the middle of the stage, my mike turned down, the band blasting away behind me. The applause which followed was unrestrained. Why? Did they think I was a comedienne?

Tex whispered to me, "'How Deep.'"

The music started again. Tears rolled down my face. I was being debased in front of this huge crowd. I hated the studio for pushing me into this humiliation. Except for Vic Damone, everyone was my enemy. My voice was shaking. I couldn't continue. I bent my head and stopped singing. The song was only three-quarters over, but Tex Beneke cut it short. The crowd was applauding. I would not sing the other songs. But don't forget, I said to myself. Even if a queen cries she never runs away. I must walk off with poise, and I did, all the way to the safety of Vic Damone, whose arms extended toward me. I ran into my dressing room, and closed the door. I shook as I waited. Where was John? Could he really have stayed in the audience to see the chorus line closing the show?

"I need you John, please," I cried out.

There was a knock on the door.

"Come in."

Four men with vaguely familiar faces came in one by one, followed by my husband. No one spoke. The silence was heavy and embarrassing. There were endless introductions, and then nothing else was said. The insult of silence was more than I could take. I knew I had failed, but the cruel stupidity of these men, studio exeutives who had not even been considerate enough to

have the band rehearse in my own key, was too much. I had had
it.

"Gentlemen," I said. "Take your damn flowers and get the
hell out of my dressing room."

They were stunned. No one moved.

"Now," I said.

I picked up a cardboard vase full of roses. As I prepared to
throw it against the door, someone grabbed it out of my hand and
they all departed, leaving the flowers and John behind. John was
in a complete state of consternation.

"Now you've done it," he sneered. "They were all top brass
from Paramount. How could you be so rude to them?"

"Get the hell out of here yourself," I screamed.

He left without another word. My mascara, my false eye-
lashes, everything seemed to be caught in my eyes. They were
burning and excruciatingly painful. I washed my face, changed,
and sat down with my eyes closed, not knowing what to do next.
Should I just walk out of the dressing room? I was ashamed of my
explosion. There was a sprightly knock at the door. It was Vic,
again dressed in his street clothes. Once more he had become a
handsome, shy boy.

"I was talking to John," he said. "And we thought maybe
you'd like to go and have lunch at an Italian restaurant in my
section of town."

"Yes, I would." I answered.

The small restaurant was warm and cheery. Vic radiated a
sense of ease among his Italian friends. We talked in a relaxed
mood. No one mentioned the morning's experience. Then it was
time to go back to the theater.

"I won't go," I said.

"Well maybe what you can do is just take a bow," John suggested, not very helpfully.

"No," Vic broke in. "I think you'll find that the first show is
always like that, off track a little bit. But suddenly in the second
show everything fits into place and it works out beautifully."

I wanted to believe it, but my doubts kept me silent.

"Didn't you hear the applause?" Vic continued. "They loved
you."

"Yes, they really did clap loudly, that's true," John added.

When we got to the theater one of the men who had been in

my dressing room earlier was pacing up and down impatiently. Near him stood the comic who was also on the bill.

"Where have you been?" He addressed himself to John.

"We took Corinne to lunch."

"Well, that's too bad. It's obvious that she can't continue singing. Have you met our comic?"

He was tall and gaunt, and I had not found an ounce of humor in the act he had performed earlier on stage. The audience had laughed, but I hadn't understood why. The man from Paramount was telling the comic to find a few jokes he could do with me.

"Let's see," the funny man said. "Do you know this one?"

It meant nothing to me.

"No."

"How about this one?"

"No." The second was equally obscure.

"This one I'm sure you know. It comes from your country."

I did not recognize the gag.

"Sorry."

He turned around, lifting his shoulders in a gesture of blank resignation as if to say, what can I do with her?

"Well, write something, something she can learn," the Paramount executive said.

"I can't do it fast enough. I go on in five minutes."

"All right, Miss Calvet. You'll just have to sing again in this show, and before the next one you two can get together and dream up a sketch."

The Paramount brass had spoken, and now disappeared. After announcing how bad I was, they ordered me to go on. I stormed into my dressing room. It's inhuman, I thought. How can I go out there in front of all those people thinking that I'm the worst singer in the world? Still, I found myself putting on make-up. John came in, and seeing what I was doing, smiled.

"It's only one more time, darling. Then you'll have a cute sketch to do and everything will be all right."

"John? You too? Do you know how I feel?"

"Don't worry." He patted me on the back. "You look like a cute little bug out there, and the orchestra is playing so loud no one can hear you."

There was fire in my eyes when I turned to look at him.

"I'll stay backstage. I'll be waiting for you," John said, leaving rapidly.

If I walk out right now, I reasoned with myself, not only will I have the reputation of being a lousy singer, but I will also be seen as someone who walks out on an engagement. I did the show. I was better. Tex Beneke had been able to transpose the arrangements into my key and it actually went quite well. I would have liked to continue singing, but it was now out of the question. The decision had been made for me to do a mediocre vaudeville routine with the old-fashioned comic. It was years before I sang again in public.

Two weeks went by quickly. John and I spent a lot of time with Vic and his Italian family. It was the closest European feeling I had experienced since leaving France. Love was shared openly in the Damone household. People were not afraid of displaying their affections. What a difference between Vic's family and John's, with his domineering mother and browbeaten father.

When Paramount called to give us our flight number to Canada and John announced that I was afraid of flying, there was consternation on the end of the line. But they had no choice. Hurriedly, a limousine came to take us to the station, where we boarded a train for Montreal. We had left the hotel in a hurry, and had thrown our clothes into our suitcases. Now in the train compartment I busied myself with repacking. Before closing the suitcase, I grabbed my new mink wrap, threw it around my shoulders, and hugged myself.

"John," I said. "Thank you for letting me buy this. I love it so. It was worth every penny we paid for it. It really does make me feel like a star." Hoping to give John a sense of importance, I never bought anything without asking his opinion first.

"You look very pretty in it." My handsome husband threw a kiss at me. "Are you looking forward to staying by that river where we've been invited after the opening in Montreal? I heard they have the best kind of bass fishing up there. It's going to be nice and relaxing."

"Sure." I was still not crazy about fishing, but it was John's favorite pastime.

I snuggled on his lap.

"My poor baby," he said, caressing my hair. "You deserve a few days of fishing. It's been very hard for you, hasn't it?"

In Montreal, I was photographed pushing the lever on the huge machine that installed the first pilings for the new subway. That night there was an immense crowd lined up outside the movie house. When I was introduced the applause went right through me like a wave of powerful appreciation. It was intoxicating. There was a delirium in the stomping and shouting around me. I was a star. After the show the theater manager wanted to get a shot of me surrounded by the crowd, so he asked us to go out the front door of the theater instead of sneaking out the back. I was walking between the theater manager and John as we started through the mob, and at first they shielded me from my enthusiastic fans. But the hysteria began to peak. Everyone was pushing against us. John was pulling me by the hand. The crowd filled in between us. I clutched my fur wrap. People were touching me, touching my hair, my clothes, screaming how much they loved me. They pulled at my fur. Finally we were rescued by a group of policemen and shoved into a limousine.

"My God, look at your fur," John said with sudden concern. I took it off. It was all ripped apart. Only the lining was intact. Little pieces of fur were missing all over the garment. The wrap lay in my lap, ripped, ruined. I could not take another emotional wrench. I pulled back inside myself and remained silent.

Outside of Montreal, I slept while John fished. I ate, John kissed me, I slept, and John fished some more. And so it went for a full week. When I awoke on the day of our departure I felt like a new woman. When the tour finally came to its conclusion, and I looked back, I decided that much of it had been fun. After seventeen cities we found ourselves back in our heaven, our little house in Beverly Glen. I had everything a young woman could want: a gracious home, a handsome husband, recognition on the screen, a loving black cocker spaniel, floating chairs in the pool, and two cars in the garage.

Still something was missing.

In the months that followed, whenever a new French actress was mentioned in the paper John would cut out the article and place it under my water glass at dinner as a reminder that I should not get pregnant.

One afternoon near the pool, I was thinking about how many months I would be unable to work if I got pregnant while I played with the remains of a red balloon left over from the decorations for our last barbecue. I was stretching the rubber between my fingers, making it taut, when a defect appeared, producing a small hole. I tiptoed into the house like a thief, making certain no one saw me as I went into the bathroom. I took the barrier that stood between my womb and John's sperm out of its case, and with a pin from a brooch, pierced a minuscule hole in my diaphragm.

"It's up to you now, God. If you want one of John's sperm to be strong enough to get through this hole then it will be Your Will, not mine."

A few days later, sitting outside Hal Wallis's office, I waited for his secretary to get off the phone. I was lost in reverie.

"Is everything all right, Corinne? You feel OK?" Louise, Wallis's secretary, inquired.

"Yes," I answered, taking a deep breath.

She proceeded to tell me that Wallis was preparing two new films, one starring Anna Magnani.

"There's a small but great part you could do in that one," she said.

"A dramatic part?" I asked.

"Yes."

"Oh good!" I was enthusiastic.

"And then we're doing a picture called *My Friend Irma Goes West* to introduce the new comedy team of Martin and Lewis."

"Who's going to be in that one?"

"So far John Lund and Marie Wilson. That's all up to now."

"What kind of film is it?"

"Slapstick comedy."

"Oh well, there won't be anything in that for me."

Wallis came out of his office with a pleased expression.

"I didn't know you were here. I was just thinking about you. Please come in."

Taken by surprise, I walked in, leaving the door open.

"Sit down," Wallis said. "I haven't seen you since your publicity trip up north."

"Yes. It was very successful. They even gave me the key to the city in Toronto."

"The picture is going to make you a big star. We have to be

careful what we follow it with. It's imperative that I get to know you better."

"Would you like to come to dinner at the house on Saturday night?" I suggested.

"Is the honeymoon over yet?" Wallis said cynically.

"The marriage is getting better every day." I forced myself to hide my apprehension.

"Here's a script," Wallis said, handing me a bound copy. "Sit here and read it. I'm thinking of you for the part of Françoise."

It was the slapstick comedy. I read it with all of my attention, but its humor escaped me completely. Françoise was a bleached blonde singer who was panting after an orange juice salesman. Her constant escort was a chimpanzee dressed in clothes identical to hers. It was ridiculous! When Wallis returned I heard him speaking to his secretary.

"Hold all calls, I don't want to be disturbed." It was the first time I was alone with him since the night he had come to my apartment in Westwood.

I could not believe that he would cast me in such a script. *Rope of Sand* had made me a valuable property. Doing this film would ruin my chances of rising higher as a dramatic star.

"How do you like the script?" Wallis asked.

"I don't."

"Really? Why?"

I told him.

"You have another picture you're doing," I said. "Why not give me a part in that one?"

"Well, I could, but . . ."

He had reached the place where I was standing, and put his arms around me.

"Mr. Wallis, please, no. I'm sorry, but I love John, and I'm faithful to him."

"Very well, I'll let you know my decision." His voice turned to ice.

Two days later I received a script and an official notice. I was to appear with Martin and Lewis and the chimpanzee in the picture *My Friend Irma Goes West*, playing the part of Françoise. I stormed into Wallis's office. He agreed that the picture would not do much to advance my career.

"One picture like this won't do much to hurt you too badly," he told me, "but two or three of these kinds of parts and good-by stardom."

"So why are you casting me in it?"

He opened the office door and with a slap on my behind I was dismissed.

I would have liked to confide in John about Wallis, but I couldn't without admitting I had known all along about the circumstances behind our marriage. I failed to understand that we were both guilty of dissimulation. We were living our marriage within a bond of lies.

I was now overwhelmed with the idea that my father would have an attack if he saw me in a film that insinuated that a chimpanzee was my boyfriend. My own upbringing rendered me incapable of appreciating any humor in the part.

I called the studio, and told Louise that I could not do the film.

"You'll be put on suspension, and that means thirteen weeks without pay," she warned me.

I would have to tell John my decision, since our income would be partially interrupted.

"I'm going on suspension," I told him. "I just can't do this part."

"I never understood how that works," he said, shaking his head.

"Well, the way I understand it, if an actor or actress doesn't want to do a script offered to them, they can be put on thirteen weeks' suspension without pay. Then since we only get paid for forty-two weeks out of the year, there would be ten more weeks without pay."

"So that means that Wallis doesn't have to pay you any money for twenty-three weeks. With the money we owe the studio that would wipe out all of our savings." John was incredulous that I would even think of putting us in such a position.

"John, it's a question of honor. I'm being blackmailed into doing this picture."

My face had turned crimson as I uttered the word blackmail, but John was busy with a pencil, figuring out what our loss would be, and didn't notice.

"Look John, he can't keep me six months without putting me

in another film, so don't worry about it. It'll only be for a few weeks. We'll tell the maid to go on vacation, and after all, we still have your salary."

"You're a big star now; how can he do that to you?"

"That's what I mean. He's trying to manipulate me; the role is undignified. If I don't stand up for myself now it'll be all over."

"You're right." John was swept up into my anger. "Turn the picture down," he ordered.

Our agreement in this matter was gratifying, but there was one small item that we had failed to consider in our calculations. In our contract with Wallis was a clause stating that full payment on the loan he carried on our house could be demanded at any time. When my agent pointed this out, the fear that Wallis would call in the loan made me agree to do the film. I decided that I would treat the part as a learning experience and be perfect in it.

Wallis was on the set the first morning. He introduced me to Dean Martin and Jerry Lewis.

I found Dean friendly, a man of the world, self-assured and quiet. Lewis was the exact opposite, nervous, and trying to override his innate shyness by flattering and entertaining everyone around him. He seemed to be afraid of silence, to feel compelled to fill the empty spaces. I was sensitive to his great anxiety, his wanting to be liked by everyone. I was poised, prepared for any eventuality. So I thought. Wallis watched with a smug expression as we started rehearsing.

The chimpanzee was brought onstage, and looked amenable in his velvet suit and pillbox leopard hat, replicas of what I was wearing. The trainer brought him close to me. He took a deep breath, cocked his head to one side, raised his eyebrows, and curled his lips up in a smile.

It soon became evident that for the chimp it was a question of love at first sight. Making jungle sounds, he pranced around me, reaching for my legs as the trainer held him back.

"He's going to be OK. He likes you. I can let him loose for awhile."

Then it started. The chimp followed me everywhere on the set, making obscene gestures and sticking his tongue in and out rapidly. His eyes would turn up in his head, his lips curl open, then close with a loud smack. I was mortified.

"What's the matter with him?" I asked the trainer.

"Well, Miss," he said hesitantly, "could you be in your monthly cycle?"

I blushed and nodded.

"To him," he pointed to the chimp, "it's the time when the female is ready for reproduction."

"I don't understand."

"He's making sexual advances toward you."

"Make him stop."

"He wouldn't understand. He'll stop as soon as your period's over."

I took the director into my confidence. I asked him if they could shoot around me for the next couple of days. My request was turned down by an amused Wallis. Everyone was having a great time with this situation, everyone but me, and I demanded in no uncertain terms that the chimp be kept on a leash and off-stage when he wasn't working. Lewis couldn't resist the urge to imitate the chimp, and turned into a human monkey, harassing me without restraint. Controlling my mounting hysteria, I could do nothing but pretend to be a good sport about it.

Dean Martin, watching my predicament, rescued me when he saw that I was at the end of my rope.

"Come to my dressing room," he said. "No one will bother you there, and I would appreciate it if you could run some lines with me." I hesitated a moment—another dressing room! But the choice was clear: Dean Martin or the chimp. It turned out that Dean was apprehensive; he had never acted before. He really did want me to help him with his lines. It made me feel important, so I took him under my wing the way Burt Lancaster had for me.

The second week's shooting found us at the Flamingo hotel in Las Vegas. I was decked out in a white stage version of a cowboy outfit. It was in this costume that I posed for publicity pictures with a mugging Lewis, who never let up. My discomfort had been painful enough on the set, but now around the hotel pool Lewis had an audience, a chance to go wild. How I managed to smile during that photo session is beyond me now.

John and I were unprepared when Helen Ainsworth called from Los Angeles to announce that Wallis had not picked up John's option, and was dropping his contract. John had answered the phone. He looked at me, then back at the phone. He was bewildered.

"John, darling, what is it?"

"Wallis dropped my contract."

Without another word he stormed out of the suite, banging the door. I had to get back to the set. I kept calling the room and having John paged in the hotel without success. At midnight, when we were finished, I found him asleep, passed out on the bed with his coat on. I was overcome with compassion. I could imagine how he felt. He had ridden high on the belief of an assured future, and among the dues he had paid was giving up his bachelor life. Disregarding his mother's wishes had been the hardest part. He had enjoyed helping the lonely foreign girl in the hospital. It made him feel like a big, powerful, loving man. When I was happy he saw me as a little girl playing with my toy animals. When I was tender, he compared me to a little monkey with caressing hands, hanging on, pleading for kisses. Little monkey. It took me awhile to overcome a negative feeling each time he used the term, even after he explained that he meant it to be endearing, something he thought cute.

In bed, John made sure that I had an orgasm before he released himself, and his passion was always nocturnal. Sex took place every night to relieve the day's tensions, an addiction he needed to satisfy in order to sleep. He resented my monthly period, because he felt it gave me the right to deprive him. Over the years, as soon as he saw the upcoming signs, he became more attentive, like a little boy, demanding more of my presence. John had discovered women were incapable of resisting their maternal feelings for him, and often wanted to erase the hurt look on his face by taking care of his needs.

Now in our hotel room I took off his shoes and clothing, covering him gently. Sitting on the floor I reviewed our situation. Wallis's move had put more pressure on us, eliminating income and bringing tension in our marriage. Like a chess player, he was moving in for a checkmate.

Wallis knew that John would feel like a failure, and that his lack of self-respect would push him into the wrong move. He no longer needed John. We had been married for more than a year. My resident visa was totally secure.

"Oh John," I said aloud. "We can't let him checkmate us."

"What?" John mumbled. "Anna, why don't you leave me alone?"

"Anna?" Who was he talking about? Who was Anna? If John was seeing another woman it changed the whole picture. Jealousy took possession of me and I began to watch his every move.

Back in Los Angeles, I was erratic, unable to complete anything I started. I waited for John to return from his trips to the other studios under the guidance of Helen Ainsworth. There was no interest in him anywhere. There was talk about a Hollywood blacklist, but a list was unnecessary. A negative rumor in the appropriate ear at the top executive level was all it took. All were in fear of opposing the will of the big moguls. They were too powerful to cross; no degree of interest or dedication could lead a motion picture producer to cut his own throat by helping someone who had fallen out of grace.

Studios controlled the distribution of films, and some producers who tried to go it alone soon discovered that there were no avenues open to them for the release of their productions. This situation was partially remedied when the government broke up the studios' monopoly over distribution, but the alliances in the moguls' club remained unbroken.

One afternoon I was feeling somehow happy as I played with the dog in the pool. The day before I had seen some of the dailies of *My Friend Irma Goes West*, and I had to admit that I looked good. The clothes were stunning, and the relationship between the chimp and me was funny. Under duress I had rediscovered my natural qualities as a comedienne. I lost my fear that the film would destroy me totally. I was allowing the sun's rays to penetrate the pores of my skin when the phone rang. I answered automatically.

"Allo."

"May I speak to Farron please?"

"Who?"

"Farron Bromfield."

"There is no one here by the name of Farron. There is a John Bromfield."

"Oh yes, excuse me." It was a female voice. "I knew him before he changed his name to become a movie star. May I speak to John then?"

"He's not here. May I take a message?"

"This is Anna. . . ."

Anna. That was the name John had mumbled in his sleep.

"Excuse me . . ." I broke in. I was distracted. "I didn't hear what you said."

"John ordered a special fishing reel and he hasn't come to pick it up yet. I've left messages at his mother's. I don't have any use in my shop for such a professional reel. It's too expensive for my customers."

Shaking my head at the insanity behind all the moments that had been spoiled by my suspicion, I asked her for the address of the shop. I would surprise John by picking up the reel.

When he came home from deep sea fishing that day, his shoulders were rounded in defeat.

"I didn't even get a bite," he said, outraged, as if that had been the last straw.

"You taste good," I announced, as I kissed his salty lips. "I have a surprise for you over there on the sofa."

He opened the package and saw the reel box.

"How did that thing get here?" he exclaimed.

"Anna called, and I went to pick it up."

"Anna called here? What did she say?"

"That she was stuck with the reel you had ordered some time ago."

"That's it?" John questioned.

"Yes, so I went to pick it up for you. It sure is a big one. Anna said it was used for tuna."

Defeated, he said, "Let's hope I won't need it, because if I don't get work soon I'll have to go back to professional fishing."

Christmas was approaching and I wanted to make a gesture that would improve my relationship with Wallis. An expensive gift was out of the question, since we were barely surviving. I had noticed a collection of clown paintings in his office. That's it, I decided. My present will be my talent as a painter. I obtained one of his photos and carefully reproduced his features, since portraits had been my forte at the art school.

I thought the result was excellent when, after letting three coats of varnish dry, I lightly painted clown make-up on top of the portrait. When I had finished I stood back and felt that I had created a masterpiece. I was smiling radiantly when I left the present with Louise, Wallis's secretary.

Since I had not received an acknowledgment, a few weeks after Christmas I inquired to see if my painting was hanging in Wallis's office.

"No it's not," Louise replied. "Corinne, whatever possessed you to insult him that way?"

"What do you mean?" I was earnest.

"Well, letting your boss know that you think of him as a clown is not the way to get in his good graces."

"But that's not what I meant at all; we all have other personality traits that we hide. I wanted him to know that behind his coolness I knew there was someone very loving. It took me twenty-eight hours to paint that portrait. Do you really think I would have spent that much time just to insult him?"

"The only thing I know," said Paul Nathan, an associate of Wallis who walked in on our conversation, "is that he came out of his office in a cold rage and asked me to get rid of it, make sure it was destroyed."

"So what did you do with it?" I said, hoping to salvage my work.

"I burned it in my fireplace. Don't tell anyone, but I thoroughly enjoyed the painting. I think it was perfect."

I went home beaten. There was no way for me to fit into this society. There was no use even trying.

I was in the middle of a depression when another script was delivered to the house, *Sailor Beware*, again with Dean Martin and Jerry Lewis.

Two slapstick films like these and you can say good-by to Academy Award stardom, I remember Wallis saying. I couldn't turn it down; we had no savings left. We were dependent on my weekly salary to eat.

I complained to Edith Head, the Academy Award-winning dress designer, who was once more doing my clothes for the film.

"Look Edith, they're not even billing me above the title. I'm only a co-star."

"It's not Wallis," she said. "It's because of Martin and Lewis's manager. Just like Hope and Crosby, they demand that they're the only ones above the title. Anyway, look at these sketches Wallis okayed for you. That hardly makes it look like he's trying to

destroy you. That dress alone will cost over a thousand dollars."
She was pointing to a sketch of a white, off-shoulder, full-length
dress covered with silk fringes that were caught in a crisscross
fashion over the breast. The drawing took my breath away. I
could see myself singing the duet with Dean for which I would
wear this dress, moving my body imperceptibly so that the fringes
would undulate. One after the other the sketches were passed
before me, each more extravagant than the last. There was even a
gold lamé sarong that would have made Dorothy Lamour envious.

Walking out of the wardrobe department I remembered the
words of my dramatic teacher in Paris, Charles Dullin.

"There are no small parts, only small actors."

I will survive this film, I decided. I will be so vibrant that the
public will not notice that I am only billed as a co-star.

On the set one morning as Dean and I were rehearsing our
duet, Wallis stopped the routine. The playback had stopped. The
set was silent.

"Corinne," Wallis's voice boomed. "I've told you, I don't want
my actresses to wear falsies."

"I'm not wearing any."

"Go and take them out," he ordered.

"Mr. Wallis, are you calling me a liar?"

I spoke in a menacing tone as I approached him. I grabbed
his hand, and in front of everyone, put it inside my dress and
made sure he felt that I had nothing there but my own breasts.

"Are you finding anything there but my flesh? No? Then
thank you."

Dropping his hand, I returned to stand next to Dean Martin,
who looked extremely amused.

"Bravo," he said softly. "That was magnificent."

The act of standing up to Wallis in front of the whole crew
made me regain my pride. I made a decision. I was no longer
dependent on Hal Wallis. I was going to get other producers to
offer me parts.

Helen Ainsworth, aware that the feud between Wallis and me
had gotten completely out of hand, contacted independent companies.

"Wallis may be resentful, but he'll never be able to turn down the money he'll get for you if you are loaned to someone else," she said.

Allan May had written a story for his protégé, John Barrymore, Junior. It was set in Quebec City during the late eighteenth century. The French were organizing a campaign to recapture a castle held by the English. As a young girl I had had an affair with a country boy, and the child of this union had been kidnapped and raised by his father, who was now a leader of the French revolutionaries. Unbeknownst to the young man, their contact in the English city happened to be his mother, and as his mother, my eyes radiated the pleasure I felt upon seeing my absent son, softening the resentment I had felt toward his father.

John Barrymore, playing my son, is confused in the script by the attraction he feels toward me, an older woman, who he does not know to be his mother. At the end, of course, I, as the mother, sacrifice myself, and stand in front of a bullet meant for my son.

I was filled with excitement at the prospect of doing this film. It did not have a high budget, but it would give me a chance to display my dramatic talent. My mid-twenties freshness was concealed by dark circles under my eyes and a streak of gray hair. I enjoyed being in Quebec, and I appreciated a chance to speak French. The atmosphere of the city reminded me of my own French roots. It was also the first time I had traveled without my husband. John had decided to visit his relatives in Indiana before he came to join me. I had forgotten about my conflict with Wallis, and was happy to be using my craft.

We had one week's work left when John arrived. That night we were to shoot the climax of the film. Three hundred soldiers were to arrive by canoe to attack the citadel from the river. Explosive charges had been set up, boats were to overturn, and the men were to swim to the walls and climb to the top. It had been impossible to fly three hundred stuntmen from Hollywood, so the production hired Canadian soldiers who said they knew how to swim, and since the pay for one night's work corresponded to one month's salary for a member of the Canadian armed forces, many signed up.

Everything was set. The cameras were rolling, charges detonated, canoes overturned. Horribly, a number of men were drowned in the icy waters of the St. Lawrence River. Many had lied about their ability to swim. The town was in an uproar, and there was talk of a lynching. We were told by the producer to leave immediately and to reconvene in Hollywood in three weeks.

Sneaking out of the hotel through the employees' entrance, we departed in our station wagon in the early morning hours. Putting aside my own personality, I decided to cross the country acting the part of a soft-spoken, amiable wife. John bloomed in the face of my new behavior. I had not been conscious of what an intellectual threat to him I had become as my English had progressed.

As soon as we arrived back in Los Angeles my nightmares returned. I would wake up at night sweating, poisoned by hatred. In a recurring dream I saw myself standing in the company of other actors under contract to Wallis around a freshly dug grave. Quietly first, then more insistently, Wallis's voice beckoned me to him from that hole in the ground. Even in death he wanted my body. I leaned over to look down at the dead Wallis, whose face slowly changed into that of my father. I always awoke from the dream as I tumbled into the gaping black grave.

I was losing my grip on my own mind. The hatred was driving me insane. I had to eliminate it. I had to find a way to make peace. I needed to understand Wallis. I inquired about his background. The answers I received were always dominated by an undertone of fearful reverence. The picture of a clever, politically motivated genius emerged. The mention of his past successes carried references to films that meant little to me. I had never seen *Sergeant York, Casablanca, The Maltese Falcon,* or *Watch on the Rhine,* which came out during the war and were unavailable in France. The more I learned about him, the greater became my feelings of inferiority.

"Helen," I begged. "I have to get out of my contract."

"Well, he's not a fool," she replied. "Why would he let go of a money maker? Could be, however, that he'd like to have your contract shared by another studio." Helen acknowledged my smile of approval by continuing, "While you were gone the production company showed me some of your dailies from Canada. I got a copy, and showed them to Zanuck at Fox. He wants you for *When Willie Comes Marching Home.* Altogether, Zanuck will be sharing your contract with Wallis for four projects."

"Oh Helen," I was crying and laughing at the same time. I

felt that the vise that had immobilized my future was being loosened, and that I was being freed.

"Call me after you read the script for *When Willie Comes Marching Home*, and Corinne, if Wallis takes credit for making the deal with Zanuck, let him. Don't use his misrepresentation in your vendetta. Sometimes knowing the truth and watching others hide behind lies gives the same feeling of superiority one gets from winning."

I opened the script, *When Willie Comes Marching Home*, by Richard Sale. As my eyes ran over the pages I visualized the film. An American soldier, Dan Dailey, needs help returning to his army unit. The daughter of the leader of the French Underground in a village in Occupied France, me, after several unsuccessful attempts to help him cross over to join his regiment, becomes involved in a strange scheme. My father in the film decides that I will marry the American in plain view of the German soldiers. Our procession to the wedding will pass the escape route.

John Ford was to direct, but since he was on his yacht in Tahiti, Richard Sale, the scriptwriter, would do my test. What a joy for a performer to tune to the writer's vision, and be directed by that person. The test went exceedingly well.

When work began on the film I felt totally confident for the first time since coming to America, but I soon found myself a pawn again between two large egos, just as I had been between Wallis and Paramount.

John Ford had a group of actors with whom he always worked, and he had wanted Maureen O'Hara for my part in the picture. Ford was not a man who would let anyone make choices for him, and Zanuck was not one to back down from a decision. I walked onto the set knowing that I had earned Zanuck's praise for the test. The assistant director walked with me over to where John Ford was standing, chewing on a cigar.

"Mr. Ford, may I introduce Miss Calvet?"

All the admiration I had gained from seeing the classic films Ford had made must have shone in my eyes. Ford looked at me, his cigar traveling from one side of his mouth to the other.

"I saw your test. Very good. But of course it's a totally wrong interpretation of the part."

He turned his back and walked away.

I was shattered and lost. I followed him.

"Mr. Ford, excuse me, sir. Mr. Zanuck was enthusiastic about my interpretation. How would you like me to change it?"

"Look, since you're not my choice for the part, let's just hope for the best."

I reached Zanuck by telephone. I was close to tears.

"Corinne, do exactly as you did on the test. He's annoyed because on the strength of that test I have just given Richard Sale a script to direct that Ford thought he might like to do."

I was in trouble. Zanuck wanted me to play the girl I had played in the test, and Ford wanted me to play the part in another way. The undercurrent of emotion in the test was based on the girl falling in love with the American during his numerous attempts to escape, and her devotion was checked only by the knowledge of his imminent departure. When she learned that she had to dress as a bride in this final escape attempt, and go through a mock ceremony, she was being asked to pretend to be something she really wanted to be. Such an interpretation gave the part an added dimension. Ford wanted this whole emotional element eliminated. He wanted me to play a tough, emotionless guerrilla fighter. Once more I called Zanuck and told him my dilemma. After watching a rehearsal, Zanuck put his arm around Ford's shoulder and walked away with him. The result of their long conference was a compromise between my interpretation and the one Ford wanted. As we proceeded, Ford removed most of my sensitive lines from the script.

The film had been completed for a few weeks when I got a call from Zanuck's secretary telling me that he wanted to see me in his office at 5 P.M. that afternoon.

As I drove to the studio, I could not shake an uncomfortable feeling about going to see Zanuck in his office. I had heard gossip about these late afternoon meetings. When I arrived I was hustled past two secretaries into the inner sanctum of this small, dynamic man with a blonde moustache. Zanuck got up from behind his desk. I sat down, and he started to pace up and down in front of me, making small talk.

"Wasn't the weather cold this week in Los Angeles," he said, looking out the window. "The Palm Springs sun should be very pleasant." Dramatically, he turned on his heels and stood a few feet away from me with his erect penis standing proudly out of his unzipped pants.

"How do you like that?" He was smiling proudly.

My eyeballs felt as if they were popping out of their sockets. It was a classic, a real moment of burlesque. Zanuck was making the head of his organ bob up and down while he repeated the question.

"How do you like it?"

His behavior had taken me so much by surprise that the only sounds I could utter were incoherent stuttering. Taking my reaction as a positive response to his malehood, he stepped forward and stood right in front of me. As I stood up to move away my cheek bumped into his erect penis. More flustered than ever, and trying to regain my composure, I finally managed some words.

"Please Mr. Zanuck, I know your daughter."

Was I naïve enough to think that this would alter his conduct?

"Yes," he whispered, readjusting his pants, "and we know she is very bright, and capable of keeping secrets."

What does that have to do with it? I wondered. What am I supposed to do or say now? Again I was speechless.

"Your husband John is a very handsome boy," Zanuck went on. "I feel Hal Wallis made a mistake in not keeping him under contract. We could use a leading man like John at our studio."

My God, thank you. I smiled to myself. Zanuck, the big movie mogul, just enjoyed being a flasher. John was the reason he had wanted to see me.

"I think you're right," I spoke in ready agreement. "John was an All-American left end at Saint Mary's College. I think he would have that same All-American appeal to the public."

"Can you get out of town this weekend for a few days without him?" Zanuck walked back to his desk. He was smiling. I didn't like the question. Nevertheless, I did not present him with a negative answer.

"I don't see why not. It would all depend on the reason. If it's good enough, I am sure John would not object."

"It's good enough, I assure you," Zanuck interrupted. "It would be greatly to John's advantage." He was walking toward me again. He held my chin in his hands and looked straight into my eyes. "I like the way you handle your vibrant sexuality. Come to Palm Springs for a weekend of sunny sex play."

I was stunned at what Zanuck had proposed. Perplexed about what to say, I could only shake my head slightly. He pulled me to him, and kissing me gently on the lips, he ushered me out the side door of his office.

"Let me know your decision tomorrow morning. I want to get John's contracts ready so he can sign them when we get back."

The door closed behind me. I was alone in the corridor. Leaning against the wall, I slipped down to the floor. I had been handed the magic wand that could solve my husband's frustration as an actor. It was in my power to give him a chance at stardom. His manly pride would never again have to be wounded at a Hollywood premiere as our car was referred to as "Miss Calvet's." The price I had to pay for John's success was to go to bed with a man I did not love. For John, the price was his wife's infidelity. Driving home, I pounded my fist on the steering wheel.

"Why? Why? Why?" I said aloud. "Why do they all want to have sex with me anyway?"

Offering security in exchange for sex. This time it was John's future. What's the matter with all those big tycoons? My mind was racing. Am I being a puritan? Yes, probably. Why do I put so much value on sex? Without love, sex for me was revolting. If John was drowning would I jump in to rescue him? Even if the water was icy cold? Of course I would do all I could to save him. Is sacrifice the automatic reaction of love? But how would John accept my being unfaithful? What if I didn't tell him? That would be worse. Through gossip he would soon find out, and until he did, people would look at him smugly. He wouldn't know why. That would be destructive. And then one day he'd find out the truth and it would crush him. He would never forgive me for making him a fool. What was I supposed to do?

I got out of the car in a daze. John was frying some fish he had caught that day. From the kitchen he called out, "There's a script from the studio on the cocktail table. How about a beer?"

"OK," I answered automatically. Picking up the script, I started reading.

Peking Express had all the qualities of the films I wanted to do, the kind Wallis had dangled before me on previous occasions. As I put down the script I sat numb.

"I really had a good day. I even made the jackpot on the boat. You haven't touched your beer. Want a martini instead?"

"No John, I don't think so."

"Hey, what's the matter? You've got tears in your eyes. I read the script. It's very good. The studio wants you next Wednesday for wardrobe fitting. They're starting to shoot in two weeks. And guess who's going to be your leading man?" I shook my head sadly. John whistled the theme from *The Third Man.*

"Mr. Joseph Cotten himself," he said, clowning.

During dinner I kept looking at John. I had his destiny between my legs. I could see him as a star, his name in lights. He would have to break the habit of sniffling a now imaginary chronic running nose, a mannerism acceptable on a commercial fishing boat but definitely out as a movie star. I was smiling at him, a motherly smile. If he was my child what would I do? Without hesitation I would sacrifice myself for his future. But even for a child I would not bargain with my body. With material possessions, yes, but not with my body.

After dinner, while brushing my teeth, I thought about the problem. If I told John about Zanuck's offer, there would be no deceit because I would be doing it with his content.

John was in bed, calling me.

"Come to bed. I miss you. Come here," he said, as he held the covers open for me to snuggle against him. "Daddy is going to make his little monkey feel good."

During our love-making I fantasized that John was a big box office star.

"Call me Mrs. Bromfield," I whispered.

"Well, Mrs. Bromfield, how do you feel?"

"Isn't my husband John Bromfield marvelous. . . ." In his last film, I added silently.

"You'd better know it, baby," he said as he ended my fantasy. "Goodnight," he muttered, stretching his body. He turned his back, waiting for me to hug him and lie next to him as if we were silver spoons in a drawer.

I couldn't sleep. I had to call Zanuck with my decision in the morning, and John was going fishing at 6 A.M.

"John," I said softly. "Please wake up. There is a decision that we must make, and I need your help. It can't wait."

He sat up, his arms folded across his body, a frown on his face, while I related Zanuck's proposition. His frown deepened when I mentioned what was in it for him. And when I finished saying that I was willing to do it with his consent he looked at me in total disgust.

"You bitch. You could have done it without telling me." Grabbing his pillow he pretended to go back to sleep.

I got up, covered myself with his robe, and walked into the living room. The dinner candles were about to burn out. Automatically, I extinguished them. It's strange, I thought; I should feel something. What he had been saying was, bitch, when I was asked to help your future I sacrificed my single life, and the amorous activities that went with it. Now for my future you're not willing to make a sacrifice for me. And it was true. Opening the refrigerator, I was tempted by a cold, fried chicken breast. Munching, I walked back into the living room. I had expected John to be angry at Zanuck's proposition. Instead, he was furious with me. For me the marriage was over. I was going to call Zanuck in the morning and turn him down. I held the script for *Peking Express* to my chest. I was at peace, even as I wondered if this somehow was not yet another one of Hal Wallis's tricks.

Paris **CORINNE CALVAY**

Above: Excited, hopeful, and frightened. *Opposite above:* This photo was taken at the Hotel Pierre in New York City. I was just off the boat. *Opposite right:* Arriving in Pasadena and glad to be off the Super Chief, 1947.

Right: What a difference between Paramount's photos and Sam's. (I didn't recognize myself). *Below:* At the time of this photograph, I was distraught over the studio's spelling of my name, Calvay. *Paramount Pictures*

Right: My first husband, John Bromfield. *Paramount Pictures. Below:* The young married couple posing for the fan magazines. *Movie Star News*

Just before I got sick on Burt's back in *Rope of Sand.* *Paramount Pictures*

What a beginning! My first American film *Rope of Sand* with Burt Lancaster, Paul Henreid, and Claude Rains. *Paramount Pictures*

Trying to rebuff Paul Henreid, the bad guy in *Rope of Sand*.

Below: With Hal Wallis on the set of *Sailor Beware*.

A publicity shot for *Rope o Sand. Paramount Pictures*

Feeling foxy in a pale green velvet robe. *Paramount Pictures*

Above: Clowning with John at the County Fair. *Right:* One of the costumes in *Sailor Beware* with Dean Martin and Jerry Lewis. *Below:* Dean Martin, the amorous chimp, me, and the mocking Jerry Lewis in *My Friend Irma Goes West. Paramount Pictures*

My favorite pose. I always
felt very feminine when I
put my arm up to my hair.
20th Century-Fox

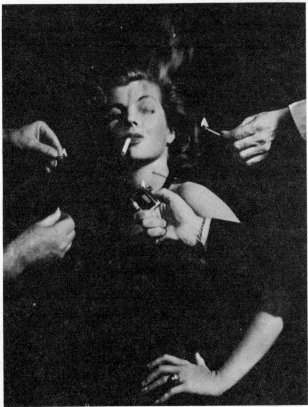

Above: Dan Dailey is imitating Hitler in *Willie Comes Marching Home.* *20th Century-Fox. Left:* A photograph by the great glamor photographer Georges Hurrell.

Above: This time I had Dean as a boyfriend and I liked it. Marian Marshall sits between me and Jerry Lewis. *Paramount Pictures.* *Right:* It was our last day of shooting for *Peking Express.* We knew we would no longer see each other every day. *Paramount Pictures*

Left: Happy in the arms of the talented Danny Kaye in *On the Riviera.* 20th Century-Fox. *Below:* Telling off Danny in *On the Riviera.* 20th Century Fox

Above: Protecting a drunk James
Cagney in *What Price Glory? 20th
Century-Fox. Right:* The bride of
Dan Dailey for the second time
in *What Price Glory? 20th
Century-Fox*

Above: In this photo taken by Bernard of Hollywood, I was wearing a great negligee that I kept for years and only wore on special occasions. *Below:* John Barrymore, Jr.'s attraction to me in *Quebec* had a touch of incest as he did know I was his mother. *Paramount Pictures*

Above: I would have liked more closeness with my compatriot, but Charles Boyer was very distant with everyone on the film *Thunder in the East. The Critt Davis Cinema Collection. Left:* With Deborah Kerr and Alan Ladd in *Thunder in the East.* I thought Alan and I made a very attractive couple. *The Critt Davis Cinema Collection. Below:* I really enjoyed acting in this film, *Flight to Tangiers. Paramount Pictures*

Twice I made the cover of *Look* magazine, once by myself and
once with Bob Hope.

Waiting for the playback of the ballad I was to sing to Cameron
Mitchell in *Powder River. 20th Century-Fox*

The "Colgate Comedy Hour" with host Donald O'Connor. *NBC photo*

In awe of Jimmy Stewart in *The Far Country*.

This publicity shot for *This Is Paris* was taken just before I learned John was in love with another woman.

The morning after the suicide attempt. *United Press Telephoto*

Chapter 9

I sat by the pool studying my part for *Peking Express,* a remake of *Shanghai Express,* originally filmed in 1932 with Marlene Dietrich. My conceptualization of the role had been completed with my final wardrobe fitting. The genius Edith Head had once more used the design and texture of the clothes to merge the outer form of the actress with the inner personality of the part. But my enthusiasm was restricted by a lingering tension, wondering when Wallis would make his demands. I smiled, remembering the morning a few days ago when we bumped into each other in the corridor.

"You're looking very good in those wardrobe tests, Corinne. Zanuck has great plans for you."

I did not flinch under his piercing look.

"Yes, but he had to forget his plans for a Palm Springs weekend." A broad smile illuminated my face.

"I heard. Corinne," he was shaking his head, smiling, "you're undirectable."

"What do you mean? I always know my lines. I'm always on time, and under a director's guidance I'm very pliable. What else am I supposed to do?" I was half begging for understanding, half rebelling at the unjust accusation.

"Undirectable means you are not going to do anything you don't want to do, even under great pressure."

"Mr. Wallis, it has nothing to do with will. Am I supposed to do things against my conscience?"

His eyes turned upward in a gesture of mock religious devotion. He sighed.

"Too bad."

That's it, I thought. Here comes the bad news. My face dropped.

Patting my cheek, he said:

"You're going to be very good in this film."

Feeling as if I had just come off a roller coaster ride, I drove home that day with hope in my heart.

My refusal to accept Zanuck's proposition must have convinced Wallis that my rejection of his advances was not personal, but consistent with my standards. My professional future was looking up.

John had become deeply resentful. He lay around the pool each day talking on the telephone, accepting every invitation we received. Each night we went out to cocktail parties. In the swing of this social life, there was a great deal of flirtation. I recognized John's half-smile as an invitation to the ladies he saw, as if to say, "Look over here, I'm available."

At a reception for *Modern Screen,* the fan magazine, we ran into our friends Guy Madison and his wife Gail Russell. It was one of their rare public appearances. Gail was a delicate little bird, afraid of noises and crowds. She was intelligent and uncomplicated, a person who should never have had a career as an actress. Apart from a pathological stage fright, she was extremely sensitive to the crass motives of the studios, and unable to overcome deep feelings of loneliness. I feel very sad whenever I think of Gail Russell and the desolate way in which she ended her life some years later just a few houses away from the one we lived in on Beverly Glen. Close to twenty empty bottles of liquor surrounded her in her small bedroom. She had not been seen for a week, and had not answered her phone. She had lain there drinking herself to death. How could all of us who knew this incredibly talented and beautiful woman have failed her so drastically?

Guy's arm was guiding Gail toward us. Gail habitually kept her eyes down, and it was always a shock when she lifted her glance, her childlike expression filled with innocent vulnerability. Hers was the beauty of a Madonna, and it threw everyone off balance. She did not understand the effect she had on people, and in fear she would drop her eyes again, as if someone else's interest in her was more than she could bear. She later solved this dilemma by wearing dark glasses constantly.

I slipped my arm into John's as we chattered together. One would never have guessed their marriage was headed for divorce. Guy's arm was around her shoulder, her cheek leaning against his hand.

"By the way," Guy asked, "how's Rhonda? I'm sorry I was in such a hurry and couldn't stop. I haven't seen her in a long time."

Rhonda? That would be Rhonda Fleming. We had not seen her in a long time either. John seemed embarrassed. I thought he acted as if he had been caught.

"Oh, she's fine," he answered. "I met Rhonda in Helen's office." John had recovered from his initial discomfort. "When you saw us I was walking her to an appointment at a beauty parlor. By the way, Helen was complaining that she doesn't see enough of either of you."

Helen Ainsworth had us all under contract. John's explanation made sense. He could have met Rhonda in Helen's office, but then why had he blushed? Though I knew our marriage was on shaky ground, my jealousy still flared up, and I was unable to reason intelligently. It didn't occur to me that perhaps John had omitted telling me of the chance meeting with Rhonda Fleming just to save us from another scene.

There was a split in my personality. In my personal life I was an emotional mess, but at the same time nothing was going to interfere with the opportunity I had in *Peking Express* to establish my credentials as a serious actress.

As I drove through the gate at the studio I was Corinne Calvet, the movie star. I loved the man who smiled with friendly respect as I parked my car in the row reserved for the stars. He never failed to make me feel great. It was a status symbol that did more for me than premieres, or any compliments I received. That day I brought my personal belongings so that I could turn the assigned dressing room into a familiar place, a place to relax during the shooting. A tall, blondish, slender and elegant man was standing near the dressing room entrance stairs. He was speaking with Paul Nathan, the gentle, small man who was Hal Wallis's assistant.

"Corinne," said Paul, "I don't think you've met Joe Cotten."

As my eyes looked into Joe's, some inner recognition made us both break into slow, warm smiles. My heart jumped upward; an artery in my neck pulsated tumultuously. I blushed. Orson Welles had the greatest respect for Joe's intellect, Errol Flynn had talked about his gentlemanly manners, and William Demarest, just the day before, had commented on how much he was like a European.

"I was in Paris a few months ago," he said, "and Marcel Marceau asked me to send you his good thoughts."

My smile grew bigger.

"He's preparing a one man show for the United States. We should see him soon."

"Mime," I heard myself say. "He's such a master of silent communication. I studied mime for awhile, but I was not very good. I was too embarrassed to move with the exaggerated gestures it required."

Joe laughed, a deep, resonant laugh. His voice was one of the attributes most appreciated by his audiences.

"Yes," he agreed. "That's the price one has to pay for a stern upbringing."

"Well, I have to run," said Paul.

"Let me help you," Joe offered, picking up the suitcase I had placed by my feet. It was the start of a romance never to be resolved.

Every morning the dapper Joe Cotten would walk into the make-up room with a different ascot, an interesting compliment to me on yesterday's dailies, and one morning a single rose that I kept for years, pressed and dried in a book.

Joe's valet was a midget, always running errands for him. This touch of eccentricity was a humorous accent on Joe's impeccable behavior. Soon, we found ourselves coming to the studio earlier than necessary, sharing our morning coffee. I was starved for conversation. Joe understood my existentialist philosophical positions. He considered their real implications, rather than dismissing them because they were politically suspect. I had been afraid to associate with many of the more intellectual members of the movie community because it was surmised that they had left-wing associations, and with the hearings of the House Un-American Activities Committee going on, and the previous problems I had with my visa, I was paranoid. I was afraid any relationship with this group might be misinterpreted. Playing it safe had landed me in an intellectual desert. When the day's shooting was over I could hardly wait for the morning, so Joe and I could continue our conversations. Sometimes, before we went to our respective homes, we would rendezvous on a deserted street behind the Beverly Hills Hotel, and like secret lovers we would exchange sweet, gentle, loving kisses of appreciation.

One day Hal Wallis approached me with the temptation of a $5,000 bonus if I could make Joe Cotten have an erection during a scene. I frowned and then laughed at this rather absurd offer. "It's all arranged," Wallis said. "Tomorrow you are doing the scene in the train corridor. Sam, the lighting technician, will be holding a screen in front of the arc light. Wink at him when you've succeeded, and he'll pretend to trip so he can check Joe. I'll take Sam's word for it." Wallis walked a few steps away.

I'll never understand this society, I thought. I was thinking about how long it would take to save $5,000 on a salary of $500 per week. If I get the bonus I can go back to Paris for a visit. I longed to see family and my old friends. I walked over to where Wallis was standing.

"Why do you want me to do this?"

"Well," Wallis said, "Joe is such a gentleman. He's made no approach to his leading ladies, and he's played opposite everybody from Loretta Young and Ginger Rogers to Jennifer Jones, Ingrid Bergman, Linda Darnell, and Joan Fontaine. Some of us have been wondering about his sexuality. Maybe he's a homosexual."

"He's not." I laughed.

"Prove it."

The fools. Joe a homosexual. How could they think so? Just because he wasn't rude, crude, and macho. How small minded they were. I would help clear Joe's reputation and walk again in the streets of Paris.

I thought of telling Joe what was going on, but I felt that his indignation might render him impotent. During the shooting of our love scene I leaned against him, but I could not feel any swelling of his organ. William Dieterle, the director, who was in on the quest, kept asking us to do take after take. Eyebrows were being raised in my direction as I flirted with Joe. Nothing doing. The cameraman kept checking the light intensity on Joe's face; the blood was running to my co-star's head, making his make-up look darker.

Seeing the chance to bathe in a Parisian atmosphere slipping away, I took a desperate initiative, and my tongue intensely searched Joe's mouth. Behind his closed eyes I could see him react with shock to my impudence. When I separated from our embrace Joe had a line in the script.

"You think that. . . ." Suddenly teeth flew out of his mouth in my direction. In my ardor I had dislodged his partial bridge.

"Cut!" Dieterle screamed at the top of his lungs. After an embarrassing silence Joe started to laugh. The tension was broken. We moved away from the restricting set and took a break. When we returned, each time we were about to start shooting we were overcome with uncontrollable giggles. It was decided to switch to another scene. Even the next day we had trouble keeping our composure, and in the movie I had to do the scene with my face mostly turned away from the camera. Wallis's proposal was forgotten.

The picture continued shooting through the Christmas season, and John was rarely home when I called from the set to check on his activities.

"I went out shopping for Christmas," he would say when I questioned him. "I want it to be the best Christmas you've ever had."

Every afternoon he went shopping? I was consumed by my suspicions and emotional distress, but despite these difficulties the picture had gone well through its concluding weeks. Although Dieterle was not exactly showing me a great deal of respect, at least he was not as disagreeable as he had been during the filming of *Rope of Sand*.

Christmas came and I could not believe the tree that John had brought home while I was at the studio. It was a vision, the biggest tree I had ever seen. By the time we finished decorating it, it was magic, a million little worlds of light reflected in its shiny ornaments.

I had stopped counting the number of presents accumulating under the tree; there were too many of them. Christmas Eve, after all of our friends had gone, John sat me down in my favorite chair, and while Christmas carols were playing he handed me his presents one by one. There were ninety-nine in all. The hundredth present was a big kiss when he had finished. Some of the gifts were not expensive, maybe no more than a few dollars, but they all had the same thing in common, they had been magnificently wrapped.

We went to sleep happily. I woke up, however, in the midst of a terrible nightmare. Someone was trying to push me over a cliff. I went to the kitchen to get a glass of water, and along the way I noticed the remains of the expensive wrapping paper lying all over the floor. I stopped in my tracks. John was no gift wrapper. Who had done it? Who took the time to wrap ninety-nine presents? They had all been different. It could not have been done by a professional gift wrapping service. Someone had taken the time to create individually the right color and the right type of bow to prepare me for what was inside. It had been a labor of love. Love for me? I knew no one who loved me with that much devotion.

I lay awake the rest of the night, stiff and cold, shivering with torment, punishing myself, refusing to join John in the security his warm sleeping body could have given me. I was afraid all during the next day to mention what was on my mind. John's mother and father had come that afternoon, and stayed most of the evening for the traditional Christmas dinner. They had just left when the phone rang at about ten o'clock in the evening. John answered.

"Yes. Oh yes. She loved it. We had a beautiful time. Thanks for calling."

"Who was that?" I called in from the kitchen.

John mumbled something. I repeated the question insistently.

"Who was that, darling?"

"No one."

"Now come on. There was someone on the line. I heard you talking."

"It was a girl."

"Who?"

"A friend of Steve Crane." He told me her real name, but here I will call her "Virginia."

Steve Crane, the former husband of Lana Turner, was the owner of a restaurant that was popular with the movie crowd. My face questioned John, but he stayed silent.

"Why did you say she loved it?"

"Because she helped me wrap your presents."

Virginia, that beautiful girl of whom Steve Crane was so enamored. She was the one who loved me enough to wrap the presents with such care! Ridiculous. She hardly knew me.

"It must have taken her a long time."

"Almost three weeks." John said.

I made a rapid calculation. It coincided with the times when I was most suspicious.

"Every day I dropped by what I bought for you."

He had dropped by her apartment every day for three weeks? Just to drop off little presents? What else had happened there? The demon of suspicion was growing within me.

"What else did you do together every day?"

"Nothing," he answered. "Just wrap presents."

It was clear that it was not for the love of me that Virginia had wrapped the gifts with such care. It must have been for love of John. The shock of this realization brought a feeling that I had hit upon the truth, and gave me a sense of relief. I wasn't being crazy.

John was glad that I didn't make a scene. We went to bed. Soon he was asleep. I lay awake, and stayed awake all night. What was I going to do? What should I do about Virginia? Why did I want to save a marriage I no longer believed in? Was I afraid to find myself alone without the security of marriage?

During the shooting of *Peking Express*, John had stopped making love to me every night. Had he gone to bed every afternoon with Virginia? By morning I had concluded that a counterattack might be necessary to blow the competition away.

That night my mind had flashed back to France, to Gilbert Lafitte and his wife Louise. After Louise confronted Gilbert with both of us, I lost all interest in her husband. I cared for him after that as a friend, but as a lover he had totally lost his appeal.

John was still asleep when I left for the studio. I called just before the lunch break.

"What do you want to do this weekend?" I asked.

"I don't know," he said laconically.

"How about giving a small dinner party for the people who gave us presents?"

"That sounds like a good idea. Do you want me to make the calls?"

"You don't have to. I'll make them myself on my lunch hour."

"All right."

There was silence. I knew John was waiting for me to ask what he was going to do that day. I did not.

"See you when you get home."

"Yes darling." I hung up.

I was proud of myself. I was in control. I had a plan. I found Virginia's phone number, called a few other people first, then called her.

"Virginia, this is Corinne Calvet. It was so sweet of you to help John with all those presents. You did such an incredible job. They were so beautifully done. I really don't know how to thank you. I'd like to get to know you better. Maybe some day you could teach me how to wrap presents that way."

"Sure." Virginia sounded cautious.

"John and I are giving a small dinner party Saturday. We would both like to have you come."

"Well, I don't know." There was a moment's hesitation before she continued. "I guess it'll be all right."

"Good, we'll be expecting you at seven."

When I came home John wanted to know whom I had invited. When I mentioned Virginia he did not act surprised. I concluded that he must have talked to her about it.

"How did you get her number? Why did you invite her?" he asked, keeping his feelings under control.

Saturday, the dinner was perfect. The music, the candles, the food, the after-dinner liqueur.

Virginia came alone. I had invited three other couples and they all left early. Virginia wanted to leave with them.

"Don't go," I said. "Stay awhile longer. We haven't really had a chance to talk."

The three of us were sitting in the living room. I was scared. I busied myself taking the remains of the party back to the kitchen. I needed time to think. Should I go forward with my plans? I peeked into the living room. They were sitting on the sofa looking at each other without saying a word. John got up to get himself another brandy. He sat down again. No words were exchanged. For two people who had spent hours together wrapping presents it was strange to see them behaving as if they were total strangers. I was right. It has gone further than I thought. They may even be in love, I said to myself, as I poured another glass of brandy, swallowed it, went back into the room, and sat next to John. I turned to Virginia.

"Well," I said. "I really want to thank you for the help you gave John. It must have taken you hours. I don't know how to show my gratitude."

"It was my pleasure," Virginia answered, giggling nervously. "I really enjoyed it."

"You're so beautiful, Virginia, and John is so handsome. Did you fall in love with him?"

"Corinne, what are you doing?" John's voice was harsh.

"Darling, please. Everything is all right. You two have spent so many beautiful hours together the last few weeks, you can't tell me that you don't feel attracted to one another. It wouldn't be normal. You're a very handsome pair." I was smiling. There was no anger in my voice. Somehow I was enjoying the bewilderment on their faces.

"You see, Virginia," I said, "I'm French, and in France when a wife realizes that her husband is attracted to another woman she invites that woman to come and share her husband with her."

"They do what?" The look on John's face was comical.

The brandy was having its effect on me. I felt a warm daring, as if I were a sophisticated woman of the world.

"Sooner or later, if you have not already, the two of you will go to bed together. If you have to hide it, it will add an element of mystery that can be dangerous to my marriage. So darling, let me give you a late Christmas present. . . ."

It was many months before I could even bear to think about the events that followed. I could hardly force myself to remember. In the morning I was the first to wake up. I went into the bathroom and took a shower, washing my hair, trying to eradicate all memory of what had happened. When I returned to the bedroom Virginia was gone. I felt that what had happened was irreparable. John and I never looked at each other all that day. Our conversation was monosyllabic. That night I pretended to be asleep when he came to bed.

On Monday I was glad to get back to the studio. I did not call John. I did not want to know if he had stayed home or gone out. If he was not home he might have gone to see her. It was turning into a waking nightmare.

We never did talk about what had happened between us that night. John went back to fishing every day while I was working, and slowly we returned to our routine of making love each night before going to sleep. We both wanted to forget the past. A deep sadness settled over me.

With the conclusion of *Peking Express* Joe Cotten and I had no further reason to see each other. I missed our sharing, and once more I felt the lack of intellectual companionship.

Wallis and Zanuck both had the vision to see the influence of television on the public, and arranged for me to appear on a number of television shows, the "Bob Hope Special," the "Red Skelton Show," and the "Donald O'Connor Comedy Hour," among others. Between Zanuck's Fox Studio publicity department and that of Wallis, I was kept extremely busy. I had won both the annual *Look* award and the Golden Globe awards for my work in *Rope of Sand,* and consequently I was in demand. The publicity push was on, and I welcomed more and more reasons to be away, since I would have to go deep sea fishing each day I was at home. More and more my stomach rebelled at the deep, slow swells of the early morning sea.

Helen Ainsworth, who had long suffered from a glandular disorder, had taken a turn for the worse, and I was forced to find representation elsewhere. I signed with Harold Rose, an agent who had broken away from Charlie Feldman to open his own agency.

One day Paul Nathan called to ask if I wanted to go to Europe and do advance publicity for the release of *Rope of Sand* in London and Paris, all expenses paid. I would get the trip after all, and John was looking forward to meeting my family. The train, the luxury crossing of the Atlantic, the return of the prodigal daughter bearing gifts were all part of that long ago dream. I had to pinch myself. I was now living this vision of returning as a heroine. I was full of excitement. Could we make it a second honeymoon, forgetting the past for the time being? Our closeness returned amid the pleasures of first class travel. During our marriage I had been adapting to the American ways of doing things; now I anticipated guiding John through the ways of Europe.

When we arrived, Papa and Isabelle went out of their way to make John feel at ease. In preparation for our coming visit, Papa had gone to the trouble of reviewing his English, looking forward to conversing with my American husband.

We were visiting my sister Chantal and her husband Claude

at their home in Neuilly, a suburb of Paris. Isabelle, Chantal, and I were in the kitchen getting dinner ready.

"Well, at least you don't have anybody to make you feel intellectually inferior," Chantal said crisply. She had married a super-intellectual who wrote philosophical books.

"What do you mean?" I said with the exasperation that had been my childhood manner of reacting to her.

"He's a good-looking GI type," she answered. "But his brain. Even for an American, he isn't very bright."

"How would you know? Your English isn't that good," I replied.

"It's good enough. Anyway, intellectual people have their brain developed more than their muscles."

I was silent for a moment before I tried to refute her.

"Take me, for example, I'm an intellectual, and yet I also have a good body."

"Corinne, you have never done anything physical in your life, except you know what," Chantal said dryly. "The fact that people find you . . . what they call in America sexy, has nothing to do with it. You live in your brain."

"Now, stop, you two," Isabelle ordered. "Take those dishes out to the dining room."

In the dark paneled room the men were waiting for dinner. Papa, using the English employed by the European elite of the 1920s, was discussing the pros and cons of the new philosophies of the day with my husband, whose interests were reserved to football and fishing. Their valiant effort to communicate warmed my heart. They both needed guidance, Papa because his focus in the scientific sphere had left him no time to comprehend or feel at ease with ordinary human behavior, and John because his limited education and experience had not been conducive to thinking widely on any subject.

As I watched them, I remembered the time years ago when Papa had announced his desire to marry Isabelle, our nanny. The suggestion had created total chaos.

"You can't bring a servant into the family, Papa. She can never be a countess. What will people say? It will ruin us socially," I could still hear them saying. When I saw Papa's head go back into his shoulders, I took his defense.

"How do you dare," I had said, getting up and planting myself in the middle of the room. "Papa doesn't even have to ask us. You are just a bunch of resentful snobs. Let me remind you that you would have gone hungry after Maman died if Isabelle had not used all of her savings to support the family before Papa got on his feet again. And who gets up at three-thirty in the morning in the freezing cold to go out in the street and wait in line for four hours before the store opens to get us butter and eggs? Who is always there to iron what you need to wear, and who has devoted over thirty years of her life to this family without ever taking a weekend off? Who? Isabelle. And now we have the chance to let her know our appreciation. You can do that without any cost to yourselves except overcoming some undignified pride." I had made a small turn during my speech, so that I looked straight into my brother's and sisters' eyes. Then I looked at Papa, letting my tone become warmer, still speaking powerfully.

"We would be honored if you would give Isabelle our name and make her our official stepmother."

There was silence. Papa's gaze had fallen to the floor. I moved toward him. He reached for my hand, squeezed it, before he dropped it.

"And," I continued, "we're all going to show enthusiasm and affection for Isabelle. I'm going to get her now."

I left the room before they could react, and was back, holding Isabelle by the hand. She was flushed with excitement, and from my smile she thought that they had accepted the idea, but she was still holding back, not quite sure that she was finally going to be rewarded for her total devotion to our family.

Madame Pierre Dibos she became, but she was never called a countess.

"You didn't marry in the Catholic church did you?" a concerned Isabelle asked when we were alone.

"No, I wanted to wait and make sure it would work before I did that. What do you think of him?" I asked Isabelle.

"He's like a big teddy bear. He must be nice to fall asleep with."

I nodded, thinking that not only did I fall asleep with John physically, but that my intellect was also slumbering.

My letters from America had been infrequent before our visit, although Papa continued to write to me faithfully every two weeks, sending me a detailed report on the activities of the family and their acquaintances. I would glance at these letters, and send a wave of love to wherever he was. Papa's act of devotion in writing often went mostly unanswered, for I had left my Parisian childhood behind and it was too painful to recall my roots. I regret not having appreciated those amusing letters from that wonderful, sensitive man. He had only a few more years to live. Papa died at the age of 69. He died in bed—of a heart attack while making love. I remember that he had joked that that was the way he'd like to go. I am glad he got his wish.

A few days after our return from Paris, a big envelope came from France. My father's letter in it was a kind attempt to cushion the shock I felt upon reading the article he had enclosed. There was an extensive piece on me in *Paris Match*. In it I was accused of playing "movie star." I was sneered at for having an American husband, and condemned for my American accent when I spoke French. They even mocked Papa, showing him in "before" and "after" photos, the first in an old suit that was too tight for him as he said good-by to me, and the second in a new suit, saying hello to me on my return. The implication was that he had let my success go to his head.

Letting oneself change with success was considered tactless in France. In America it was the opposite. Changes in one's lifestyle were an acceptable sign of success.

It was time for me to start a new picture, the second in Wallis's agreement to loan my services to Zanuck.

"We're redoing a picture called *What Price Glory?* We've decided to have you play the part of Charmaine. It's a great challenge. Two big female stars have played the part before you. I'll be glad to run those pictures for you," Zanuck told me.

"No, Mr. Zanuck. I would prefer not. I don't want to be influenced by other performances. It would limit my own freedom of expression. Please let me do it my way. The way I feel from reading the script is the way I want Charmaine to be. Who's the director?"

"John Ford."

I was overtaken with consternation. John Ford, the director of *When Willie Comes Marching Home*. No, I was not going to go through that kind of putdown again.

"I'm sorry, Mr. Zanuck. I don't want the picture, not with Mr. Ford."

"Look Corinne, I know you've had your problems with him, but we've talked about it, and he's promised to be courteous and behave kindly toward you. You have James Cagney and Dan Dailey as your co-stars. This picture will do it for you, Corinne."

I was still hesitant.

"My secretary will have orders to put you right through to me instantly if you call because of any trouble on the set."

I read the script. It was a good part. I decided to do the film.

John Ford was not cordial, but he had accepted me. He would sit just under the camera lens, chewing on a corner of a white handkerchief all day long. It looked disgusting. It seemed to an outsider that he was engaging in rather strange and childish behavior for a man of his age. Gossip had it that he was getting senile. Soon I understood what he was doing. Ford had discovered a way for his pictures to appear on the screen the way he intended them to be.

Because of the need to create movement on the screen, the same scene is shot and recorded on film from different angles and distances with different lenses. The choice of the moment at which one shifts from one shot to another is the most sensitive part of the completed product. When watching a play onstage the audience can choose to direct their attention as they like, concentrating visually wherever they prefer. Not so with film. The choices are predetermined. The final editing of the various shots determines how the film will be seen by the public.

After this film was finished Ford never went to the cutting room to protect its integrity. He did not have to. He had held the corner of his handkerchief a little higher into the camera frame so that when the film dailies were screened only certain frames out of each day's shooting could be used. In the rest a white piece of cloth in the corner rendered the film useless.

It was difficult but enjoyable keeping up with two of the most brilliant scene stealers in the business, Cagney and Dailey. Actors of this period tried to draw the attention of the audience to themselves at all times, whether or not they had any lines. Stars were made that way. It was considered more important for the public to leave the theater engrossed in the performance of a single actor or actress, rather than moved by the overall impact of the story. Queries to the audience at sneak previews became guide posts for the studio. If the audience mentioned an actor or actress when asked to recall what they liked about a picture, the studios were inclined to put money behind promoting the pictures starring these artists.

Both James Cagney and Dan Dailey were masters at scene stealing. It was a game with them, for they were both renowned stars. It was a challenge for me too, because I had to call upon a great deal of power even to be noticed in the picture, caught as I was in the middle of this championship test of magnetic mannerisms. They totally ignored me when they were both in a scene with me.

One of Dan Dailey's visitors was a young actor under a minimum contract to Fox. Robert Wagner had a crush on me, the movie star. It was so obvious, and so fresh and beautiful, that his charm made me want to cuddle him warmly. It was tempting. I wanted to hug and kiss him, rest my head on his masculine chest. I recognized the impulse only too well. It was too dangerous to give in to the attraction.

The film was a big success and my popularity continued to grow. John's ego took a terrible beating, particularly at the Hollywood premieres where screaming fans were always in evidence. Outbursts of recognition were deafening as we emerged from our car at each new appearance, and I was very conscious of how much John must dread these occasions, and the lack of recognition or consideration shown him. The doorman would call on the loudspeaker for "Miss Calvet's car," and my husband would cringe. In restaurants it was "Miss Calvet's table." Mine was the only name anybody remembered, doormen, the maître d', the fans. I was careful to introduce John as my husband, but nobody seemed to care. The name Bromfield all but disappeared.

Occasionally John did get some recognition through our marriage. The studio publicity department set up a lot of magazine coverage for me immediately after I finished *What Price Glory?* Photographers and journalists would come over to our house and treat us as a couple. We were sent on weekend vacations where we could be photographed in various hotels and spas, engaging in whatever activities were available to their customers. I was feeling important, more secure. It was easy at such times to pretend that everything was perfect, and that our marriage could go on forever.

Chapter 10

"I am starring in *On the Riviera* with Danny Kaye . . . whew!" I let the air out of my lungs as I drove along Santa Monica Boulevard toward the Twentieth Century-Fox studio. I was thrilled—in working with a gentle genius like Danny Kaye I had finally realized one of my Hollywood hopes. Danny's career had been in low gear. His last two pictures had fallen flat at the box office and the blame had been placed on Danny's wife Sylvia, who had written the scripts and been very much in control of those pictures. So when Zanuck wanted Danny for *On the Riviera*, there was one stipulation: no Sylvia on the set.

I remained on the set whether I was working or not. Watching Danny do one of his routines reminded me of watching another genius in Paris—Marcel Marceau. I was very impressed with Danny's control over his movements. His routines were timed so beautifully that he seemed to expend no effort.

Billy Travillas's costume sketches for the film were magnificent and I was kept happily busy running between clothes fittings and dance rehearsals for numbers that were staged by Jack Cole. My dance coach was Gwen Verdon. I had never seen a dancer who could create such an electric field of energy around her. She was then still a relatively unknown Broadway actress, singer, and dancer, but her brilliance was already evident. She had authority, even in the tips of her fingers, and she was cute, with her red hair and freckles.

When we started the actual shooting, I would get as close as I could behind the camera next to Charlie Lang, the director of photography. Danny would stare at me with a question in his eyes after each take and I found myself letting my face express my reaction to his work. Soon I was winking at him whenever I felt something was perfect. Danny had never asked me to do this; it just happened. I was taking the place that his wife had occupied.

The more he depended on me, the more rewarded I felt. His acceptance of my reactions flattered me into feeling good about myself, my talent, and my future. Danny was discreetly flirtatious and, childlike, I enjoyed every moment I spent near him.

One night as John was drowsing in front of the television the phone rang. I answered and heard Danny's voice telling me how attracted to me he was. I was speechless.

"Who was it?" asked a sleepy John.

"It was a wrong number," I answered, hitting my pillow with my fist—disappointed again. Why couldn't this have been a friendship that did not involve sex?

Since I was not needed on the set the next day I stayed home, afraid that my presence there would be for Danny an acceptance of sexual possibility. When it was time for me to go back on the set, I still admired him, enjoyed and respected his work, but I watched from the side where he could not see me. Nothing was ever said about the phone call.

Shortly after the completion of *On the Riviera* John and I were invited to the first Mexican film festival, held in Acapulco. On the way to Mexico we spent a great deal of time with Herb Jeffries, a talented singer who became internationally famous for his renditions of exotic songs like "Flamingo," and who later married the dancer Tempest Storm. I was struck by Herb's incredibly blue eyes, the kind that radiate light. Herb had told me how he had chosen to identify with his black heritage in high school when he decided to join Duke Ellington's band, even though he could pass for white. What I did not know then was that he was also a devotee of the late Paramahansa Yogananda, an Indian sage and teacher of Kriya Yoga, who had exercised a great influence on Herb.

Herb's presence gave me a feeling of peace and protection. When he was with us I found that I did not experience negative thoughts, and got a reprieve from all the problems on my mind. Something about him gave me the power to protect myself with a veil of detachment. Nothing seemed to matter, nothing seemed to interfere with the sensation of total security I felt in his presence.

A star-studded assemblage gathered in Mexico City on the way to the festival in Acapulco: Gary Cooper, Hedda Hopper, Rhonda Fleming, Debbie Reynolds, Lex Barker, to mention only a few. It was a very gay and explosive group. Except for Gary

Cooper, we were all terrified of Hedda Hopper's power to make or break a career through her daily gossip column in *The Los Angeles Times*. We were all on our best behavior until the whole group was taken to a luxurious restaurant outside the city, with magnificent gardens and a mosaic swimming pool. Cocktails in the warm sun helped us all to relax, and the formidable Hedda was the life of the party. She handled her liquor remarkably well, and to my surprise there was nothing very fearful about her, especially when after lunch she went to the pool, sat down on the edge, kicked off her sandals, pulled her skirt high around her, and dangled her feet in the cool water, lifting her skirt high enough to reveal the fact that she was wearing no panties. She was taking pleasure in the attention she attracted from the male audience, who watched her exhibition from the other side of the pool. Hedda's unorthodox behavior turned our uptight group into a little tribe of giggling children.

Some of the group flew from Mexico City directly to Acapulco. Gary Cooper, Lex Barker, John, and I drove in a gray Lincoln Continental. The whole trip had a sense of unreality about it. It was like being caught in a movie. Cooper was an actor who had the same personality on and off the screen. His words were the same monosyllables, his actions straightforward; his look, his hesitation, they were all there. The magnificent setting of the semicircular highrise hotel on the bay of Acapulco added to my feeling that I was having a marvelous dream.

When we returned home from Acapulco all my doubts and troubles returned. I began losing weight, and I was plagued with migraine headaches. The doctor's tests were all negative, and there was nothing wrong with me. But the recollection of my mother's sudden death from a brain hemorrhage haunted me constantly. It was difficult for me to accept the doctor's judgment that there was nothing wrong with me physically, and that the headaches were brought on by an emotional disturbance. I resented his suggestion that I see a psychiatrist. I still loved and cared for my husband, even after some difficult times. I was successful. I was a star. What could be wrong?

Since the incident with Virginia I had been living with only part of my mind and body. The other part had gone dead that night. I could not talk about what had happened with anybody. It was locked inside me like a cancer. I was living in shadows. The part of me I had destroyed was eating me up, I constantly reviewed the events of the last few years. Black thoughts were my constant companions.

I was relieved when I received word that Hal Wallis had made a deal with Paramount for me to appear in a picture starring Charles Boyer, Alan Ladd, and Deborah Kerr, but the necessary enthusiasm was lacking. All of my shattered illusions made me realize that stardom was not going to give me security, happiness, or peace of mind. *Thunder in the East* was just another picture to do with the same dialogue and the same kind of part. I was to play a prostitute who wants to get out of India, and tries to seduce a celibate Nehru type of character into giving her a visa in exchange for sexual favors.

I loved being at the studio while that picture was being made. The set had a library full of information about India. The prop men had filled shelves with real books on Yoga and the spiritual philosophy of the East. I had never felt so much intense joy as when reading some of those volumes. In a way it was the same intensity I had felt many years ago when I perused my father's collection of erotic literature, except that these books spoke of the energy of spirit rather than flesh.

From the *Bhagavad-Gita* to the lives of various Indian sages, I devoured these books page after page. I seemed to recognize in them knowledge with which I could identify.

Charles Boyer, who played the Nehru character, acted toward me like someone much older who felt no rapport with my generation. The fact that we were both French did not seem to help him bridge the gulf. Perhaps his reserved, cool mood was induced by the role he was playing. Alan Ladd was also distant. His whole personality came oozing out with obvious warmth and sincerity only when he was before the camera, and when the scene was over he retreated into a shy posture. His wife was always with him on the set. Some years earlier, when she was an agent, she had found him working at odd jobs, and she had made him a star. He now seemed to depend on her totally. I thought this was wonderful, a woman who had fallen so much in love with a man that she had given up her business, and now lived only for him. Once again I felt the desire to try to make my marriage work. I returned home each night from the studio gay and happy, full of love and tenderness for my husband. The headaches disappeared.

It was not long after the completion of *Thunder in the East* that I got a call from Zanuck's secretary.

"I have a script for you, Corinne," she said.

"Did you clear it with Hal Wallis?"

"Mr. Zanuck wants you to agree to it first."

All was well. Zanuck was protecting me from suspension in the event that I did not want to do the film, called *Powder River*.

"Who's the leading man?" I asked.

"Cameron Mitchell and Rory Calhoun."

Rory. My knees started to shake. I can't do it, I thought. I wonder how I feel about him now. Since we broke up, every time I had seen his name in print my heart seemed to skip and lift inside my chest. When I saw the picture of his wedding to Lita Baron, a fiery Mexican singer, I had some regret as I toasted them with a dry martini.

The last time I had any real contact with Rory was when the Bromfields, married for three years, met the Calhouns, who had been married for a year and a half, a meeting that had been arranged by Henry Willson, still Rory's agent.

"Corinne, Rory and John were good friends, and Rory is lonely," Henry had said to me. "The only friends he and Lita have now are Lita's family. Why don't you bury the hatchet and let Rory and John be friends again. Every young couple needs another young couple to be friends with. I also think that if the four of you go to events where the press is present you'll all benefit from the publicity. The photographers will go wild."

We arrived at Willson's house early. I looked around the room and chose a good vantage point, a place from which we could see everyone coming in, and where sooner or later everyone would have to pass.

"John, look who came in. Rory and his wife Lita. We haven't seen them in ages."

"You keep cool," John said, putting his hand on my elbow as if it would be necessary to restrain me. He knew about the tempestuous romance between Calhoun and Calvet. When I felt there was only a few feet separating us, I turned to face them. Like a frame in a movie, we all stood frozen. Rory was looking at John, I was looking at Lita.

"Hello, Lita," I said, breaking the ice, walking over to her and kissing her lightly on the cheek. "You look beautiful. I think it's wonderful that we're both happily married." I threw a rapid glance in Rory's direction. "Hello, Rory."

His eyes were laughing in anticipation of whatever might be about to happen. Lita had stiffened at my touch.

"Look, Lita," I pressed on, "Hollywood is really a small town. Let's agree to let bygones be bygones. After all, it would make it very difficult if everbody was jealous of their mate's past lovers."

Her mouth dropped open, but no sound came out.

"Rory would not be unfriendly to your past lovers. Right, Rory?"

Before her marriage, she had had a long relationship with the leader of the band for which she sang.

"Talk for yourself, but for me, I was a virgin when I met Rory."

"You have a great sense of humor; that's funny," I said in disbelief.

"Rory, let's move," Lita said.

I stood there laughing at the absurdity of her statement.

As Rory left he looked at me, his eyebrows drawn into a frown that ordered me to let it go. Henry's experiment had failed. The gap between us had widened. From then on whenever the Calhouns found themselves at the same opening they kept as far away from the Bromfields as possible.

Zanuck's secretary said, "We're sending you the script."

I felt breathless. I was going to do a film, play love scenes, and spend every day for weeks with Rory on the set. The prospect was tempting. I wondered what Lita's reaction would be.

The first day on the set Rory was cold and distant. Lita had set rules, he told me, and he had promised not to spend any time with me, not to share any meals, not even to talk to me on the set, and never, under any circumstances, to be alone with me. She had even hired a part-time boxer as Rory's valet and bodyguard to make sure the promise was kept.

A bodyguard to protect Rory from me? At first I found it funny, but it soon became inconvenient. Then the little game began. I sent little notes to Rory, telling him what I liked about his performance. The bodyguard had relaxed when he saw that Rory had no apparent interest in me.

We were in our sixth week of shooting when one day the bodyguard did not show up. Like kids who had not been permitted to eat candy all day, we played flirtatious games, our eyes always on the alert for the arrival of Lita's spy.

It was four o'clock and the production needed to change sets. We had an hour off. As I was leaving my dressing room I found Rory waiting for me. I passed by, and he looked straight above me and spoke.

"Come and join me in ten minutes in 106."

For a moment I was furious because he had taken for granted that I would meet him, but I was caught up in the game.

We hugged when I came into the room, letting out repressed giggles like two children enjoying a chance to be naughty. Not wanting to disturb our make-up we did not kiss, but disrobed from the waist down. The pleasure came from the fear of being caught. It was done quickly. When it was over I left. We met again on the set, shot our next scene, and for the rest of the filming ignored each other. There was no longer any need for a bodyguard.

I was amazed that I felt no guilt where John was concerned. It had been like ringing the doorbell of a former residence and walking through the rooms, ill at east with the changes made by the new inhabitants.

It was during that period that I received a telegram informing me of Papa's death. The studio could only give me 48 hours off to go to the funeral in Paris, so I decided not to go. That way I could keep my memory of him as alive as the last time I saw him.

Since Hal Wallis continued to be sensitive to the opportunities presented by television, I was due for an exciting experience. Television, soon to become a monstrous threat to the film industry, was no longer in its infancy. It had a strong voice, and the masses were heeding it. No need to pay for it, find a baby sitter, or worry about parking. They could be warm in bed, lazy, sick, or bored, and by just turning a switch they would be entertained and influenced. Hollywood tried to deny television's importance. It was a dirty word, a disease that they hoped would pass, and in their fantasy world the moguls were hoping for a miracle cure.

Not so with Wallis. All of us under contract to him were asked about our stage experience. I had already done a number of variety shows, but he wanted to know who could do live drama. Few Hollywood actors had ever worked on the stage, and most were threatened by the prospect. My experience as a stage actress in France now proved useful, and a week after the shooting of *Powder River* was completed, I went to New York to appear in an episode of "Lux Video Theater."

Though I don't remember the teleplay, one incident remains fresh in my mind. The show was live. I had to make one of those rapid costume changes from a dress to a negligee—and the wardrobe department failed to bring the nightgown that went under the very transparent clothing. There was no time to lose so I put on the filmy garment and held my arm across my chest to hide my nudity. Marty Milner was my leading man. Not knowing what had happened, he kept trying to pull my arm away to reach me for the final embrace that would close the show. Of course I resisted—it was a very awkward final kiss we exchanged. But those days of live TV were exciting, and I was in demand because I loved working in front of a live audience.

In Hollywood the panic continued. Studios cut back on personnel as movies lost money. They were trying to stem the tide running against the studio system—television; the court decision which declared illegal the production, distribution and exhibition of a film by a single entity, the studio; and the rising cost of studio payrolls. Powerful stars were forming their own production companies, independent of big studios, and by cutting down on the overhead sustained by a large corporation they were able to make films that earned a profit. More and more big stars were not available to the studios unless they were offered a generous percentage of the picture's profits.

It was now that I learned that Wallis had sold me for two films to Paramount. The first one had been *Thunder in the East,* and now I was to do a second, *Flight to Tangier.* In order for the studio to rid itself of outstanding commitments, they decided to take a mediocre script and cast all the actors and actresses to whom they were obligated.

Joan Fontaine, Jack Palance, Robert Douglas, and I found ourselves running through the vineyards of Bakersfield, a poor man's version of the outskirts of Tangier. Edith Head had designed a pale green skirt and embroidered pearl sweater for me to wear in the film.

"You are going to be a refreshing sight on the screen running away from the authorities in the midst of all that hot desert dust," she said. "And here is a scarf that you can wrap around you in different ways."

On our way to Bakersfield I discovered that I was going to have a lot of fun with Joan Fontaine. She was extremely friendly, with a great sense of humor. We laughed and joked as we rode. She had brought books to read, and I had brought a chess set. There was no place to go at night, and we spent our evenings together in our Bakersfield room. Like two girls we giggled, gossiping about people we knew.

One night Jack Palance kept walking by my window. He had approached me earlier during the day, and suggested that we take a moonlight walk. When he finally knocked on the door, I went out to join my co-star for what I hoped would be a brief, innocent stroll. Without a word, Jack took my arm and guided me to a rock that overlooked the valley. He was silent, looking into the distance, his jaw tense, his eyes squinting. I was apprehensive. I complained of the cold. Jack took off his sweater and dropped it over my shoulders without uttering a word.

"I want to go back," I said.

Like a flood over a broken dam, words gushed out. He needed me to listen, he said. He had a lot on his mind. He talked about his relationship with his wife, about how he had boxed professionally. He had the vulnerability I found irresistible in a man. Suddenly he was like a little boy needing reassurance and comfort. I stroked his bowed head. He started to sob. I held him and rocked him gently, silently, back and forth.

When his distress subsided I told him that I needed my rest for the next day's shooting. At the door of my room he took back his sweater, his eyes squinting with embarrassment over his outburst. Without saying goodnight he left.

The following days Jack acted as if he had never confided in me. When the filming was over I finished *Flight to Tangier* with great hope for my career. The movie was not a success. In the final analysis the script was poor, full of redundant dialogue. Still, I felt that my performance had been excellent. On a spring morning in 1953, Paul Nathan called to tell me that Hal Wallis was not picking up my option, which had three more years to go. I was shocked.

"Don't feel too bad, Corinne. He's not picking up the options of Wendell Corey, Vince Edwards, Don Defore, Polly Bergen, Dolores Hart, or Lizabeth Scott," Paul told me. "So you're not the only one."

"But Paul, why?"

"I don't even know if I'm going to be working for him. He's closing Hal Wallis productions, and I think he'll be merging with someone."

I put the phone down and walked around the pool, stopping to smell the flowers blooming on the hill. It was strange. I felt no emotion. I had no financial panic. Everyone had told me how well I would do if I freelanced. Thinking how I would feel if I had given in to Wallis, I smiled to myself. One stage of my career was over, but I didn't realize then just how thoroughly.

Joe Pasternak had opened his Bel Air mansion to the friends of his young wife, Dorothy. John and I soon became regular guests, and when Pasternak saw my husband playing in the pool, his muscles accentuated by the rippling water, he decided that John would be perfect with Esther Williams in the film Joe was planning. *Easy to Love* would contain elaborate water ballets, choreographed by Busby Berkeley, who was coming out of retirement to take charge of the production numbers in the luxurious setting of Cypress Gardens.

It was a big break for John, the first good part he'd had since he appeared in *Paid in Full,* starring Lizabeth Scott, before Wallis dropped his contract. He had a supporting role in *Flat Top* starring Sterling Hayden and Richard Crenna.

The picture was rehearsed in the studio before going on location in Florida, and within a few days John was walking taller, his head held high. When I saw John returning happily from rehearsals I suddenly knew that until he was successful in his own career, our marriage would continue to be unbalanced.

It was about this time that I was offered a second "Lux Video" television drama. Paul Nathan said Wallis would let me keep the salary I was getting for it. I was happy. The first show I did for this series, about six months earlier, had been the closest experience I had ever had before a camera to the sense of heightening excitement I felt during a stage performance.

"I'll come down to Cypress Gardens as soon as I finish the show in New York," I told John, almost apologetically.

"You know, I've been thinking," he replied, speaking rapidly, "with the money we're making this month there is no reason why you couldn't treat yourself to a trip to Paris. After all, you've not seen your family since your father died."

I was hesitant. I did not want to let him know that I didn't want to go anywhere alone. He went on.

"It's all right, darling. You can spend the money now that I'm working."

I said nothing. I could not know he had another motivation. I closed my eyes. I pictured myself coming out of the George V in Paris, all heads turning to watch me as I graciously answered questions and posed for the European press.

The faraway look on my face convinced John that I had accepted his suggestion. I would go to Paris right after the show in New York, and return to meet John in California after he finished filming in Florida.

That spring New York looked radiant. My thoughts were of John in Florida. In my reverie I concentrated on sending him the support I thought he needed.

My old friend, Murvyn Vye, whom I had not seen for a few years, arrived at the "Lux Video" rehearsal in a West Side theater. I waited for the first break to run to Murvyn and throw my arms around his neck. Murvyn, dignified as he was, gleefully accepted my exuberant expression of delight at seeing him.

That night there was no rehearsal for the television drama, so Murvyn suggested going to the Village to hear one of the entertainer heroes of the intellectual minority, Lenny Bruce. Lenny was not yet vulgar, as he later became, but was a brilliant political cynic.

Years later in Chicago I opened my nightclub act following Lenny's closing, and was there on the last night of his performance. He confided in me that one night in a club like this he began to insult the audience, which had become rude and impatient while clamoring for the return of the showgirls who opened and closed the show.

"I thought I was kissing off my career," he said, "and I was really ready for it, but you know what those ignoramus bastards did? They loved it. They came back the next day for more. They brought friends. For awhile I loved it, but then I wanted to go back to my typical sarcastic shtick. The club owners wanted me to keep on being a dirty-mouthed insult artist. Now I don't know which one is the real me, no shit." He finished his drink in one gulp. "Don't let them change you."

He got up and left the club. I followed Lenny's advice. When the club owner handed me some off-color jokes to add to my act, I refused, and it became obvious that my material had no appeal for his customers. We amicably canceled my engagement after the second show.

Lenny was like a frail bamboo and he finally cracked under the persecution constantly leveled against him.

On this occasion I saw Lenny in New York with Murvyn Vye and Murvyn's friend Kem Dibbs. Kem was a handsome struggling actor of Armenian extraction, supporting himself through a multitude of small business deals. The conversation turned to a woman they both knew. Anne Bates was a model, out of work, depressed, too ill even to call the doctor, and unable to pay if she did.

"I think on top of her cold she's suffering from malnutrition, trying to be as thin as the new models coming on the scene," Kem said.

"Well, why don't you help?" I couldn't understand how they could remain so unconcerned.

The next day I went with Kem to visit the sick girl.

Four days later Anne, a small blonde with incredibly long, slender fingers, was with me on the flight to Paris as my secretary. She would be my companion. I was going to Paris in style, traveling with my own secretary, filled with a sense of having sanctioned my feelings as a person of importance with this addition to my retinue. I was on top of the world as we landed in Paris at Orly. Extravagantly, I took the presidential suite at the Hotel George V.

The two bedrooms were separated by a spacious, luxurious living room. The decor was fit for royalty. I called Isabelle, Chantal, Hughes, and my niece Marie Terese (Christiane's daughter), and invited them all to come and have champagne with us.

I had come back to Paris as a star in the Hollywood pantheon. I disregarded Isabelle's attempt to question the expense of all this opulence. After they had all left I flopped on my bed, with

Anne on the one next to mine. Pushing the air out of my lungs energetically I felt a great relief, and laughed at my family's obvious admiration of my success. Little did they know what a great emotional price I had paid to see my fantasy fulfilled.

The next day was busy with interviews and photographers. They seemed pleased that I had not traveled with my American husband, and wondered if I intended to stay and marry a Frenchman. I was light, gay, and noncommittal. I could feel Anne watching this new part of my personality with a quizzical look on her face. About five in the evening she asked me if she could go out by herself for a few hours.

I was glad to be alone in the immense suite. I bathed, dressed carefully, and put on make-up. I needed to be alone. Since John and I had married I had never felt free the way I did now.

The only shadow over my happiness was that my attempts to reach John in Florida had been frustrating. I had attempted to leave numerous messages, but the desk clerk who answered the telephone at his motel refused to write them down. I was about to go to bed when John called.

"How are you, little monkey? It's good to see your family, right? . . . But of course I missed you. . . . But they keep us very busy. . . . I know they won't take messages. Too many actors staying here. Look, a month won't be that long. Enjoy yourself, have a good time . . . and go out on dates—platonic of course. Listen, I have to go, talk to you next week. Just a minute."

I heard him partially cover the phone with his hand and tell someone he was speaking to Paris. "OK darling," he was speaking to me again, "have a beautiful time. So do I." I heard the click of the phone disconnecting. I felt the old suspicions stabbing at me again.

I had to return to the States right away. After making plane reservations I called Kem Dibbs in New York and asked him to meet me with a limousine at the airport.

He was waiting for me when the plane arrived in New York, his curly, dark hair groomed in place. I was momentarily taken by his good looks. He guided me to the waiting limousine and handed the ticket stubs for my luggage to the driver.

"I'm glad you've come back," he said, taking my face in his hands. "I haven't been able to chase you out of my mind since you left."

"Kem, can I confide in you?" I asked.

"Only if you promise to have dinner with me after we drop your luggage off at the hotel. I'll be all ears."

Over some fresh mussels, I presented my fear and suspicion. "Corinne, there isn't one man in the world who wouldn't be proud to be your man. Don't worry, nobody can take your place. If John's having a little flirtation, I'm sure it's just that." In the face of my somber silence he continued, "Listen, a little romantic excitement is a good diversion, even in the happiest of marriages. It gives you the feeling of being desirable and beautiful again."

"I'm tired, Kem. Thank you for your friendship." I was not pleased with his analysis. "Please take me back to my hotel."

Back in my room I noted that it was now 11:30 P.M. in Florida. Once again John's room did not answer.

The next morning I bathed and shaved my legs with care. I powdered and perfumed, looking forward to my coming reunion with my husband. The door buzzer rang, jarring me back from my contemplation. I quickly draped my dressing gown around my body. It was room service with the breakfast I had ordered. Right behind was Kem, holding a single rose. He tipped the waiter, and closed the door.

"What are you doing here?" I asked.

"I just came to take you to the airport. Do you mind? Every minute I spend with you is a cherished memory."

"Oh Kem," I said, putting my cup down on the coffee table. Before I could realize what was happening, Kem's face was pressed between my legs. He had opened my robe, and with his mouth on my thigh gently forced apart my knees. Almost immediately I was in the ecstasy of a long, totally encompassing orgasm.

When Kem placed his head on my trembling stomach, I pushed him quietly away. In a daze, without looking at him, I went into the bathroom. With trembling hands I attempted to put on make-up, gave up, and gathered up my toilet articles to put in my suitcase. Without a word, Kem helped me close the bag. I went to the phone, summoned two bellboys for my luggage, and told the desk to ready my bill. I went to the window to look out. Kem handled the details. My luggage was gone. The door was closed. There were only the two of us in the room. Kem caressed my hair and looked at me adoringly.

"Whatever happens, Corinne, just remember, I love you, and I'll come to you wherever you are. You only have to call."

"Nothing like this has ever happened to me," I muttered. "I'm very confused. Please understand, I want to go to the airport alone."

"I understand," he said.

Outside the hotel as the limousine prepared to leave, he gently placed the single rose on my lap and left.

On the plane I realized that I had been on automatic, totally disconnected from what was going on around me. I was overtaken with guilt by the time we were over North Carolina. How could that have happened? I thought. How could I have gotten so aroused? Listening to the roar of the plane's motors, I caught the reflection of my face in the double pane of glass covering the small window. It was some other ugly me. I carried on a silent conversation with the reflection.

"You were aroused because it excited you to think of John with another woman."

"Ridiculous," I replied haughtily to my ugly self.

"Well, now look at it this way. You never came that fast before. And why do you think you invited Virginia into your matrimonial bed?" the face went on, laughing cynically.

"Get away from me, you're evil."

The interior voice changed into that of Kem, repeating what he had said on the phone when he paged me at the airport.

"I love you, Corinne. Don't forget that I love you. Have a safe journey."

"Go away," I said to these voices. The image I saw in the window faded.

Kem's words sang in my ears, becoming a symphony scored by the roar of the DC-7 engines. I knew I was hallucinating, and I resisted entering further into the world of illusion. I welcomed the sleep that overcame me for the rest of the flight.

I woke as we landed, deciding to forget the whole incident with Kem.

When I called John's room from the airport in Tampa there was still no answer. I took an interminable taxi ride to the motel, which was located on one of the lakes near Cypress Gardens. The desk clerk informed me that John was not working that day, and that he could not tell me anything about my husband's whereabouts.

"I'm his wife," I said authoritatively. "Can you let me into his room?"

Once in the room I noticd that the bed had not been slept in. There was a phone number written on a match box. The name Terry was written beside the number. I called and asked for Terry, hoping to find John with him.

"Terry is not here," a woman's voice answered. "She went out and did not tell me when she would be back."

"Thanks," I whispered.

So Terry was a woman. Was I in time? Or was my worst nightmare already reality? I did not want to believe that it was so. Maybe he's fishing on the lake. I went back to the desk and found out where I could rent a motorboat. It died twice before I could carry my investigation very far, and realizing the futility of my efforts I went back to the motel, took a bath, and went to bed.

It was dark when John woke me up. No doubt he had been told of my presence by the hotel manager. He did not seem surprised to see me. Instead he was angry.

"What are you doing here? Trying to catch me doing something wrong?"

"No, darling. I tried and tried to reach you, but I couldn't. I was miserable in Paris without you. I couldn't stand being alone."

I asked him to take me in his arms and he did, but he did not attempt to make love.

The next day when I woke up I saw him standing by the window with a faraway look.

"Do you have to work today?" I asked.

"Not until this afternoon. I've got a dance rehearsal."

"Then why don't we go fishing this morning," I suggested.

"You really want to?" He seemed surprised.

"Why not?"

I was afraid that his hostility was an instinctive reaction caused by what had happened between Kem and me in New York. We had been basking in solitude in the middle of the lake for some time when I spoke.

"John," I said hesitantly. "I need your help. I'm so confused.

I have to tell you what happened to me yesterday. I don't understand it. You're a man. Maybe you can explain it to me."

I told him as simply as I could what had happened with Kem. When I finished he did not say a word. He started the boat motor. I began to sob.

"John, please help me to understand."

"What is it about you," he said angrily. "What is it that makes you say the truth, the whole truth? Who do you think I am? Your father confessor? Well, I'm not. I'm a furious husband who does not want my wife to come and bug me on location on my own picture."

He said nothing further, but took me to the room and left. He did not return until very late. I had cried myself out.

"The director wants you to come on the set tomorrow. They want to take some publicity pictures."

He took off his clothes and turned out the light. Once again he fell asleep beside me without making love. We never again brought up the subject of Kem Dibbs.

The next day we were all smiles for the cameras that followed Esther Williams and her husband of that time, Ben Gage, Van and Evie Johnson, and John and me. We walked through the flowery gardens, had lunch, and went dining and dancing under the stars.

John spoke to me only in monosyllables for the next three days.

"Would you prefer for me to go back to Los Angeles and wait for you there?" I offered.

"Yes," he replied coldly.

My pride wounded, I left for California.

When John arrived in Los Angeles after completing *Easy to Love,* he was always out of the house for one reason or another. He had taken over the job of paying bills and signing the checks on our joint checking account. It was strange. It had been a job he said he hated, and appreciated having me do. He also complained all the time. After almost five years of marriage he complained that I was not a real woman because I didn't cook or make my own clothes. I found it difficult even to respond to these ridiculous charges, but the idea gnawed at me. I decided to busy myself in the kitchen. For Christmas I asked John to buy me a sewing machine. I made one slipcover for the bed in the guest room, and proved to myself that I was capable of being the kind of wife he wanted. Afterward, the sewing machine went into the closet, never to be used again.

My efforts did not help the situation. John's complaints continued. Harold Rose had not been able to get me any work. Wallis had applied the clause in my contract which permitted him to retain me for twelve final weeks without pay, though he agreed to let me do a "Playhouse 90" television show.

For some time the agent Bill Schiffren had been anxious to represent me. He was a hard-driving character of the "What Makes Sammy Run" mold, and I decided that it was time to give him the chance he wanted. It paid off almost immediately. Aaron Rosenberg was producing a film, *The Far Country,* for Jimmy Stewart. It was to be shot in Canada, and in it there was a part for a French girl, a sixteen-year-old virgin who was in love with Stewart. When Bill mentioned my name to Rosenberg he just stood there and laughed.

"Look Bill," I said when Schiffren called me, "the part is mine. I can feel it. Let's try to do something. Make an appointment for tomorrow afternoon with Rosenberg for yourself and a Mademoiselle Dibos. I'll go buy a white dress that will flatten my bust, I'll put my hair in pigtails, and if Aaron doesn't recognize me in the first three minutes we'll have a chance. I want this part. I want to prove to Wallis that he made a mistake in letting me go."

It was a crazy scheme, but it worked. Rosenberg, who had met me a year before, received me with great charm. He appraised me for a long time before he spoke.

"How long have you been in Hollywood, Miss Dibos?"

"A few years."

Even though I spoke in a little girl's voice I gave myself away. The tonality of my speech was impossible to disguise. Rosenberg, an intelligent man, was not easily swayed, but he listened to us and was willing to be persuaded. We signed the contract that afternoon, and Schiffren convinced Rosenberg to keep the deal secret until a week before shooting was to begin, the last day of Wallis's contract with me.

I soon found myself on the way to Canada with Walter Brennan, Ruth Roman, and Jimmy Stewart. John didn't want to come with me, and I really did not want him along. I did not want to hear his continuous put-downs.

The Far Country was done in some very beautiful locations. Since it was an independent production, the film was not released for over a year, and although it received mixed reviews, I was praised as a dramatic actress. Reviewers had been surprised to see me as a convincing ingenue.

It was amazing. As a freelance actress I had made more money in six weeks than I had made under Wallis's contract in the last two years. When I returned to Los Angeles Bill Schiffren had numerous scripts for me to read. Each time the negotiations went beautifully until the moment came for signing the contract. Then, without explanation, the deal would be off.

I found out later that many of my co-workers whose contracts had been dropped had difficulty finding work over the next several years. They would inexplicably lose film offers at the last minute. Lizabeth Scott drifted quickly out of films, becoming a recluse. Vince Edwards struggled for years before he got his role as Ben Casey, M.D., the television part that relaunched his career. Wendell Corey dabbled in politics, and finally died prematurely, an alcoholic. Dolores Hart became a nun. It was not an easy period for any of us.

From this constant professional rejection and the rejection I was receiving from my husband, I found myself sinking into a very bad state of mind. John had now totally discarded me as a sexual partner. Matters between us quickly became impossible. John told me that he wanted to separate and move into his own apartment in Westwood. He argued that he would do better as an actor if he were single.

When John moved out I invited Anne Bates, who now lived in Los Angeles, to move in with me and be my secretary. She soon observed that I was torturing myself. My mental state was deteriorating rapidly. In her view there was only one way to save my sanity, and that was to see that I learned the truth, a truth that everyone else knew. Somehow, someone had to tell me that John had fallen in love with another woman eight months ago in Florida during the shooting of *Easy to Love*.

Anne could not tell me herself. She must have known that I would resist the truth unless I was confronted with incontrovertible evidence.

Imitating my voice, she called a detective agency and asked them to provide a report on John's activities, giving them enough details to make their job an easy one. It was a prescription for driving out of my head the final illusions I might have had about my marriage, and the medicine proved strong and effective.

One evening I opened my door to find a man representing the agency Anne had employed. He introduced himself and began in polite, decisive tones.

"We have your report, Miss Calvet. You have the goods on him all right. Red-handed, and it didn't take long either."

Anne handed me a check which had already been filled out. I signed it and gave it to the detective without a word.

I sat on the sofa, the report on my lap. Here was the evidence that would help me regain my strength and self-confidence. Stunned, I sat there thinking that I could not bring myself to read the insidious details. My heart was pounding. For the first time in many months I was conscious of hearing the birds singing outside. The truth cures all, I repeated to myself as I read the report.

"I'm sorry, Corinne, but I thought you ought to know. This was the only way."

"It's okay, Anne, I'm all right," I said as I retired to my room. I lay sprawled on our marital bed. There were no tears.

After a while I went to the garage to look for Donald and my toy animals that John put away some years before.

"When people come to visit and photograph our home it's really undignified to have toy animals in the bedroom. It doesn't go with the sophisticated image the studio is creating for you," John had said a few years back.

Donald Duck and my other toy friends stayed for awhile in the guest room before John removed them to the garage.

Large, slow tears rolled down my face as I searched through the mementos of our life together. In a corner, in a cardboard box under discarded fishing equipment, I found my friends, reduced to tatters by rats. The sight caused me to break down.

"Rats, they're all rats." Sobbing, I ran back into my bedroom and mourned.

For a few days I was overwhelmed with the pain of knowing John loved someone else. Sad and beaten, I decided to make some changes to cheer myself up. I went to have my hair bleached platinum blonde. I then bought a new, metallic Cadillac El Dorado convertible. Driving down Fairfax I searched for John's girlfriend's apartment. It was a mediocre building. I could picture John living there.

The extravagance of the changes I made gave only temporary relief to my battered ego. I settled down to live with Anne, a recluse, silent, morose.

It was Anne's suggestion that I go out and meet new friends, but I had no interest in doing so. Finally she suggested giving a party so I could meet some people she knew.

"Anne, I know I've been unpleasant to be around. I'm sorry I have had nothing to say to anyone. Do you understand? Please give the party for your friends. I'll turn the place over to you," was my response to the idea of a party.

I did not know it, but there was a new man on my horizon, a man who would lead me down twisted paths of joy and sorrow far more complicated, devious, and ecstatic than any I had traveled with John Bromfield.

PART THREE

The Last of the Big Spenders

Chapter 11

Kem Dibbs had arrived from New York to do a film. He helped me regain my confidence by making me feel like a desirable woman again as he escorted me to some of the fabulous Hollywood parties. He was a lot of fun and a great dancer. For a moment I thought of renewing the romance that had brought us so very close during my stay in New York. But Kem was a confirmed bachelor and I instinctively knew that he was a man to enjoy but not to fall in love with. Our attraction mellowed into a friendship that has lasted to this day.

I was starting to feel alive again and thought it was time for me to find a new romance. Kem suggested that I give a party and offered to invite the most eligible bachelors in town.

It was getting dark in Beverly Glen, time to turn the lights on. There was still an hour before the guests were to arrive. I was smiling, pleased at the way the house looked, but my heart was heavy with the memory of other successful parties John and I had given over the six years of our marriage. Anne couldn't understand that I didn't want to meet anyone. I could hardly keep from bursting into tears whenever someone spoke to me. The doorbell rang. Anne was still in the bathtub. The maid was busy making hors d'oeuvres in the kitchen.

"I'll get it," I called out. "It must be the twenty pounds of ice cubes we ordered."

I opened the door.

Adonis stood before me smiling. My whole being fluttered. Inside, I was caressed by the wings of butterflies. I felt a phoenix rising within me. A choir was singing in my brain.

"*C'est lui, c'est lui,*" I heard the lyrics.

Johnny Fontaine was an actor I had met only once, before I married John. I had been embarrassed for him. His inebriated wife had verbally torn him apart during dinner, yet he had remained quiet, his anger running deep beneath his dignity. It was obvious to me that it was a condemned marriage. He was even more handsome than Rory or John. I wanted him, but I would not approach him until he was separated. Watching the papers every day for the announcement of their divorce, I had given up when the Wallis contract made me John Bromfield's bride.

Now Johnny Fontaine stood there before me, framed by the porch light. If I'm dreaming I don't want to wake up, I thought. I felt a bit faint.

"I thought I'd come earlier in case you need help. May I come in?" Johnny said.

I flattened myself against the wall to let him pass by.

"Corinne, who is it?" Anne called.

"It's me, Johnny," he answered.

"Oh, good. I'll be right out."

He walked into the living room. In a trance, I followed and eased myself onto a stool in front of the circular bar. Just outside the wide bay window, cork trays carrying candles surrounded by white gardenias were floating on the pool. I felt myself becoming one of the dancing flames.

"Come," Johnny said, taking my hand and walking me into the garden. "I fell transported into a fairy tale, and you, m'lady," he bowed in deep reverence, "you are the princess of the gentle burning light in the kingdom of the flower's heart."

"I guess you've already introduced yourselves," Anne said as she joined us.

"We've met before," Johnny replied.

"Yes, we have." I heard my own voice, powerful with a tender intensity.

"Anne, is there anything I can do?" Johnny offered.

"No," she answered. "Everything is perfect. Just fix yourselves a drink while I finish getting ready."

With his arms around my waist, Johnny guided me back to the bar.

A new sensation arose in me; a part of myself that had been pushed aside was being awakened. When Johnny gently kissed my lips I felt I was Sleeping Beauty.

The overhead light of the bar made a halo around his head. He called me a princess, and he made me feel like one. Prince Charming. Johnny sat beside me on the bar stool, his knees surrounding mine. Silently, we toasted each other. I was no longer lonely.

People began to arrive. They complimented me on the house, but I was oblivious. I was held in the magnetism of Johnny's eyes, his words, his laughter.

When the food was served I went to phone my agent, wondering why he was late.

"Hurry up. The one I've been waiting for is here."

"We're on our way now, but be careful," he said; "you know what love on the rebound is like."

I laughed.

"See you soon," I said.

When I returned Johnny was sitting on the sofa with food in hand, laughing with an attractive brunette. Back on the barstool I watched him.

"There was salt in the air the day I was born," he had said earlier. I didn't understand what he meant but it sounded magical. He could have said "night is really day." It wouldn't have mattered. There was such a powerful caress in his deep voice. I wonder what he's saying to that girl, I thought. She's hanging too close to him. Their eyes are locked. That should not be happening. I crossed the room quickly and stood in front of them.

"Corinne, this is Jackie Fontaine." Johnny introduced me suavely.

"Are you his sister?"

"No," Johnny was laughing. "Our names are just coincidentally the same. Jackie is a great comedienne."

"Why did you kiss him?" I asked petulantly.

"Because I love him," Jackie answered, laughing.

"Does he love you?" I pressed on intently.

"I think that he did once maybe, a little. But not anymore." She sighed. "He liked me a lot though."

My hand moved possessively across Johnny's knee.

"He's mine," I said.

What am I doing? I thought. What am I saying?

"He's mine," I said again, lovingly.

"I can see that," Jackie said in serious agreement.

Johnny's arms now went around me. With silent recognition I accepted the commitment. Safe and secure, I left them alone and went to join the other guests. "Now Corinne," Kem said. "I have invited all these guys who are panting to meet you; give them a chance. When Johnny Fontaine enters the picture, he seems to take over."

I smiled joyfully.

"I must admit," he continued, "you two look exquisite together."

"Oh Kem, stop it," Anne insisted. "She's just finished with one bastard. Johnny's fine for a little fooling around, but he is definitely the wrong person to fall in love with."

"Why?" I asked defensively.

"Because he's left a chain of broken hearts all the way across the country. He's the biggest Casanova in town."

"That's what I told you when you first met him," Kem reminded her. "Did that stop you from falling in love with him?"

"Not me," Anne said sharply. "I thought he was a great lover, but I was never in love with him."

"Well I am," I said, smiling.

When the guests left Johnny stayed.

The next afternoon he moved in with his belongings, two suits, three pairs of pants, a few pairs of jeans, five elegant shirts and a copy of *The Prophet* by Kahlil Gibran. I was ecstatic. I floated around the house wearing the negligees I had bought in an effort to rekindle John Bromfield's sexual interest.

Johnny was an attentive listener, probing into my personal life in a way that was supportive and compassionate. He was sitting on the long sofa with music playing softly. I was lying down, my head resting in his lap.

"I'm sure glad people don't call you John. Johnny . . . Johnny . . . Johnny." Behind the name I was putting all the emotion of my needs.

"You make it sound like a symphony. I like it a lot."

"Johnny. . . ." There was a moment of silence. "I'm insanely jealous. I don't want to share my man," I admitted.

"Maybe you have a good reason to be jealous." He was caressing my hair. "Do you feel like telling me about it?"

"Well . . . I don't know if I should."

"Tell me the most outrageous thing you did when the monster of jealousy took over," he said, clowning.

With my finger between my teeth like a mischievous gamine, I thought for a moment, then told him about the time a girl had flirted with John and I had slashed her cheek with lipstick, telling her that next time it would be a knife if she didn't leave my husband alone.

"You did that?" Johnny looked surprised.

"Do you know that she said I was supposed to be a sex queen, and if she could go to bed with my husband and steal him from me it would make her superior to me, and when the newspapers got hold of the story it would make her a star?"

"Time to go to bed," Johnny said, picking me up in his arms. "You're the most adorable, exciting, mysterious woman in the whole world. I'm your humble servant."

I abandoned myself to Johnny's sensuous ritual. I was a queen; my inner sanctum was his for whatever worship he chose. He was my king.

Every afternoon he would leave for a few hours. His return would be enhanced with roses, funny little cards, or candy. Now as we were lying in bed, the breakfast tray on the floor, Johnny was reading the newpaper aloud. My head resting on his bare shoulder, I was hardly listening. I was lost in contemplation in the mirrored wall of what a perfect couple we made, he dark and bronzed by the sun, me very blonde and pale in my lace nightgown. The words he was reading were like a melody from a distant world.

I had not seen John Bromfield for days. I had only talked to him on the phone since Johnny entered my life. His curiosity aroused by the fact that I had let days go by without calling him, my husband decided to pay me an early morning visit on his way back from fishing. He entered the kitchen carrying his morning catch.

"Good morning, Clarice; is she awake yet?" he asked the maid.

"You'd better not go in," Clarice said, attempting to bar the way.

"It's all right. I'll wake her up." He handed her some fresh fish, pushed her aside, and started on his way to the bedroom. Upon opening the door he saw me in bed with Johnny. With the anguished sound of a wounded animal he ran back into the living room. I had hurriedly pulled the sheet over myself and sat frozen.

"You'd better go to him," Johnny said.

I had never before seen a man cry the way I saw my husband crying now. He was leaning on the tree that grew out of the center of our living room. I stood close to him and stroked his hair.

"I'm sorry, darling."

"When?" His voice had the sound of a cracked bell.

"Four days ago."

"Why?" There was no hope in the voice asking the question, only a cry of anguish. Johnny had put on a pair of slacks and a shirt, and walked into the living room.

'John," he said. "I'm sorry we meet again in this difficult situation."

"Do you love her?" my husband asked.

"Yes. Don't you?"

My husband's eyes seemed to open wide. He stumbled toward me. Johnny put his arm protectively around my shoulders. John closed his eyes as if to chase away the image before him. He staggered out of the house like a drunk. Something in me went dead.

"He'll get over it," Johnny said. "He was pretty sure of your love."

"He didn't want my love anymore," I said coldly.

"It didn't look that way to me," Johnny spoke softly. "Maybe he wanted your love plus someone else's."

"Well, that's too bad. I want a hundred percent, because that's what I want to give."

"I'm going to shower," Johnny said, without commenting. I sat there frustrated, unresolved about his views on love.

Anne handed me the phone. It was John. The tables were turned. Now he was begging me to tell him I was not serious about Johnny. He wanted to have dinner with me.

A few weeks later Anne was worried about the seriousness of my infatuation with Johnny. "Corinne, you must stop seeing him. He'll end up hurting you."

"I haven't felt alive in years, Anne. When we're together I feel as if I have never known what love is—the kind I have been looking for, romantic, interesting. I feel beautiful again."

After Johnny asked me to stop seeing my husband on Thursday nights and I refused, he changed, becoming moody and making me jealous with his many long phone calls. I hated feeling insecure about him. Maybe Anne was right. John's attentions confused me. I found myself hesitant to let my husband go. After dinner on Thursdays when he took me home, John never wanted to come into the house. I would spend the night lonely, knowing he was with Terry and wondering where and with whom Johnny was spending the night.

"Well, how was your evening?" Johnny would say when he returned on Friday.

When I asked him why he hadn't come home Thursday night he said he wanted to give me the freedom to choose between them. I was being torn apart.

One Thursday we were having lunch in an Italian restaurant in Beverly Hills when Johnny spoke softly.

"I'm in love with you. Do you love me?"

"You know I do."

"Then come with me now. Let's drive to Tijuana and get your divorce so we can get married."

He was watching my reactions intensely. I hid my head on his shoulder.

"Please." He spoke ardently, gently forcing me to look into his eyes.

"I can't," I said stupidly. "I have to go to dinner with John tonight."

"Then go to him."

He got up abruptly and left.

Feeling sure that Johnny would be back on Friday morning, I picked John up at his apartment. It was the first time since we had separated that the conversation was not charged with our problems. Johnny's proposal had healed the wound of my insecurity. After dinner we went to Mocambo's, our favorite dancing haunt. The maître d', seeing us laughing, welcomed us exuberantly.

"How nice to see you, Mr. and Mrs. Bromfield."

Charlie Morrison, the owner of the club, sent a bottle of champagne to our table. We were being treated as if we had just reconciled. We had already drunk too much brandy. Nobody asked questions, but photographers appeared and took pictures because it seemed to everyone present that if two young, handsome people like us could dance so close, so well together, smiling at each other as we did, they couldn't possibly be heading for a divorce.

John drove us back to the apartment he was sharing with Terry. He parked and we were silent. He looked away from me.

"John, I love you. I've never stopped loving you." He smiled sadly, and we kissed. Tears gathered in my eyes. Kissing me on the forehead, he opened the door of the car.

"I'll call you in the morning," he said as he got out.

"Darling, please . . . don't leave me right now." I leaned across the car seat toward him.

"It's no use. Don't you know?"

"Please, don't talk this way. I'll go now, but call me when I get home."

"Good night, little monkey. I'll talk to you tomorrow."

I watched him enter the building across the street. The door closed behind him. The noise was like a slap in the face. I sat for a few minutes more, completely paralyzed. Tears streamed down my face. I had no perspective on what had happened. It was the final rejection. I drove away in deep despair.

It was past one in the morning. The streets were deserted. Cooling sprinklers profusely watered the grass margin dividing Sunset Boulevard. Some of the water had overflowed onto the road. It was dangerously slippery.

Ahead of me as I drove was a young couple in a little Volkswagen convertible with the top down. I could see how much in love they were. The girl was intent on the driver's profile. She could not resist kissing his ear. They were almost enveloped by the headlights of my massive car. Suddenly they skidded uncontrollably. There was no way for me to miss them. My heavy Cadillac was about to pulverize their car with them in it. They had love. They had to live. There was no other choice possible. It took the merest fraction of a moment for me to decide. I turned my wheel sharply, jumping my car over the divider, certain I was going to give up my life for theirs. The car was out of control. I closed my eyes and smiled, waiting for the impact of death. Round and round the car skidded. When it came to a stop I was facing in the opposite direction from the one in which I had been traveling. Was I dead? I didn't know. I had no feelings in my body, and no emotion in my heart. The car door was being opened. I was being pulled out, sandwiched between the grateful young lovers. Hugging and crying, they thanked me profusely.

"We saw what you did. You saved our lives. How can we ever thank you?"

How strange, I thought. Why do people cry when they're happy? What is there to cry about? There isn't anything to cry about. It's all . . .

"Are you all right?" they asked anxiously. I managed a smiling nod.

"Can't we do anything for you? Is your car all right? Can we drop you anyplace?"

I was shaking my head no. There was no need for words. I would never need words again.

"God be with you. Thank you again." They went back to their car.

Going home I didn't feel as if I was driving at all. I felt strange, yet at the same time I didn't feel anything. It was a sensation I wanted always to feel, a sensation of emptiness, a void. I was happy because there was nothing to be happy about. I thought I was at peace.

At home, the face reflecting me in the bathroom mirror was me but I thought I looked different in an attractive way. It's funny for me to look at me. My face looked so relaxed, like a wax mask. Why am I visible? That's funny. I don't need to laugh, but it's silly. I don't need to be visible. I don't need to be. This is bliss. I have no past, no future. I don't feel any pain or elation. This is the state I want to stay in forever. Suicide. Yes, I'm going to leave this body, kill this funny, visible thing I am. Get rid of this encumbrance, this form. Far away, echoing, reverberating, I heard the voice of Isabelle. "Look around this house. It's messy; your running mascara has made a mess of your face. You must clean the house. You must make yourself beautiful and clean. You don't want them to find you and think you did it because you were despondent."

"Thank you, Isabelle, you're right."

I vacuumed the house, paid my bills, and put clean sheets on the bed. I opened the closet to choose my final attire, my last wardrobe change for my final appearance. There were two possibilities. One was what Ginger Rogers would have worn on her wedding night in a film with Fred Astaire, but it was too cute and too virginal. The other was better, what a young Barbara Stan-wyck might have worn, dignified, and discreetly sexual.

I put the negligee on the bed, laid out the sleeping pills side by side on the sink, and stepped into a bubble bath. I washed, perfumed my body, and put on fresh make-up. I was in total bliss, preparing myself for the ultimate lover. I knelt in front of the sink and prayed.

"Dear God, if what I'm doing is wrong, then have me saved,"

I swallowed the pills, walked to the bedroom, and looked around. The stage was set. It was perfect. I lay down on the bed, checking in the mirror so that I could assume the most attractive posture for the photographers. They will come in from that door, I thought. From that angle. Yes, this position is good. I was set. I was breathing the name of God, in and out, then nothing, out and in, then nothing, waiting, a smile on my face.

I abandoned myself, enjoying the feeling of approaching sleep.

In the depths of my languor I felt a troubling sensation. What's happening now? Oh my God, I'm getting cramps. After all this they are going to find me in a bed full of *merde*. Diarrhea. I can't let this happen. I struggled to my feet, and gathering all my energies together, I managed to grope my way back to the bath-room. I reached the toilet. It's impossible. How can I have so much waste in me? I was holding onto the wall, clawing at the plaster, breathing more slowly and deeply. It was coming to an end, everything. I stood up and fell, collapsing on the floor.

"Walk, walk, come on. You have to walk. Anne, go and get some more coffee," It was a man's voice. "Try to open your eyes, Corinne."

I didn't recognize the voice, but it sounded like John's. Then all went silent around me. I felt a sharp pain in my throat. What was it, what was causing that pain? I could not open my eyes. Why is there so much light around me, so much artificial light? My body was convulsing. Why am I crying? Why am I sobbing? Why am I screaming?

Someone was holding my hand. It was a man's hand. It felt good, strong, secure. I wondered whose it was.

"John?" I whispered.

"Sssssh baby, everthing's going to be all right."

I opened my eyes. The room and everything in it was out of focus. Still, the person standing next to me looked like John.

"John, you're back. You're here with me," I said. "Thank you, thank you."

I kept moving in and out of consciousness for a long time. And then I woke up. It was morning. I was back in Beverly Glen, alone in my bed. Anne was standing at the door.

"All the reporters are out in the driveway. Are you up to seeing them?"

"What reporters? What's going on, Anne?"

"It's all over the news that you tried to kill yourself."

"I didn't try to kill myself, I just didn't want to go on being who I was. What happened?"

"I decided not to stay out all night. I had a funny feeling and when I got home I found you on the floor of the bathroom."

"Where's John?"

"He's not here."

"Why?"

"Don't worry about that now. What do I say to the reporters?"

"Let me get dressed and put on some make-up. I'll see them in half an hour."

Anne looked startled at my attitude.

"Do you feel all right? Are you sure you're up to it?"

"How do I look?"

"Beautiful," she answered. "Listen Corinne, we brought you home after you had your stomach pumped out, and were out of danger. I don't think you should admit to having tried to commit suicide. Think of your insurance. Your premiums are going to triple."

Back in this life and already it was going to be the same game again of deception.

"I want John," I demanded. Without answering, Anne walked out.

I believed that it had been John who had stayed with me in the hospital, pulling me back to life, just as he had watched over me when we first met after my car accident. I called; Terry answered, and said John wanted nothing to do with me. My insistence did not bring him to the phone. I did not know until seven years later, when Anne finally told me the truth, that John had not been with me in the hospital. In my coma, I had confused Vince Edwards with John Bromfield. They looked very much alike at the time. Anne and Vince decided to allow me to believe what I wanted, and Vince had played John Bromfield for me all that night. The future Ben Casey had accomplished his first merciful, life-saving act.

When I went out to face the journalist from UPI, James Bacon, who had come to interview me, I was unemotional, wrapped in a white lace dressing gown, looking virginal and at peace. I denied trying to take my life. I was not lying, I decided. I had only tried to give it back to God.

Bacon questioned me further.

"What are the chances of a reconciliation with John Bromfield?"

"None," I said. "I'll be applying for a divorce as soon as possible."

"How about Johnny Fontaine?"

"We will be married as soon as my California divorce is final."

"That takes a long time, a year or so, doesn't it?"

I guess Bacon didn't believe me about Johnny Fontaine. The newspapers did not carry the story of my marriage plans. The photographers took their pictures, everyone wished me well, and then they were gone.

"What do you mean?" Anne asked in disbelief. "Marrying Johnny? Are you crazy?"

"He asked me yesterday afternoon. Why isn't he here?" Anne was silent. She looked guilty.

"Did he call?"

"Yes."

"Then why isn't he here?"

"I knew when I introduced you that I had made a mistake," Anne said ruefully.

"What are you talking about?"

"I knew he was going to push you into suicide." She seemed genuinely distraught.

"Anne, where is he?"

"He's right here." Johnny was standing at the door, smiling. I ran to him. He held me tight. Not a word was said. It was as if a magic spell surrounded us. We were breathing in unison. My ecstasy was broken by the sound of a door banging loudly. Anne had slammed into her room.

"What happened, darling?" Johnny said. "I called as soon as I heard the news on the radio. Anne told me to get lost. She said that she didn't want me to come around anymore, that I was the reason for what happened."

"It was an accident, darling. Too much brandy mixed with drama. You had nothing to do with it. Hold me tight, don't let me go. I love you." Johnny was looking at me with concerned adoration.

"I thought about what you said yesterday," I went on gaily, referring to his proposal of marriage. "I'm going to see a lawyer tomorrow and start proceedings for a divorce."

Our happiness became an irritant for Anne. She took every opportunity to put Johnny down. The situation became impossible. Of course Johnny stayed and Anne departed, angry and bitter.

My attempted suicide had me back in the news. Bill Schiffren, the agent who had gotten me *Far Country* with Jimmy Stewart, called with a film offer, and I was soon driving through the gates of Universal to star with Tony Curtis, Gloria De Haven, and Gene Nelson in *So This Is Paris*.

Corinne Calvet, the "love goddess," and Johnny Fontaine, the debonair man-about-town, were highly publicized. He was the perfect D'Artagnan producer Leonard Goldstein had been looking for. The American film of Dumas' *Three Musketeers* was to be followed by a television series of the same name.

The American–Italian co-production was going to be shot entirely in Italy, and my joy was only tempered because Johnny had to leave before I finished *So This Is Paris*.

On the Universal set I played the part of a singer entertaining in a chic Parisian nightclub. In my Rolls, driven by my sometime lover, Pierre, on a set representing a street in Paris, we have a small accident, running into Tony Curtis, a GI on leave. Punishing Pierre for some displeasure he has caused me, I flirt outrageously with Tony, and take pleasure in making Pierre drive us around the city. Tony then meets an American girl (Gloria) involved in a French orphanage, and through a benefit I help them raise money.

On the set of *So This Is Paris,* both Gene Nelson and Tony Curtis were wonderful to me with their courtesy and attention.

Johnny had already left for Rome. It was at Universal that I met a magnificent man with prematurely gray hair, Jeff Chandler, so elegant in manner and thought. Sitting on the steps leading to the dressing rooms, we shared our knowledge. He spoke of his understanding of the American Indian culture, which he had studied because he was so often cast as an Indian, and I spoke of my experience with existentialism. In many ways they were different interpretations of the same understanding. I was outraged and saddened some years later when I learned he had died from a medical mistake in a hospital while I was in Europe.

It was a little less than three weeks before I could join Johnny. In June 1954 we met at the airport in Rome under the eyes of the infamous paparazzi. Lenses clicked and flashbulbs popped frantically. Johnny Fontaine, however, was no more. His producer, Leonard Goldstein, was afraid that the name Johnny Fontaine would be confused with that of the actress Joan Fontaine. Johnny was so happy to be getting a break in his career that he would have accepted any conditions Goldstein imposed, and it was finally decided to christen him Jeffrey Stone. So Jeffrey Stone, formerly Johnny Fontaine, exchanged his first kiss with Corinne Calvet, formerly Corinne Bromfield, with a year to wait before they could officially join their names under California law.

I was spellbound under Jeff's charm, overwhelmed by his savoir faire. After a few days, however, I felt a slight strain, which I later knew to be caused by Jeff's annoyance at having only a few weeks to taste the ripe fruit of Italy's fair sex. Nevertheless, he soon forgot his disappointment, and we settled down in an apartment on the Viale dei Parioli in the Rome of the American movie stars. It was the period of "Hollywood on the Tiber," during which a number of American producers congregated in Rome to make films at the Cinecittá studios and on Italian locations, using up reserves of foreign currency that had accumulated since the war. In the midst of this influx, we became a new king and queen of Rome, with heaps of that large, beautiful Italian folding money stuffed in every corner of the apartment. Our friend Herb Jeffries was living in Rome and appearing at a nightclub. His poise was great enough to attract sexually-minded Jeff Stone to the discipline of Yoga. I was in heaven. It seemed that my sex life with

Jeff was better than any I had ever known, and at intervals we were able to join together in silent meditation through which we could reach a level of communication where we could also share our spiritual love. It was what I had been searching for.

Another friend, Jack Lambert, one of the great Hollywood villains, was in Jeff's series. We appreciated his brilliant thoughts on metaphysics, and for years, until he married and moved to Palm Springs, he was on our guest list whenever we wanted to give an interesting dinner party. The combination in Rome of Jack's intellect and Herb's Western adaptation of Eastern philosophy was so irresistible that I knew I would be leaving Jeff in good hands when I went to Paris to make the film *Bonnes a Tuer*, or *One Step to Eternity*. I called my French love, Jean-Pierre, and asked him if he could pick me up at the airport.

On my arrival, Jean-Pierre's arms surrounded me with the shield of security I remembered so well. He was still handsome, just a little older. His receding hairline shone under a film of perspiration as he attempted to fit my luggage into his minuscule Renault. It was cloudy and cold outside. As I watched him work at the task a familiar sorrow mounted in my throat. He would have made such a wonderful husband, I thought. I wondered if we would have married if I had stayed in France. I sighed as he squeezed my hanging bag next to me on the front seat and slammed the car door closed.

"Jean-Pierre, isn't it wonderful? I'll be here a full five weeks. We're going to spend a lot of time together. It'll be like old times, well almost. . . ." I suddenly felt embarrassed.

He pulled up at a small corner cafe.

"I'd like a brandy. What about you?"

I was soon standing at the zinc bar sipping an espresso into which he had poured a cognac. I was waiting for him to speak.

"I never know what to expect from you, Corinne. One phone call and you reappear in my life as if nothing has changed. You need me and I'm there."

"Cheri. I can never forget the closeness we shared. I'll always love you. I'm sorry if it was unpleasant for you to see me with John the last time we were in Paris. And then when I came back alone you were in Timbuktu."

"If you had let me know that you were coming I would have flown back."

"And if you had been here I wouldn't have felt so lonely. I would have stayed longer. And now at last we're here together."

"So how is John?"

"We're getting a divorce."

'Why?" He was frowning.

"He fell in love with someone else." I smiled, relieved that I could now make that statement as a fact, without emotion.

Jean-Pierre was silent for a moment.

"And you?" he asked. "Are you in love?"

"Yes."

"Where is he?" The knuckles of his hand turned white as he gripped the rail of the bar.

"In Rome. He's an actor, playing D'Artagnan." The words spilled out of me feverishly. What am I doing? Almost apologizing, I thought reflectively. I put my hand over his and was silent.

"What have you done to your hair?"

"Bleached it. Do you like it?"

"I liked you the way you were. Damn you, I like you every way you are. You're staying with Isabelle this time?" Jean-Pierre asked.

"Yes. It'll be good to be in my little bed. Did I ever thank you for not letting me get away with pretending in our love-making?"

"I don't remember."

"Well, I'm really grateful. Whatever pleasure I have in love-making I owe to you."

"Stop it, Corinne. Can't you see I love you, and that I've been doing my best to forget?"

"How can you stop loving? Can't you take it to another level where we can be the closest of friends?" In the silence that followed I smiled hopefully.

"No, I can't. And I'm going to be very busy at the television station. So don't count on me too much."

We left the cafe and drove to Isabelle's apartment. I was now puffing as we climbed the stairs. I turned back to ask him. "Are you in love with someone else?"

"I love a lot of women."

"Well, well, the Don Juan in you has come out."

"I wouldn't call it that. It's just that we're a group of grown individuals who enjoy the pleasure of our bodies without getting caught up in sentimentality."

As I had done so often, I rang the doorbell three times. Leaning against Jean-Pierre, I turned my head up into his face and whispered, "Yes, comrade, sex without emotion, pure physical lust." I exaggerated the shiver that had taken hold of me at the mere thought of primitive animal sex without emotion.

Isabelle opened the door. I threw my arms around her.

"I'm so excited. Can I stay in my old room?" I spoke like a happy child.

"Well, I gave you the one Papa and I used to sleep in. I don't sleep there anymore. You'll be more comfortable there, and there's more room in the armoire for your clothes."

I turned and looked at Jean-Pierre, disappointment written on my face.

"You can't turn the clock back at will," he said.

"I can do anything I want," I answered arrogantly.

"Well, ladies, I have to go back to the television station. Goodby for now." Jean-Pierre was very successful in his career as a news commentator, taking advantage of his trained voice.

"Good-by, Jean-Pierre, thank you for everything."

The door was closed.

Soon I was facing the French cameras for *One Step to Eternity* with Michel Auclair and Danielle Darrieux. During the first week's shooting everyone on the set watched to see if I had gone Hollywood. The view of me held by my French colleagues had been shaped by reports in the French press, mainly hostile and all ill-informed. The journalists continued to react sarcastically to my return. I decided that the only way I could be accepted was to report some of the film capital's deficiencies. I hinted at my dissatisfaction with my American career, and rumors soon spread through the courtesy of my leading man and the first assistant director.

Two days later, Danielle Darrieux's attitude toward me had changed. In the make-up room she confided the humiliating experience she had suffered in Hollywood, when the studios refused to recognize her box office potential. I countered with my story about William Meiklejohn, and explained that I had stuck it out to show them how wrong they were about me. Before long I was plagued by people who wanted to hear my stories. Eventually, I put a stop to their endless curiosity by stating that Hollywood was behind me, and that I was back in Europe to stay. With nodding appreciation, they responded positively. I became for a time France's prodigious, prodigal daughter.

I liked my performance in *One Step to Eternity*. In many ways it was the best role I had ever played. The script was good, and acting in my own language was wonderful, permitting me to experience what I could have been had I stayed in France, a dramatic actress respected and secure for life. I didn't want to leave Jeff alone in Rome long enough for him to have a serious romance with an Italian beauty. Had I accepted the fact that his "serious romances" were no more than temporary sexual flings, as ephemeral as the gratification of any other bodily function, I might have remained in Paris to take advantage of the renewed interest in my career. But as a child I had been influenced to think that a man was more important than a career, so when there was a choice to be made, I always asked myself (that is, I did until much later in life) what good is success if you don't have a man to enjoy it with?

Finding Jeff hard at work on his series, I accepted an offer to go to Venice to do *The Loves of Casanova*. It was to be shot on location, using the Doge's Palace and the famous dungeons over the Bridge of Sighs, from which Casanova escaped the clutches of his enemies by dropping into the cold waters of the canal below.

Back in Rome again I accompanied Jeff to his work every day. One of the things that seemed to drive the Italian producers insane was our sexual activity whenever we stayed on location overnight. The fact that there was no actors' union in Italy, and that actors were being worked sixteen to eighteen hours a day, with only a few hours for sleep, made them furious at the time Jeff and I spent together making love. (We had not realized how thin the walls were in our hotel room.) In their view, Jeff should be resting for the next day of shooting. Finally, they informed Jeff in a written dispatch that his nightly activities indicated that he was not giving his work the attention it required, considering the great opportunity it afforded him to launch his career.

This edict was greeted with hysterical laughter by the American cast members with whom we shared the note. The flippancy with which we received their order drove the producers to coun-

ter with the announcement that there would be no more room in
their vehicles to and from the location for anyone not directly
engaged in the production.

I had been offered a guest appearance in a French remake of
Napoléon. (The film ran so long that my guest appearance, among
many others, was never seen in the released version.) So back to
Paris I went, where I bought a racing Alpine Lodge convertible.
Jack Lambert flew in from Rome to drive it across the Alps.

I flew back to Italy, and in Rome, a taxi took me to the set
where Jeff, as D'Artagnan, was rehearsing a scene with Cardinal
Richelieu. I stood quietly in the shadows, smiling proudly at the
elegance with which Jeff gestured as he removed his hat and
bowed deeply in homage to the most powerful prelate of the seventeenth century.

When Jeff saw me he pushed everyone gently aside. He
swept me off my feet and carried me in front of the whole crew to
his dressing room.

"I really missed you," he said. "You should have seen the
scene we shot last week. As a matter of fact, you're going to see it.
It just came back from the lab in England. We're viewing it
tonight."

My fingers were touching his face. It was shining with excitement. Even the make-up could not hide the glow.

"I have to go back to the set," he said. "Can you wait until I'm
finished?"

I nodded. A few steps away he turned.

"How did it go in Paris?"

"Fine." I nodded affirmatively.

He smiled. With panache he settled his plumed hat on his
long, black, curly hair.

Jack's arrival with the car was timed perfectly, since Jeff was
due to leave for location again. Gleefully we drove our Alpine
past the slower Fiats of the production staff. Our laughter, the
exhilaration of the wind in our faces, was conducive to the subject
of marriage, which Jeff brought up when we stopped to have
lunch in a romantic roadside trattoria.

"I don't want to wait four more months until your divorce is
final. Why don't you go and get a Mexican divorce, and when you
get back we can start on that baby we've been talking about."

"But I don't want to leave you," I protested, "even for a moment."

"Look darling, it can't take you more than a month, and then we can have a big wedding in Rome."

"That's a lot of money to spend for just a gain of three months."

"Well, if that's what you think." He walked back to the car, brooding.

Although I did not feel safe leaving Jeff alone in Rome, I decided to go. I gave a letter for John Bromfield to someone who was returning that night to Los Angeles, telling why I wanted a Mexican divorce, and another letter for my lawyers, requesting that they prepare the necessary papers. That would at least set things in motion and shorten the time I would be gone.

The flight from Rome to New York was sleepless, and when I boarded a plane for Los Angeles in the late afternoon, I began to feel depressed. After one drink, watching the magnificent sunset blazing across the horizon, I found myself crying as I reflected on the failure of my marriage to John Bromfield.

From behind me a piece of paper came flying onto my tray. "Hello beautiful," it said. The signature was unreadable. I did not turn around. Leave me alone, I thought. Another note followed. "Let's make it, why don't we?" followed by the same illegible signature. I was tired. In New York, between planes, I had felt pulled apart. Jeff was in Rome, and I wanted to be with him. John was in Los Angeles, and by now maybe had grown tired of Terry. I had never really given him up. I had just run away to Europe. I felt that if I wanted to I could somehow get him back. But I had to let go of one to attach myself to the other. The thought that I might end up with no one again panicked me. Anxiety again tore at the edge of every nerve in my body. My fear of belonging to no one was chronic. I was critically lonely without a mate. I needed the security of marriage. I was in limbo and it terrified me. A paper airplane now landed in my empty glass. If I close my eyes, I thought, maybe whoever is bothering me will think I'm asleep.

I felt someone sitting down beside me.

"Corinne, I'm Daniel Mann. Hal Wallis and I are sitting right behind you." Daniel Mann had been a noted stage and television director, and was now moving on to films.

"Wallis is sending those notes?" I inquired without turning around.

"I'm going to direct his next film. Would you like another drink?"

"Yes." Back in America two hours and I find myself on the same plane with Hal Wallis. What's going on?

Two martinis later, I was sharing my sorrow with Daniel Mann. His understanding and compassion, in combination with the alcohol, made me feel that he was the most sensitive American man I had ever met. Three hours later, I fell asleep on Mann's shoulder.

When we landed in Los Angeles Daniel Mann had gone back to his seat. I remained on the plane until I was certain that they had disembarked, then stayed in the lavatory long enough for them to pick up their luggage. What was I doing? Hiding from Wallis? Did I still fear him that much?

Events moved swiftly. John Bromfield gave his consent without a quibble, and I soon crossed the Mexican border back to El Paso, Texas, an unmarried woman. Only three days had elapsed, and I was on my way back to Rome. It was 9:30 P.M. My attempt to call Jeff from Texas had been fruitless. When I tried again in New York, the telephone ringing in our empty Rome apartment sounded like a hollow cry for attention. At the Rome airport the telephone booths were all occupied by agitated Romans. I decided that I could get to our apartment before those tender lovers and hard-driving businessmen finished their conversations. In the taxi, the driver sang ballads, auditioning for me, the American movie star he had recognized. What an accomplishment, getting a divorce in three days! I felt like a victorious warrior. I had left Rome on Friday morning, and it was only Tuesday evening now. It had been miraculous. Everywhere I went, like the parting of the sea, the way seemed to have been prepared for me. My purse contained the document Jeff had sent me to obtain. Surely I had earned his applause for a well-executed plan. Clutching two cartons of his favorite cigarettes, which I had bought on the plane, I was greeted by the doorman, Pietro. He knew everything that went on in the Parioli apartments. He also knew where to obtain, for a fee of course, anything necessary for his tenants' needs. These services had made Rome a haven for American stars. They were paid extravagant sums of money for appearing in Italian films. The scenes with Americans were shot first, then the production would return to do close-ups of the Italian actors with stand-ins for the Americans. Since the films were all dubbed anyway, it seemed to work out.

"Signorina Calvet," said Pietro, "we didn't expect you back so soon."

"My keys please, Pietro. Mr. Stone home yet?"

"No, Signorina. Mr. Stone has changed apartments since you have gone. He is now in the new wing."

"In the new wing?"

"Yes. Let me help you up."

What was going on? An insidious fear sneaked up my body again. I was trembling. As the elevator doors closed, I told myself to disregard my feelings. I would let nothing spoil the pleasure of Jeff's surprise at seeing me. I'll have time to take a bath and get ready for him, I thought. Thinking about his touch made my heart skip a beat. Pietro, using his passkey, put my luggage inside the door of our new apartment. Standing there, I felt as if I were entering a stranger's home. Our plants, ashtrays, large floor coverings all seemed out of place in this new setting.

"Your princess, your love has returned," I shouted. Whirling around, I noticed dirty brandy glasses and overflowing ashtrays. Laughing, I took them to the kitchen. For every man there is a woman. My singing accompanied the sound of water removing the traces of yesterday.

A black poodle puppy came out of the bedroom wagging its tail feverishly. "Well, who are you?" I said, crouched on the floor, letting him cover me with kisses.

"I don't know who you belong to, but you're cute."

Before I left we had ordered from a Roman kennel a miniature white poodle that I had always wanted.

"Are you a miniature?" I asked the black puppy.

No way, I thought. Look at those big paws.

"You're going to be a big one. You can't be mine. You're really cute though," I added, not wanting the dog to feel rejected.

Looking at the clock, I tried to imagine in what restaurant Jeff would be eating, wondering what he was wearing. Followed by the dog, I went to look in the closet. I froze in my steps. The bedroom was a shambles. The antique wood tilting mirror had been moved closer to the bed. The covers were crumpled on the floor, an empty brandy bottle lay on a pair of socks. I shook my head in disbelief.

"How could he?" I didn't recognize my own voice, two octaves higher with whimpering indignation.

I ran back into the living room. I felt nauseated. In the bathroom I put my finger in my throat again and again, forcing up the champagne I had drunk on the plane to celebrate my forthcoming marriage. Empty, I still regurgitated my memories and disappointments. Composing myself, I looked in the mirror and watched desperation change to rage, a rage that slowly built into cold determination.

I was ready for battle. Whoever had shared the bed with him did not have a chance. It was going to be his last bachelor fling. I picked up the sheets with the tips of my fingers, an expression of disgust on my face. I carried the bedding, covered with proof of sexual intimacy, to the garbage can in a gesture of disdain.

Then I cleaned the place, took a bath, put on perfume, and slipped into the negligee I had purchased in Beverly Hills. I remembered how I had gone through a similar set of activities before taking the overdose of sleeping pills. How different I feel now, I thought. This time, I was utterly committed to fight for what we had decided we wanted together.

I waited in a dark corner of the room for my man to return. It got later and later. Lying on top of the bed holding the poodle, I reviewed recent events. Speaking to the dog, I questioned:

"Do you think he wanted to get rid of me? Is that why he sent me away, thinking he would be free to play around for a month?" Maybe he stayed at someone's house and lent his apartment to a friend. That must be it, I convinced myself. I'm sure he'll have a good explanation. Cigarette after cigarette, I turned these ideas over in my head, convincing myself that even if I knew he was lying when I saw him I would let him make me believe what he said. I couldn't give him up. He was such a good liar anyway, it was never difficult to believe him. For Jeff the world was never as beautiful as he wanted it to be, so he exaggerated everything, or hid the truth from himself, especially a truth he thought might hurt someone. Piling fibs upon fibs, he charmed his way in and out of the affections of everyone he met. The man I was in love with was a ladies' man, a master manipulator. Lost in these thoughts I fell asleep.

I was awakened by voices outside on the landing. I heard a key turning in the lock, and then Jeff's deep, soft laughter. He was with a woman. He must have seen my suitcase for he was out the door again before I could decide what to do. Running, I saw him and a woman going quickly down the stairs, disappearing into an apartment on the floor below.

I stood watching in disbelief. He had run away from me. Resolutely, I walked down the stairs and knocked on the door twice. Finally, it opened. Peggy White, an English blues singer who was appearing at the same nightclub as our friend Herb Jeffries, stood barring my way.

"Hi Peggy," I said. "I saw Jeff coming in with you. I just came back sooner than planned."

Jeff was coming out of the bathroom with a big smile on his face. Deciding that I would not let him see my jealousy, I ran to him and put my arms around his neck.

"I got the divorce, darling. We can get married right away." I turned and faced Peggy. "Would you like to be maid of honor? It all went wonderfully well," I continued, not waiting for her reply. "John, my ex, didn't give me any problem. It was like a miracle. Everybody went out of their way to make it happen." I sat down on the sofa. "Oh my God, look at me, in my nightie. Excuse me, Peggy. Let's go, darling. You'll excuse us, Peggy, won't you?"

"You go back up, Corinne," Jeff said. "I'll be there in a minute. We have to make some decisions about tomorrow. I'll be right up."

I didn't want to leave, but I had no choice. The same intensity that had possessed me when I stubbornly wanted a kiss from Rory Calhoun in front of Henry Willson's house took control of me again.

I didn't have long to wait. Jeff came up almost at once. I babbled on and on, bringing up none of the evidence I had discovered upon my arrival. Jeff fell asleep as I was relating in detail all the incidents of my trip.

Sometime in the middle of the night we were awakened by someone trying to enter the apartment, stopped only by the night bolt. A flame-swallowing male Hawaiian dancer was standing at the door when we opened it.

"Sorry, Corinne came back unexpectedly last night. You can't stay here tonight," Jeff said as he closed the door. So that was it, I thought, relieved, it was the activity of the Hawaiian that had soiled the bed. But if he had stayed here, where had Jeff spent his nights? With Peggy? In her apartment? It was dawn when the alarm rang. Jeff had to go to work.

"When will you be back?" I asked.

"We have only a half day's work, so I'll be back before noon. Then I have four days off. I've planned to drive down to Capri."

"Oh, that's wonderful. I love Capri. Do you want to leave this afternoon?"

"Well. . . ."

"I've got plenty of money with me in case we want to buy that Ferrari," I said, bribing him with the possibility of buying the car he had admired.

"Corinne, I need a few days by myself to sort things out."

"Don't worry. I'll give you lots of space. I know a fabulous beach in Sorrento where you can take long walks on the most beautiful sand you ever saw. I'll tell you what. Let me drive you to the studio. I'll have the car checked, go to the bank, pack our clothing, and we can leave right after you finish working." My desperation had turned into stubborn intention. I had not fought for Bromfield but this time I was going to get my man. I had taken over. I was moving too fast for him to figure things out. He was very quiet in the car.

When I came back alone I walked down to Peggy's apartment. She was reluctant to let me in.

"I need to talk to you," I said, pushing her aside and entering. "Listen, it won't take long. Jeff sent me to get a divorce so we could marry. I don't care what has happened between the two of you. Nothing is going to come between us."

"Jeff told me you had gone back to America to reconcile with your husband."

"He lied."

"We're going away for a few days together, Corinne; our plans are made."

I was furious. "You're English, aren't you? You need a visa to come to Rome."

"Sure," Peggy looked at me suspiciously.

"I heard you always bring dope into the country. You like to sing in Rome don't you? You leave my man alone or you may find it impossible to get a new visa."

The blood drained from Peggy's face.

"If and when Jeff calls you, tell him you've changed your mind. Tell him anything you want, but don't ruin my chances with him. Do we understand each other?"

She nodded in disbelief.

I left. I was in charge. I didn't even feel guilty about using threats to get my way. I went to the bank, and when I returned to the apartment I saw Jeff getting out of a cab in front of the door. I followed him in, and hurried up to our apartment. He wasn't there. I packed, unconcerned. He came in a few moments later, and asked me what I had said to Peggy.

"Didn't she tell you?" I said.

"She only told me that I had lied to her, and that she didn't want to come between us. She's decided to return to London."

We drove away in stony silence, the puppy between us. The wine with the spaghetti at the trattoria off the road untied my tongue.

Looking out the car window I saw a sign.

"Pompeii to the left," I exclaimed. "Let's go and see the famous paintings on the wall."

Without a word Jeff followed my suggestion.

The pictures were unusual, fantastic, with a strange evocative eroticism.

"Look at this one, darling," I said, pointing in the direction of an aroused Roman. "Isn't that ridiculous? No one has that kind of penis." My feigned gaiety did not jar Jeff out of his black mood.

Later, after we registered in a beautiful whitewashed hotel in Sorrento overlooking the Tyrrhenian Sea, Jeff sat looking somberly at the fishing boats in the harbor.

"It's over," he said finally. "It's not going to work. I want to be free. I cannot tie myself to one woman."

"Jeff," I protested. "You can't do this to me now."

"I'm sorry, darling, but I thought you wouldn't be back for awhile, and it would give us both time to think. You knew I wanted to experience other European women before I settled down."

"What about the baby we wanted to have? We've already created him in our minds. We've talked about him and about all the things we would do with him, and for him."

"I want to be free. I'm going out to walk. Don't wait up for me." He was gone.

The bells were ringing in the village below. Tears rolled quietly down my face. Tying a scarf on my head I joined the pious women in their dark clothes who were walking silently toward the church for evening prayers. I kneeled in the midst of these devout mothers and grandmothers.

"Jesus, oh Holy Virgin Mary," I prayed to the statues before me, "please intercede with Our Father in Heaven and give me back my man so I can have the baby I want so much. If you do I will raise him to do your work."

I was lost in contemplation. The priest was tapping me gently on the shoulder.

"I'll be closing the front door of the church. When you're ready to leave you'll have to go through the door of the sacristy."

"I'll go now, father, thank you."

"May your prayers be answered," he said gently.

When Jeff got back to the hotel a few hours later his face was peaceful again. He smiled, taking me in his arms. "Do you really want me? I don't think I can ever cure myself of being a bachelor. I'll try but I don't think I can ever be faithful."

"I want you," I said. "I love you."

"All right then . . . but don't ever tell me that I didn't warn you."

"OK, OK, I understand. Everything is going to be perfect." After all, I thought, all men resist the idea of matrimony, but I'll make him so happy he'll soon experience the bliss of a devoted wife, a family life, and our adorable child.

Putting the nightmare of the last twenty-four hours behind us, the next day we took the ferry to Capri, playground of the jet set. I was radiant as I stepped off the boat, hanging onto the arm of my future husband.

Jeff was my king, I was his queen, our treasury was filled by the Italian producers. We had the world in our hands. The week of eating, bathing, sunning, and loving was a premarital honeymoon. We spent some happy moments with Lana Turner and Lex Barker, who were in Italy for a few days.

On our return to Rome, I heard that Peggy had already left for London, taking a miniature white poodle along with her. The one we ended up with was Flip, the magnificent black standard, who grew and grew. An innocent friend commented one night to Jeff:

"I thought you had bought the white one for Corinne, and the black one for Peggy."

So Peggy, after all, had ended up with something that had been meant for me. She got the dog. And I got Jeff.

Jeff's series returned to the medieval castle in the village of Latina, about 40 miles south of Rome. The American actors and the top production people lived in a mediocre hotel fifteen miles from the location. The Italian director was first to leave and take refuge in the only bathroom that had a tub. One by one the Italians formed a chain of users, and would keep us out until there was no more hot water.

Now that we had a faster car than the production personnel it was war. We easily passed them on the road. Our laughter must have driven them mad, and as we Americans imitated what they had done to us, the director devised another strategy. He would set up a scene and leave before dismissing the actors. We counterattacked. As the day came to a close I would stay in the Alpine, and as soon as I saw the director leave, I would blow my horn audaciously, the signal for Jeff to join me in the car. Finally, the crew moved to another hotel.

Each day D'Artagnan, the musketeers, villains, Richelieu, and ladies in their crinolines would walk through the streets inside fourteenth-century feudal walls. On lower ground stood a small village where the residents still used the same ancient bakery, forge and apothecary. Tortuous cobblestone streets led up to the residence of the feudal lord, a formidable castle with heavy gates, slim windows, and a moat with a drawbridge. Within the castle walls there were various relics including the machines used to torture the enemies of the lord, who eliminated potentially rebellious subjects through terror and punishment. It was like opening a page in a history book to see how this little medieval village had been the matrix of control over the subjects of the vast surrounding countryside.

Most of the shooting was done inside the castle on the highest crag dominating the village below. There I walked around in love, looking over the grass-covered parapets to the valley below, where highways and cars took on the look of an intimidating enemy camp. Each morning as we drove up the serpentine road, all mundane thoughts would slip from my mind. Returning to the historical realm in which this costume drama took place was like entering a time machine, where peasants, slouched under the burden of domination, stood in contrast to the feathers, lace, and jewels of those in power. The sword fights, rehearsed with stunt men, were convincing. Watching the filmed action was like watching the past. It was fascinating.

On one occasion the Italian production company had not yet procured the lightweight balsa staffs to be used in the fights. After some rehearsal, the stunt men were replaced by the actors. In what followed, instead of narrowly missing Jeff, the actor playing the villain hit him squarely with his solid wooden staff. The castle walls reverberated with the impact of the weapon on Jeff's head. I stopped breathing. Jeff lost his balance on the high parapet where the fight was taking place, and a crew member leaped up to grab his legs, saving him from falling to his death.

Blood was running down Jeff's face from the deep gash on top of his head. This was more realism than was needed. Jeff, as D'Artagnan, got up courageously, and supported by others walked through the streets erect, wiping the blood away with his lace cuff. I was pushed aside. Running behind them, I put my foot out decisively to keep the doctor's office door from slamming on my nose. Jeff refused a shot of pain killer before receiving the seven stitches required to close his wound. Pain killer did not exist in the seventeenth century, he said, staying in character; maybe a shot of brandy, and then "let's do it." He never flinched. He was D'Artagnan, the bravest of the musketeers.

We had been at the castle a month when the Italian producer walked onto the set and announced that Leonard Goldstein had died. The Italians wanted the American cast to go on working without pay until Goldstein's estate was cleared. No one trusted the Italians, and someone suggested that the whole company go on vacation until the production problems could be resolved.

"Where do you want to go?" Jeff asked, as we drove back to Rome.

"South," I said suddenly, shivering in reaction to the wind and cold that came each day with sunset.

Jeff inquired at the airline office, and found the first plane heading south. It was not long before we were fastening our seat belts. I looked at my handsome husband to be, with his shoulder-length, curly black hair. I was filled with anticipation. The plane was taxiing. Jeff took hold of my hand. We were on a flight to Casablanca, embarked on an unforgettable journey into a land totally unlike anything I had ever known.

Chapter 12

We landed in Casablanca in the late afternoon. The modern city showed no signs of the Moroccan architecture and atmosphere of which we were in search. Jeff asked a bartender in our hotel where we could find some action.

"Don't you know," he looked surprised, "don't you know we're in the midst of a revolution?"

News of the nationalist uprising against the French in Morocco had not reached our film location. I looked at Jeff apprehensively.

"What about the Kasbah?" Jeff was not deterred.

The bartender leaned over to make certain no one could hear him.

"Don't go near the old town; the revolutionaries threw some bombs there yesterday. It's one of their targets."

Jeff took on the personality of the fearless D'Artagnan.

"If we mind our business they'll mind theirs."

Shrugging his shoulders, the bartender moved away.

"Jeff, he knows what he's talking about. Did you hear how he said 'revolution' like a patriot? That's how he knows that the Kasbah is a target."

"Here." The bartender was back, and gave Jeff the name of a restaurant where we would be safe.

In the taxi, opening the window, Jeff inhaled deeply, squeezing my hand.

"A little adventure is just what we need right now," he said with panache, paying the taxi driver.

Through ornate portals we stepped into a courtyard covered in mosaics. A cascading fountain splashed in the protected silence. The beauty of the pure white floating lotus was a balm to my mind. As we followed the maître d', who was dressed in Moroccan attire, I felt refreshed and at peace. The Italian producers, the fights, the news of the revolution had all faded away.

Exchanging a joyful look of appreciative anticipation, we entered a room designed to satisfy the senses.

The silk cushions, the brass tables, the silver hanging lamps were an orgy of color. The waiters gave mouth-watering description of the many dishes available. After our hands had been rinsed with lukewarm water in an embossed basin, patting them dry with a warm towel was sensuously stimulating. Like children in paradise, we delighted in each new sensation. Jeff's hand caressed mine as we reveled in the music provided by local musicians. One after another, exquisite delicacies were placed before us.

The tempo of the music changed as we were sipping the thick, aromatic coffee we had been served. Just then an old friend of my mother, the French poet and novelist François Mauriac, sat down next to us. We soon learned that he was the leader of a pro-sultan political organization.

"Mr. Mauriac, I'm Corinne Calvet, the actress. My parents were Pierre and Juliet Dibos. This is my American fiancé, Jeffrey Stone."

Some graceful young boys were dancing sinuously, offering the gyrations of their posteriors to the men in the audience.

"Is this a homosexual club?" I whispered to Mauriac when the music returned to a less frantic level.

"They have a room upstairs for the men who enjoy 'ails,' which is the name for a boy lover." Mauriac smiled. "Sexuality between men and boys was never considered abnormal or shameful in Morocco until the imposition of European values."

"I understand," I smiled. "Some of my very good friends in Hollywood are gays."

European and Moroccan attitudes differed widely on all matters pertaining to sex, and perhaps most of all with regard to the questions of homosexuality and prostitution. To be a prostitute was in no way a dishonorable profession, or one to be ashamed of. Sexual pleasure was to be enjoyed as one of the gifts of Allah. Prostitutes wore a magic sign on their foreheads which created love and desire in men. Often a husband would ask a prostitute to visit his young bride to impart to her the knowledge of the trade. Also, a father would customarily present his son with a female slave on his first sign of puberty so that he could be initiated into the mysteries of sex.

The brothels in Morocco were located in closed quarters. The tax on prostitution had always been an important source of revenue, and it was customary for a sultan to pay his troops entirely from this tax. In this respect Mauriac commented that the sultan's soldiers had their fun, and then the sultan got their money back.

There is a section of Casablanca called the Bous-bous. It was reserved for the French and forbidden to Moroccans. Ladies were imported from Marseilles or recruited from among the prostitutes who were caught working the street or the hotels without paying the tax. We left Mauriac at the restaurant and now took another taxi to this part of the city.

As soon as we stepped behind the barbed wire which enclosed the Bous-bous, we were surrounded by a multitude of women in all sizes, shapes, colors, and ages. Some offered themselves to Jeff, others to me. They grabbed and attempted to direct us into their own cubicles until a French lieutenant dispersed them and assigned us a Moroccan police escort. The hierarchy among these officers was startling. The Moroccans did not even wear shoes while the French were extremely well attired. Walking through the small street, we could see that five or six women shared a small cubicle where they cooked, slept, and received customers. Without running water, their bathroom facilities were covered buckets. We arrived in a building that was in better condition than others. The French officers wanted to know if we would like to see a show. We said yes, and were taken to a large room where we were served warm beer and strong coffee.

We sat on cushions, our backs leaning against walls spotted with dirt. An ornate water pipe rested on the floor between us. In it hashish was placed over a small piece of burning charcoal.

"I wonder who else has sucked on these," I murmured to Jeff as I saw him reach for one of the tubes coming out of the pipe.

The officer clapped his hands, and two new tubes were brought in to replace the first ones.

Soon the dancers arrived, the eldest in her late twenties, the youngest not more than twelve. They danced languorously, removing their veils. We could hear the Arabic musicians playing behind the cloth hanging on the door. Allah did not allow them to gaze upon the naked dancers.

The coffee and smoke had put us in a euphoric mood, and we could not help giggling at the effort the fiddler was making, pushing the drapery aside with his bow in an attempt to sneak a look. For the finale, the lead singer took a newspaper, twisted it into a torch, anchored one end of it inside her vagina, and with great pomp lighted the paper flambeau. The gyrations of her abdomen became frantic as the flame moved closer and closer to her pubic hair. When it had almost disappeared the odoriferous smell of singed fuzz filled the room. With a great thrust, she pushed the remains of the burning torch out of her body and stomped out the flames with her bare feet. The officer whispered in Jeff's ear before he left.

"What did he say?" I asked.

"He wanted to know if we would enjoy some sex play."

"I wonder what the percentage of venereal disease is around here?" I mused, hoping to abort any thoughts Jeff may have about taking up the suggestion. Just then the whole building shook with a deafening detonation.

"Sorry," the officer said, running back in the room. "We thought they were finished for the night. This way please."

Through a tunnel we were ushered out into a garden, then through an unmarked door. A French officer drove us back to the hotel.

"Should we go somewhere else, Jeff," I suggested, "some quieter place, maybe the south of France?"

"No," he said. "This is exciting. Let's visit Marrakech. It should be quieter there. Go up to the room; I'll make all the arrangements."

When he returned he was aglow.

"All set. By ten tomorrow morning we will have a chauffeur and a limousine."

It had been a long day, and soon we were asleep.

In the morning, standing by an old elongated Chrysler limousine was a young, handsome chauffeur with dark, wrap-around military sunglasses and a very sharp one-button suit.

"Mr. Stone, I presume," he said.

Jeff nodded.

"Mademoiselle." He opened the car door.

We were on our way. Jeff lowered the window to enjoy a sense of freedom. A few moments later our chauffeur spoke.

"Mr. Stone, could I suggest you roll up your window for a little while? We will be going through a very poor part of town on our way out. They sometimes confuse this car for one belonging to government officials. So, just as a precaution please. We will be out of this section in just a few minutes. Thank you."

Jeff complied. I pulled the jumpseat down in front of me, resting my legs on it as I sank down into the luxury of our continuing Moroccan adventure. I felt safe in the hands of our chauffeur, who seemed to be aware of all possible danger. Within a few minutes we were rolling along a country road where all human habitation was far back from the highway. The sun shone brightly. The air was still, and the scene was very primitive. Instinctively, our hands met.

"Now it is all right to lower the window," the chauffeur said.

Smiling, I heard soft, deep, happy laughter coming out of me.

"My name is Henri. Where would you like to go?"

"It's you who are taking us, not us taking you. We don't know, you do."

Henri's eyes looked straight at Jeff in the rear view mirror. They both smiled.

It was dusty, and grew warmer. On the road coming to town were men riding on mules, and women carrying heavy loads on their backs ran barefoot, trying to keep up with the animals.

"Look at that," I burst out. "Do you think they ever change places?"

"No, and lady," Jeff said, "you better behave or I'll marry you and settle down right here."

"Oh master," I clowned. "Where are we going?"

"Henri, where are we going?" Jeff asked.

Henri proceeded to give a detailed picturesque account of our itinerary.

We were to go first to Marrakech, taking the high, Atlas mountain road, then to Quarzazate, where Henri knew a caid who would be honored to have us as his guests, then down to Bou Izakarn on our way to Goulimime to see the Camel Market festival, and then return to Casablanca via the sea, visiting Agadir and several other smaller towns en route. He finished by telling about himself.

"I was chauffeur for General Patton during part of his campaign."

When Henri stopped at the side of the road he took off his chauffeur's cap and turned to us.

"What would you like, kif, hash, opium or . . .?"

"Hmmmmm." Jeff, surprised but pleased with the suggestion, decided, "A little bit of the first two for now."

"Very good, excuse me. There's a small market behind this row of trees. I'll be right back."

When Henri returned he handed Jeff a small paper bag, put his cap back on, and started the motor. I looked at Jeff for acquiescence.

"You don't have to wear that cap," I said, smiling. "Not unless you prefer."

He didn't answer. He was looking at Jeff through the rear view mirror again.

"Sure," Jeff said. "It's going to be a long drive. Relax with us."

"Thank you."

With fascination I watched Jeff fill the pipes and light them. He handed one of them to me. I sucked in the air and choked.

"Easy," Jeff said, "take only little tokes, this stuff smells like dynamite."

"Here, Mademoiselle." Henri passed me a thermos bottle.

After the ice cold, strong, sweet tea appeased my throat, I followed Jeff's advice.

For the next few hours not a word was exchanged. On the lonely road surrounded by glistening sand, we passed small groups of veiled women in white, walking alongside donkeys loaded with produce. In front, leading the small caravan, were prancing horses, their proud riders armed with large curved knives and rifles. They never raised their eyes in the direction of the limousine. Apparently we were of no concern to them. Obviously, the revolution had not reached them.

As we crossed the river Oum er Rbia, we stopped and sat under some trees to eat roast chicken the hotel had sent along. The herbs that had been placed under the skin before it was cooked made it aromatic and savory. We watched an Arab man take Moroccan sandals called babouches, which he was carrying, and slip them onto his bare feet as he entered the water to cross the stream. When he came out close to where we were sitting he removed his babouches and slung them over his shoulders again.

"Henri," I said, "quick, ask him why he did that."

"Allah gave us eyes to see what is on the ground, but he chose not to let us see through the water. He is protecting himself from the bite of a poisonous snake or a broken piece of glass," Henri answered.

It was not long before we reached the outskirts of Marrakech. The terrain had turned from white sand to red clay. The ancient Islamic city was surrounded by a verdant palm grove. We passed low red earth structures, some of which were crumbling and decaying. Soon we saw buildings covered with wares the shops were selling. There was a multitude of people in the streets. The limousine moved at a very slow pace. Up on a hill, ramparts protected the imposing palace of the sultan. Tall gateways led into extensive, lush gardens full of fountains, behind which stood the guards and the gates of the extravagant palace. We checked into a lavish hotel. Our room had a veranda overlooking orange groves which filled our quarters with delicate perfume.

Later, in the marketplace, while we were shopping, Henri overheard a plot to separate us so my purse and the jewelry I was wearing could be stolen. Pushing us with force into one of the shops, he spoke with the owner, who took us through the back into the storeroom of another building. We waited there until Henri convinced the potential thieves that we were his friends.

By the time we got back to the hotel the cool marble floor was a welcome comfort to our weary feet. We gave Henri the night off, and looked forward to a quiet dinner in the hotel dining room.

After a refreshing shower, we lay on the turned down sheets. The antique wooden fan on the ceiling made a buzzing sound. I wore only a small, white hotel towel. Jeff was covered with his own terrycloth wrap.

"Henri told me that we're invited to stay for a few days as the guests of the caid in Quarzazate," Jeff said nonchalantly. "He says it's safe. The Berbers are on the move, going down to the plains."

"How many wives does the caid have?"

"Seventeen in his palace here in town, and a half dozen or so in his country residence." I detected a slight envy in Jeff's tone.

"He must have put the other six away to pasture, I guess." I laughed. "I think it's great. I always felt that part of me was an Arabian princess in another life," I said, looking up toward the curved wooden ceiling. "You know, whenever I look at photos of this culture, I see myself entering the picture and walking through mosaic arches. When are we going?"

"Tomorrow if we want to." Jeff's voice was neutral.

Smiling, I drifted away into my favorite childhood Moroccan fantasy, that of being stolen from my father's palace and carried away by a formidable Arabian prince who had fallen in love with me, but promised that he would not force his attentions until I begged him to come to my bed. In my fantasy, Jeff had become Valentino, the silent movie star. I imagined myself in his tent in the middle of the Sahara, slowly inhaling the narcotic smoke from the hash pipe Jeff had passed to me. Jeff spoke:

"There's one request the caid's representative made," Jeff said, his voice teasing.

"What's that," I said, sitting squarely on his navel.

"You have to stay in the women's section of the palace. Even the caid's own daughters stay in the harem."

"Do you mean I can't stay in your room?"

"No woman can live in the men's quarters."

"I'm sure they don't. Seventeen people in one room would be quite a lot."

"Well, don't worry. We'll be together anyway. I'll request your presence all the time."

"And what about when I'm not with you?"

"The rest of the time I'll sleep, shower, talk to the men and read."

I began tickling him.

"If you think I'm going to let you loose in an Arabian fantasy world with me behind locked doors, no way, unless I get you completely and totally loved out." I whispered the last words in his ear.

"Good idea." Jeff nibbled at my neck and rolled me into an embrace.

The next morning we drove to Quarzazate, full of anticipation as the limousine approached the imposing palace gates of our host, the caid. We waited while six majestic black Arabian stallions with riders in full uniforms of black and silver trotted out of the grounds toward the city. It was a scene from some remote past.

I squeezed Jeff's hand. It was heaven. We were together and having a rare adventure. When we entered the white building with its golden dome, I was taken to an interior garden surrounding a pool where fountains made perpetual music. An older French woman dressed in a simple white robe received me. Behind her, like giggling joyous children, was an array of beautiful women. Through the sculptured door I could see a huge bald man standing guard. I wondered if he was a real eunuch who fantasized that all the women in the harem were his. There were birdcages everywhere, filled with parakeets and white doves. I felt like Claudette Colbert in a De Mille spectacular, waiting for my Marc Antony to call on me.

The women's quarters consisted of a series of large rooms divided into smaller spaces by bright, shining satin draperies. Some were closed, providing a semblance of privacy. The women, dressed in loose, transparent robes, were like beautiful, exotic birds. It was about dinnertime, and I was growing tired of answering numerous questions in French, mostly about the latest fashions in Paris, when a courier appeared at the door.

When their names were read, the two ladies closest to me broke into exclamations of joy, and ran to change into magnificent Arab pajamas. The other women helped them and bedecked their hair with flowers and pearls.

I changed into a high-necked black lace dress with a revealing fitted bodice. It was my favorite, for Jeff had described my appearance in this French creation as ravishing.

Walking through a series of long corridors, with the two girls whispering and giggling, I wondered what was being said, since I saw our escort blushing under his blue turban. At the end of our journey, we were guided into a room finished in modern elegance, with oak panels and huge leather sofas, essentially a replica of the office of an international banker. Recovering from my surprise, I found myself looking at the caid. He was smiling as he walked toward me.

"Mademoiselle Calvet, it is indeed an honor to have you as

my guest. I have been a great admirer of your beauty and talent. May I introduce you to my other guests?"

Standing next to Jeff were an English diplomat and an Italian architect. The caid was dressed in European clothing, topped with a black silk turban. Only the bartender and the two concubines were, through their dress, reminders of where we were. Champagne flowed freely as the evening progressed. Dinner was served Moroccan style in the ornate dining hall. The music and dancing were better and more refined than any we had seen in the Moroccan clubs. As thick, powerful coffee was served in gold-lined porcelain demitasse cups, the caid's guests decided which of the ladies was most to their liking. A magnificent beauty I had not met before entered the room. Her complexion was golden tan. Her large brown eyes, slightly slanted, held the mystery of the Orient. A choker of rubies and diamonds bound her throat. Her long tapered fingers were laced with brilliant gems. I expected her to get up and dance like the heroic foreign slave in an Errol Flynn movie, but she remained sitting quietly at the prince's side. For a moment he placed his hand on her knee, leaving no doubt in the minds of his guests that she was untouchable as far as they were concerned.

Brandy in crystal snifters and on the flaming dessert had made me feel warm and lazy. The ladies' sparkling laughter acknowledged the men's humor. The subjects of conversation were diverse, though no one spoke of the revolution. Before the ladies arrived, the prince had requested that they should be spared the subject of politics, Jeff told me after I had asked the prince about the Berber revolts.

In the morning, exhausted after having spent most of the night talking about a movie story possibility involving the characters with whom we had spent the evening, Jeff walked me back to my harem quarters. Our steps aroused the guard, who smiled for the first time and opened the door, clapping his hands twice. The ladies had been waiting for my return. A perfumed bath was prepared. I had been the only one chosen to spend the night. I was the winner of that day. I lay on my bed, resting, with my harem companions seated on the floor around me, their long hair loose, wanting to exchange female secrets.

During the next two days the courier came three or four times a day to fetch me to join Jeff and the other guests. Each time my stock rose in the kohl-lined eyes of my beautiful companions. I received gifts of scented oil, special dance movements were demonstrated for my benefit, my feet were massaged, jewels offered, silk scarves were laid on my shoulders in an attempt to get me to impart the secret that made a man want me so much.

I could not accept these gifts, for I had no secret to reveal. They thought I was having sex each time I went to see the men. They had no idea that men might want to relate to women in any other way. Touched by their disappointed looks, I said as I was leaving:

"My secret, if there is one, I share with most Caucasian women. We don't let our men have more than one woman, and if they break this rule we make sure they feel guilty about it."

Their reaction to this disclosure was spontaneous. The idea that one woman would have to satisfy all of a man's sexual needs was hilarious. They burst into childlike, joyful laughter at my incongruous tale.

Leaving the palace at Quarzazate, we headed south. When we reached Bou Izakarn, we had to deposit a large sum of money with the French patrol before we could proceed.

"The Berbers have raided the posts at Assa and Tiglit. They are in control. You will have to return to Casablanca by sea, and in case you do not arrive at Goulimime in twenty-four hours, this money will pay for a search party."

"Why don't we wait and pay you if you need to look for us?"

"Dead people do not pay their debts," the French guard said with finality. We turned to Henri.

"The Berbers are moving toward Marrakech. They are not going south. We have time. You may be the last whites who will have a chance to see the yearly camel market."

"Let's go," said Jeff, handing the money to Henri, who demanded a receipt.

The landscape during the six-hour drive was totally denuded of vegetation, just sand dune after sand dune. My head on Jeff's lap, I fell asleep. I woke up when we had reached the land of the Blue People, the proud Berber tribe who were often dressed in blue robes, their heads wrapped in blue cloth. The plant from which indigo dye is extracted comes from that region, which is why they dye all their clothes dark blue. Even their skin looked so black that if I were to paint them I would use a dark blue for the shadows in their faces.

We had arrived at our destination. As we walked through the immense bazaar, we were fascinated with all the activity.

"Where are the camels?" I inquired.

"They're a mile away in the desert; ten thousand camels can smell pretty bad."

"Especially if you're down wind," Jeff laughed.

I had an uneasy feeling. I was being watched by a handsome man riding a black stallion. As we proceeded among the natives with their wares spread on colorful blankets, I could see him half-hidden, looking at me intensely. Henri excused himself while we watched a woman in consultation with the local doctor, who listened attentively to the words of his patient while he kept his eyes closed. Once in a while he asked the woman to point out on a drawing of a woman's body where she felt the pain. He then closed his eyes again and fell into meditation. On one occasion a question brought a flurry of excited answers from the woman. After that he again lost himself in contemplation. Nodding his head as he came into accord with his inner voices, he opened his eyes, reached under a blanket to take out various pouches, and mixed a special potion to hand to the woman.

"She'll stay there for hours," Henri explained when he returned, "arguing about twenty cents more than she's willing to pay for the consultation and cure."

As we moved toward a large tent where we sat to consume the thick, black mixture they called coffee, Henri laughingly announced that one of the wealthier caravan owners wanted to offer Jeff one hundred camels as an initial bid for the privilege of adding me to the already impressive number of his wives.

"That's an extremely high price. You must feel flattered, Mademoiselle Calvet," Henri said in response to my mock consternation.

"How much would I be offered if I let the chief check the merchandise?" Jeff asked playfully.

"Jeff," I said, only slightly amused, "don't joke. He's over there in the corner watching your reactions to his offer."

"I told him you'd let him know tomorrow. We should not antagonize him, and by tomorrow morning we'll be gone."

Besides being a center of trade, the camel market was also a social event and a place for entertainment. The men sat with their water pipes and talked for hours about all the things they had thought about since the last time they had been together. They soon ran out of mundane information like news of a sandstorm, the birth of a child, or the death of an elder, and their minds were free to dwell on more lofty matters. They shared their thoughts and ideas about life almost as if they were Greek philosophers in the marketplace of ancient Athens. The women, in the meantime, were busy looking at baubles and beads, visiting the doctor, and preparing their daughters for presentation later in the evening when the caravan chiefs would bid on the new crop of women.

There were games for the children, but the favorite source of recreation was the storyteller. The little ones were gathered in a semicircle. We too became avid listeners. The storyteller was highly skilled, and even if one didn't understand his words, which were translated by Henri, his gestures and expressions would have conveyed much of what he said.

The story he related involved a camel afraid of his own shadow. The children laughed at the silliness of the poor camel, and the storyteller deftly kept their interest with his sound and pantomime.

Henri, who had slipped away while we watched, hurried back to us. "We must leave at once," he said. "The camel chief is determined to gain Mademoiselle Calvet as his property, and his men are arming themselves. I'm afraid that if you don't accept his offer he may attempt to kidnap her."

We arrived late that night in Agadir, the Moorish city on the sea. The next morning in the sun, we looked down from a parapet to buildings like a flock of white doves resting near the deep, blue Atlantic waters. The air was pure and fresh, and the sun's rays bathed the whitewashed walls of the city and its inhabitants with a powerful light. The breakers on the shore reminded me of moving sheep in a blue pasture. Even the children were dressed in white. Veiled women hurried through the narrow market streets.

For lunch we were invited to the home of a middle-income family. In each corner of the reception room was a radio, each softly playing different music. In the middle of each of the four walls was a clock.

"Why is there a different time on each clock?" I inquired.

"While in my home it will be whatever time you choose it to be," my host replied, smiling.

"What about the radios? They're all tuned to different stations?"

"Whatever is pleasant to your ears. It is yours to choose." Since he made no attempt to lower or raise the volume on any of the stations, I came to understand that the freedom of choice was not to be imposed by any one person in the room over the others. It was up to each individual to tune out whatever did not appeal to him at the moment.

After lunch we decided to take the limousine and go to the beach by ourselves.

"Don't stay in sun too long," Henri warned us. "The sun's rays are treacherous."

Two hours later when we returned to the hotel I started to have chills. By nightfall I had to be wrapped in an ice cold wet blanket. I had severe burns all over my body. I was in agony. Jeff asked the doctor to give me a pain killer. When Henri returned with the prescribed medicine he had all the paraphernalia we needed to smoke opium.

Lying on my right side, I felt myself becoming the pain itself. I observed the cells of my flesh contracting to extract the water to form a protective shield for the layer of my epidermis that had not been burned. Witnessing the process eliminated my fear of pain, and as I let go, my body relaxed. I became the child to be born, floating in the water sac in my mother's womb. Words of a religious man were passing through my brain, the burning fires of hell, and I thought of witches, the burning of heretics, the authorities' suspicion of seers who possess intuition.

One after the other, as if I were passing through the thoughts that appeared as reality, I saw the water of the baptism, the body's percentage of water, the spiritual river of life's energies. I floated with the current through doorways in geometrical designs, into a land where the drops of dew, the blooming flowers were diamonds reflecting rainbow colors. I was home, smiling, suspended weightlessly by sleep.

Two days later we left in a hurry, because Henri told us the revolutionaries and the Berber tribes had formed a coalition. We were forty-eight hours away from a complete takeover, and he was anxious to get us all out of there and return to his family in Casablanca.

My burns had subsided. Going beyond the pain had left me nearly healed. We drove incessantly, stopping only once to refresh ourselves at a shaded oasis next to a stream. Finally, we arrived in Casablanca.

The next day we returned to Rome, where we were told that the production of *The Three Musketeers* would be shut down indefinitely due to some complications with Leonard Goldstein's estate. We had just returned from picking up Flip, the black poodle puppy we had left in Herb Jeffries' care. I was playing with Flip when Jeff asked me where I wanted to get married. Since the day I had prayed in the church at Sorrento, I had not brought up the subject.

Having loved our Moroccan experience, we were drawn back to the Arab atmosphere. There was unrest in all of North Africa except for the free port of Tangier, which played the role for this continent that Switzerland played for Europe. There we found a contingent of wealthy Americans headed by Doris Duke, and a mixture of rebels, adventurers, and exiles. Through the Comtesse de la Faye we made the arrangements for our wedding. The comtesse, known for her extensive collection of rare jade, received us in the immense house where she lived with many servants. Their primary job was to clean up the droppings of her many monkeys running free on the premises. As we entered a long hallway lined with glass cabinets, we were dazzled by her collection. In a niche next to each display was a ferocious chained dog to keep visitors at a safe distance. In honor of our coming wedding, the comtesse invited *tout* Tangier to a beach party where huge blocks of ice had been carved with indentations to hold shot glasses of vodka. The caviar was salty, the sea was salty, and the only beverage served was the potent Russian liquor. In no time the party became frantic.

My heart full of hope for our future, I watched Jeff turning down propositions from inebriated females. So he can turn down a woman after all, if he wants to, I remarked to myself. I went into the sea up to my waist close to where Jeff was standing.

"Help, Jeff," I called. "Help!" I cried, taking a big breath and staying under.

He was there, holding me up in his arms.

"I love you so very much." As we kissed we fell backward, and played in the water until, laughing and·wet, we walked back to the hotel.

It was the day of the romantic wedding of my youthful dreams. I was watching from behind the screen on the window overlooking the garden of the sultan's townhouse. The final preparations were being made for the ceremony. The American Consulate had furnished a Marine guard. I had not seen Jeff since earlier that morning. It was now three o'clock in the afternoon. Any moment now the American consul was going to escort me to join my future husband. My eyes caught sight of Jeff. He was making sure everything was in order. There was a knock at the door. I linked my arm in that of the consul, my heart beating furiously. I was an Arabian princess living my fairy tale fantasies. The sweet scent of multitudes of flowers pervaded the air as we walked to where Jeff was standing, erect, proud in a dark suit, a small white rose pinned on his lapel. His smiling, caressing brown eyes looked at me softly as I walked toward him carrying my delicate bouquet.

We had chosen to be married by a gentle old missionary. He was retired now, and his memory failed him. Forgetting to ask Jeff to kiss the bride, he looked confused for a moment, and started the ceremony all over again, afraid he had missed something. We looked at each other, beaming with happiness. Maybe we could go through a ceremony each year, I thought. Not waiting for the missionary this time, Jeff bent to kiss me. The world around me disappeared, my body melted into complete acceptance. The applause was the sweetest that I had ever heard. Flower petals had been strewn on the path we walked under the arch formed by the Marine guards. Throwing my bouquet in the direction of an unattractive teenager, I shivered as she held the flowers against her heart. I can still see vividly the smile of hope that transformed the ugly duckling into a beautiful young woman. We were steered into a limousine, the crowds outside pressing to take a look at this handsome young movie couple. The wedding feast was given at a restaurant appropriately named the Thousand and One Nights. The limousine first took us for a drive along the sea, a moment of privacy before joining our guests.

Jeff held my hand in his. We were both ecstatic, breathing

the salty air that stroked our faces. No words were needed; savoring the moment was enough.

The meal was sumptuous. The elite of Tangier savored the many dishes prepared in our honor. The five-tiered wedding cake was beyond my wildest dreams. Soon the hashish cookies we had been served along with the wine and strong sugared coffee took effect. The Arabian musicians were smoking kif, and a pouch was brought to each table. Everyone completed the celebration by smoking the pungent Moroccan cannabis mixed with opium.

When it was time for us to leave, the night sky seemed like a black velvet jewel box displaying the precious stones of heaven. We had been presented with two bronze candelabra holding large three-foot candles that we were to let burn until they were extinguished. According to Arab custom they would burn thirty-six hours, and during that period one of us must stay awake while the other slept to establish the vigilance required for a happy and productive union.

We drove to our honeymoon cottage outside of Tangier above Hercules Grotto. Our chauffeur carried a huge picnic basket filled with bread and cheese, fruits and nuts, wine and a part of our wedding cake into the room. In front of our windows overlooking the beach, night and day the natives guided donkeys with large baskets at their sides in a continual chain up and down the embankment, carrying sand from the beach to the road. Seeing the candles burning in our windows, they assumed we were Arab newlyweds. So they serenaded us as they passed, chanting, blessing our union day and night for the entire thirty-six hours without stopping. Their blessings, though we could not understand a word, were a tonic to our love. Somehow, we did not seem to require much sleep. Tenderness sealed our union as I watched my loving husband rest, sleeping like a satisfied god. When I could no longer keep my eyes open I kissed him gently, and it was his turn to watch over my ecstatic slumber. During the day we walked down to the famous grotto, reputed to be the spot where Hercules rested between his courageous feats. In one of the coves cut into the rock by the sea there was a flat slab that made a perfect resting place. Carrying blankets and pillows, we returned that evening to lie on the stone as the sun celebrated the end of day by painting the sky in glorious colors. Directly above our heads through an opening in the rocks the North Star shone.

When we returned to Rome, the city looked as if it had been invaded by Hollywood. The Italian film industry continued to cast American stars in their pictures, knowing that it would assure them an American release.

Everyone who was anyone seemed to be at our belated wedding reception. Kirk Douglas, Humphrey Bogart, Ava Gardner, Henry Fonda, and Edmond O'Brien, among others, came. All were making pictures in Rome at the time.

For the next three months Jeff and I traveled through Italy, Switzerland, and France. Dressed in white, in matched sweaters and pants, Flip riding between us, his black coat shining against the red upholstery of the white Sunbeam Alpine, we created a sensation wherever we went. We were the King and Queen of the Kingdom of Beauty, Youth, and Wealth. For the first time, I felt wealthy. Between the high salary I had been paid by the Italian producers and the excellent salary Jeff had made from his series, we were flying high!

We were treating Flip as an equal. In Europe pets are allowed in restaurants and Flip sat quietly on a chair between us, gazing at customers who looked with amazement at this elegant dog's perfect behavior. We would have his steak cut in small pieces and brought to the table at the same time as our entree. The delicate manner in which this lovable poodle would pick up a few pieces at a time and hold his head up to chew quietly was fascinating. Flip was a well-behaved child, and we were the proud parents. By now he was full grown, and we kept him clipped in the lion cut originated during the reign of Louis XIV. Toward the end of our meal Jeff would call the waiter, put Flip's leash on, and the waiter would take him outside. It was fun being able to be different, an eccentric, wealthy, young, and gorgeous movie couple doing just as we pleased.

In Madrid, Barry Mahon, the producer who wanted Jeff to play the lead in *Miracle for Chico*, kept delaying the filming of the picture while he attempted to raise money for the production. Jeff was not needed, so we returned to the United States because by now I was happily six months pregnant. And of course we wanted our baby to be born in America.

We returned to the house on Beverly Glen, and soon changed its atmosphere. The fishing net adorning the wall, a relic of my marriage to John Bromfield, was removed. Moroccan lamps, copper tables, and leather ottomans turned the place into an Arabian abode. Ballooning silk cloth gathered from the edges of the ceiling surrounded a multijeweled, colored, brass lace chandelier. Receiving guests in our Moroccan costumes, we continued to live the fantasy of our romance.

Our small gatherings became the talk of the town. Robert Stack, one of the most eligible bachelors in Hollywood, met his future wife, the exquisite Rosemary, under the flickering flame of our Aladdin's lamp. Herb Jeffries helped us sharpen our chess game. Shelley Winters was a frequent guest, and the intellectual Barry Sullivan. Richard Basehart and his wife, the matchless Valentina Cortesa, John Ireland and his entourage, Lana Turner and her various escorts, Deanna Durbin and her devoted husband were all frequently at our parties.

I was in ecstasy. I felt that my big, extended stomach was my badge of honor. I busied myself keeping everyone well cared for while my husband made himself endlessly entertaining to our guests, adding to his reputation as a raconteur.

My place in the background was secured by the unbending commitment we had made the night of our wedding. If our union was to be blessed with a baby, we would never separate and deprive our child of the combined love of a mother and a father. This false security gave me confidence in my physical beauty as a mother to be. Humor and laughter were part of our daily routine.

I was eight months pregnant when our bliss was tempered by our tax man's discovery that most of our savings had to be used to pay back taxes. Ignorant about such matters, neither Jeff nor I had planned on paying taxes on our European earnings. I had no intention, however, of letting anything mar my happiness. Jeff's series would soon be released in the United States, and the films I had done abroad would, I felt, make me a valuable actress here after the birth of our child. Money would soon be coming in to refill our horn of plenty.

Herb Jeffries, since his return from Rome, had renewed his devotion to his Yoga master, Yogananda, and was guiding our meditation according to the methods of self-realization. Each afternoon, protected by our white burnous (Arabian hooded capes) each of us in a different room, Jeff and I would meditate, turning ourselves inward to the quiet flow within us. I would tune to the child within me, seeing him, speaking with him, telling about the love I felt for him, for I was sure now that it was a boy. I interpreted his various moves in my womb as answers to my queries.

"It won't be long, my darling, and you'll be in our arms. Here," I said, passing my lips over two of my fingers and placing them on my belly. "There's a kiss for you."

Right then I gasped in pain, as if someone had pinched me inside, near my navel. Maybe it's time to go to the hospital, I thought.

The doctor's routine inspection reassured us. I still had time to wait. The last month is the longest, he said, and attributed the pain I had to an especially hard kick from the baby. He told me not to worry.

I tried to take the doctor's advice, but a lingering feeling of uneasiness had taken hold of me. For two weeks I had been hearing a very high-pitched whistle whenever I was alone in the living room. I had heard that sound the first time I had walked into the house before we bought it. It always stopped if I brought someone to listen. It disturbed me that no one but me could hear this sound, and I went around the neighborhood inquiring if anyone was using a ham radio, or some other device that would make such a whistle. But I could find no explanation. I wondered if it had some relation to the voices I had heard within me in years past. A few times I had seen from the corner of my eye a foggy kind of a figure walking through the house toward the garden. Since we returned from Europe I had seen two silent figures dressed in white robes. I would see one of them sometimes standing, smiling behind the television set, watching Jeff and me. At other times, outside, a figure would seem to be sitting on a bench in deep contemplation. They always emanated a sense of happiness. I never felt afraid but I did not share these experiences with anyone.

One night during a business meeting in our house at which Herb Jeffries was presenting to some investors the idea of building a musical review around one of his albums, the sound became deafening. I could hear nothing but the whistle.

"I hear it too," someone replied. "I thought maybe you had a tea kettle boiling on the stove."

Now that everybody heard, the business was forgotten. There was a mystery to solve. We located the sound emanating directly from behind a green plant, where there stood a small statuette of the Virgin Mary with the Christ child. I had placed it there, hidden from the guests' view, but present to protect our home. A tape recorder was brought in. Herb began asking questions.

"Whom do you want to communicate with? Do you want to speak to Jeff? To Mr. Seltzer? To Mr. Aronson? To me? To Corinne?" The sound was intermittent. It seemed almost like a Morse signal, someone observed. As we played back the tape we could hear a distinct murmur. "I have a message, I have a message." The voice seemed to speed up in anger at Herb's questions.

"Let's continue recording," Herb said to the people present. Then he addressed the voice again. "Listen, we can hear you, but it's not clear. Could you speak more clearly?"

As we listened to the answer I felt it was my unborn child trying to communicate with us.

"I don't know how, I have a message. I'm new, I have a message . . . don't wait, don't wait. Don't wait, I have a message. . . ." The voice spoke with increasing anxiety.

I fell back on the sofa, limp. It was two in the morning.

"I'll get some expert to come tomorrow and do a real seance," Herb said.

"Where will you find someone?" Mr. Aronson asked.

"I'll call Duke University. They'll advise us," Herb said, recalling the experiments in ESP that were being conducted at Duke.

The next day I was vomiting blood. The doctor could not discover the cause. When Herb called I refused to continue the experiment.

"Whoever it is, Herb, they are using my body to communicate. I don't want to hurt my baby. We'll see later on. Maybe it will happen again after the baby is born."

Jeff wanted to call our son D'Artagnan, but I could not see a child going to school and taking the ribbing he would surely get with such a name. So we settled for Robin, from Robin Hood, the role that had shown Errol Flynn's charm at its best. It's my baby, Robin, trying to communicate, telling me not to wait, I concluded. I must have him now. I remembered at six months the doctor told me after he looked at the x-ray that I would have a large baby, that his spine was very large for six months.

That night, lying in bed with Jeff asleep, I felt water running out of me. The two ectoplasmic figures were standing at the foot of the bed; their emanation was of doom.

"My water is breaking," I moaned.

"No," Jeff replied, half asleep. "It's the baby, pressing on your bladder. Don't worry, you'll know it when the water breaks. It'll be like a flood."

"What about a leak?" I asked, unconvinced.

"Try to sleep, little mother to be. Big, strong daddy needs his rest."

I woke up time and time again in the night, hearing a baby cry. But where did it come from? What was I hearing? Was it my baby?

"Doctor," I said, the next day in his office, "don't ask me why, but I know we must take my baby out or it will be dead."

"Let's not be dramatic. Yes, it should be here any day now, you're just impatient."

Standing up from my chair I planted both my hands on his desk. My protruding form pushed over his container of pens and pencils.

"If you choose not to perform a Cesarean I'll go to another doctor, someone who will." The glare in my eyes was convincing.

"All right Corinne, be at the hospital tomorrow at 10 A.M. We'll give you something to induce your labor."

In the beginning Jeff was with me in my room holding my hand. Then I went through eighteen hours of four- to five-minute intervals during which, blacked out with pain, I would return to consciousness only to hear an impatient nurse say, "You must push down, you must." No one had explained the process of birth to me. If I pushed down I would empty my colon, and I did not want my baby to be born in excrement. It was frightening. I didn't know what to expect.

Jeff had been absent from my room for what seemed like an eternity.

"I can't take any more of this," I pleaded.

"I know, Corinne," my husband said when he returned. "I just signed an authorization for the doctor to perform a Cesarean. They're going to give you a spinal. You won't feel a thing, and I'll be right there when you come out."

I was wheeled into the operating room drugged. I felt nauseous. Strange, worried faces surrounded me.

"Turn on your side and don't move. Hold her down," I heard the doctor say.

It was not long before I heard a cry. It was a cry of anguished impatience.

"He's all right?" I whispered weakly.

"Yes," the nurse said, "a very healthy boy."

I fell into a deep, comalike sleep. When I awoke Jeff was not there. Where was he? I complained.

"He must have gone home and fallen asleep," the nurse told me. "He was here a long time waiting for you to wake up."

When Jeff came he looked exhausted. Two cigars were sticking out of his breast pocket.

"He's a big, beautiful boy," he said, as he placed roses on my bed.

"Look Jeff, look at all the telegrams we've received. The publicity man is coming over with the press in half an hour to take pictures for the wire services. I wish you had been with me when I woke up," I said.

"A man has to "celebrate" the birth of his son," he replied.

I didn't like the way he said "celebrate." But I pushed the negative thoughts out of my mind as we posed for the press.

Soon after Robin and I came home from the hospital a telegram arrived summoning Jeff to Madrid. The film *Miracle for Chico* was going to start shooting. Jeff left the next day. I anxiously waited for the doctor's approval for me and Robin to join Jeff. This was not the scene I had imagined—me alone with our baby and a nurse. Where were the adoring parents bending over the child's crib? Where was the loving father, getting up to fix the formula? "I don't think you should breast feed him," Jeff had said at the hospital. "It will tie you down if you get an offer to do a picture."

I was lonely, and wrote to Jeff, sharing with him what had happened in his absence. The closest I could get to him was watching *The Three Musketeers*, which was finally shown on television, and writing love letters.

Two weeks after Jeff's departure, leaving the nurse behind, I headed for Spain and Jeff. Loaded down with diapers and formula, carrying Robin in my arms, Flip, the black poodle, in an airflight case, I changed planes in New York on my way to Madrid. When the plane was airborne I looked for my passport. While giving me the VIP treatment, the airport personnel had forgotten to return it.

I became hysterical. I had a sudden case of postpartum blues, and was biting my hand in distress. I had the pilot contact New York, and the passport was sent on the next plane.

At the airport in Madrid, I had to wait three hours. I was exhausted. The baby was cranky, and the dog would not stay still. Isabelle, who had come from Paris to assist me, could do nothing but stare helplessly through the glass that kept me in quarantine until my passport arrived. She passed a note to me saying that Jeff was working on the film, which explained his failure to meet me, and that she herself had only arrived that morning.

When we finally got to the apartment, I found a note under the door, this one addressed to Jeff. It was perfumed. I could not resist. I opened the tightly sealed envelope.

> Jeffrey, you cannot get rid of me that easy. Come and see me this afternoon at five o'clock, or I will let your wife know about us.
>
> Maria

Jeff had been here without me for only two weeks. Our baby was barely three weeks old. My husband was busy shooting a picture. How could he have worked so fast?

I reread the note twice. I paced the floor, feeling as if I were caught in the huge mouth of a carnivorous monster. I feared that I was about to be swallowed by insanity.

I walked to Robin's bed. He had his middle finger in his mouth, the same pose that had been captured in his identification picture taken in the hospital. He looked like a Buddha, surprised to be on this planet.

In my mind I addressed him silently. Your father is very successful with the ladies, he has irresistible charm, and he doesn't know how to refuse a sexual overture. He knows the pleasure he can give a woman, and he can't bear to have any of them feel rejected.

I ran to the bathroom and lay flat on the marble floor. My

forehead rested on the cold stone, my eyes were dry, there were no traces of tears. My breathing was slow and deep. I inhaled, until every part of my being expanded. Exhaling, I emptied the air from my lungs and my fears from my body.

Twenty minutes or so later, when I stood up, I was calm. There was a new me in the reflection I saw. I had only seen this person, my decisive self, once before, in the car mirror as I waited for Rory and Henry. Putting on my make-up carefully, examining my figure, I was pleased with what I saw. I'm here now, lady, I spoke in my mind to the woman who had written the note. You don't have a chance. He's the father of my child. Nothing can separate us.

Isabelle picked up the crumpled note that was lying on the floor and read it.

"I'm going to the set to surprise Jeff," I said.

"Do you think that's a good idea?" Her voice sounded resigned. "Men, they're all the same."

"I'm a formidable opponent as long as he doesn't know I know." I tore the note up. "Let her come and tell me her story. I'm curious to see who she is."

I did not find out. She did not follow up on her threat, but this experience reactivated my internal alarm that went off each time Jeff's sexual desires were aroused by another woman.

The film dailies of *Miracle for Chico* displayed a new Jeff, a sensitive actor, but the production had run out of money.

"My other investor should have the money cleared any day now. I only need $20,000 to hold us over," Barry Mahon said.

I hesitated. I had about that amount in my Swiss bank account. Jeff was excellent in this touching film. Since it was only for a week or so, after which I would get it back as soon as the investor's money cleared, I made arrangements with the representative of the Swiss bank to have $20,000 in cash delivered to our hotel suite that evening.

I was nervous about keeping that much cash in the hotel while we went out to dinner with Mahon, but only the day manager was able to make arrangements for me to place the money in a safe deposit box. When Barry Mahon stopped by to pick us up we inquired if there was a way to get around this rule and use the hotel safe.

"Well, not before tomorrow, but if you want," Mahon said, "you can put the money in my safe deposit box."

At the desk I handed Mahon the purse in which I had put the funds.

"Mr. Mahon, would you please write on this card what you are putting in," the desk clerk instructed.

"It's just routine," said Mahon, turning to me. "It's for their insurance. I can put down anything you want."

I looked up at Jeff, who shrugged his shoulders.

"Twenty thousand dollars," I said simply.

Barry handed the card and the safe deposit box back to the clerk.

We had a marvelous dinner at El Commodore, and the next morning when I joined Barry and Jeff in the lobby to retrieve my money they were having a heated argument with the manager. It seemed that Barry's safe deposit box had been sealed and the money confiscated for past due hotel bills. We were almost totally broke.

Mahon offered to pay for our return tickets to the States with his credit card. We had no other choice.

Back in Los Angeles a tax man showed us how to deduct our travel expenses and bad investments from what we had saved for the government. It gave us some months' reprieve. There was nothing to do but wait for the film offers to appear.

The Stones became style setters, discovering new restaurants and making them popular. We were never bored together; that was the extraordinary part of our relationship. We were caught in the elating fascination of our minds. I wanted to be all women for Jeff, so I devised a game. I suggested that we reserve one evening a month when we would impersonate some of our favorite historical figures. The rules of the game were simple. We each placed the name of our character in an envelope, sealed and left in our bedroom. The game would begin when Jeff went out the front door and rang the doorbell. I opened the door, and the choice of the restaurant we went to, the subjects of conversation, the beliefs we expressed, the taste and inclinations we displayed, our behavior in general were all in keeping with our characters.

One of the most memorable evenings I recall was the one when Jeff, as General MacArthur, spent a splendid evening with me as Mata Hari. General MacArthur's well-organized campaign plan took us from a Korean dinner to some intimate moments of dancing at the Luau, an elite Polynesian restaurant on Rodeo Drive. Moments of spontaneous laughter would sometimes interrupt our portrayal, but a few moments of meditative silence would bring us back into our proper characterizations.

That special night I prepared for bed and perfumed my body with exotic flower oil. After pinning a gardenia in my hair, I sinuously entered the bedroom where Jeff, the general, was pacing up and down at the foot of the bed.

Paying no attention to the positions of sexual promise I took on the bed, he looked at me with his jaw set in disappointment. His eyes small with contained anger, he announced, "I will return."

I was stunned for a moment, and waited a few minutes before I grabbed a cape and went in search of him.

My bare foot found a wet spot on the carpet. "Flip," I thought. Shaking my head, I dismissed the idea, and entered the guest bedroom. There Jeff was pretending to be asleep. His gray slacks were wet up to the calf; so were his shoes. I could not help laughing as I addressed the immobile form on the bed.

"General MacArthur, sir, excuse me for awakening you, but you should stay alert. Washington may be calling."

Pushing the bed covers back and exposing his readiness he replied.

"I thought you would never guess. After I doused myself with the garden hose my shoes were making squishy noises as I walked back and forth while you were doing all those Theda Bara poses. Well, whoever you are, come here." He moved over, making a place for me in the single bed. "Madame," he continued, back in character, "you have enticed me all night. Come and share with me the mystery of your embrace."

One of the photos seen the world over.

Above: Flip, Jeff, and me in
Italy while Jeff filmed *The
Three Musketeers. Publifoto.
Right:* My future second
husband, Jeffrey Stone.

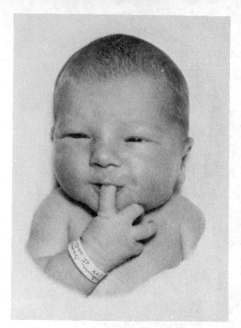

Left: A first photo of Robin taken in the hospital. *Below:* One-month-old Robin, Jeff, and me in Madrid, where Jeff was filming *Miracle for Chico. A Saiz*

Above: My painting of Robin
with his toy animals. *Below:*
Robin at four years old.

Above: In the Sultan Garden after the ceremony. *P. Alcaine, Jr. Right:* Coming back to the U.S.; feeling on top of the world. *Associated Press wirephoto.*

While expecting Robin, 1955. *Photo by Bernard*

Above: With Michel Auclair in *One Step to Eternity. Left:* Another scene from *One Step to Eternity*, a French film. *Movie Star News*

Opposite top: In Italy during the filming of *The Sins of Casanova*. It was the first time I wore wigs and antique costumes, and was lots of fun. *C. Martini. Opposite below:* A still from *The Sins of Casanova. Times Film Corporation*

Right: With Leo Gorcey and Huntz Hall. *Below:* With Skip Homier in *Plunderers of Painted Flats. Republic Pictures*

Above: The closest I ever came to becoming a nun was during a test for the *Other Face.* Jeff wrote the script, but the film was never made.
Right: Breaking more records as a nightclub entertainer, this time in San Francisco.

Left: Here I am with my hand to my hair again, this time in a publicity photo for my nightclub tour. *Below:* This photo was blown up to life size and made into a cutout for the night clubs' front doors.

Right: Baby Michael, just a few months old. *Below:* Here I am with Robin just after I was separated from Jeff. This was taken during the tour for the play *Personal Appearance.*

Above: My two handsome sons. *Opposite:* This photograph was taken by Richard F. Hodges in February 1983.

Chapter 13

Jeff and I were now signed with an agent who wanted to handle us both. With my six recent starring roles in Italian and French films, and Jeff's work in Italy for television and the movies, the agent had imagined that his ten percent of our action would amount to real money. Now, he changed his tune.

"You stayed away a long time in Europe, Corinne; then, on top of your absence, your pregnancy kept you unavailable. There's not much gratitude in this town. You turned them down when they wanted you a few times, and they don't forget that."

I decided to do something, so I took some of Jeff's footage to a studio executive I knew at Universal. A week later, Jeff signed a seven-year contract with that studio.

That is when Jeff suggested we hire a girl he knew to help with my fan mail which had accumulated while we were in Europe, as well as the mail he thought would soon be arriving for him. She had lost a leg in a motorcycle accident, and I felt sorry for her. Each morning she came to the house and worked in the dining room. One day, while shopping at Schwab's drugstore on Sunset Boulevard, I was approached by one of Jeff's acquaintances.

"You know, Corinne, you're such a wonderful, understanding wife. Europeans are so much more sophisticated than Americans. For you to hire your husband's mistress to do your fan mail, that's admirable."

"Well," I covered my shock at this disclosure, "I felt sorry for the girl, with one leg and all. The only thing I'm curious about is how they met."

"Oh," said my well-meaning friend, "the night Robin was born Jeff was distributing cigars to everyone here at Schwab's. He met her then. She invited him to come home and celebrate with her."

So, that was the answer to the mystery of Jeff's disappearance the night Robin was born. I went directly to her apartment and told her I no longer needed her services.

"Why?" she asked.

"You know why," I answered, losing my composure. "How could you, the night I gave him a son?"

"So what? Jeff told me you knew he could never be faithful to you, but you married him anyway. So what's the big deal?" she said cynically.

"Stay away from him or I'll . . ." I did not finish my threat.

"I'm really sorry, Corinne. I should have known better. Men are all the same. Liars. I won't see him again. You have my promise."

I knew that by marrying Jeff I had asked for problems, but being unfaithful the night our son was born? It was more than I could bear. I was disgusted with him, but grateful that I had not found out earlier. Now it was too late for recriminations.

A transformation in my emotions took place. I felt what Jeff had done that night was sacrilegious and showed a lack of respect for both me and his son. Somehow he was no longer my hero, my prince charming. He became Jeff, the father of my son. And Robin was going to have a successful actor as a father, a man who was going to take good care of us both financially.

Universal was keeping Jeff busy. During the first year he was under contract he made five films, *Men, Women and Guns, Damn Citizen, Girl in the Kremlin, Head That Wouldn't Die,* and a musical, *The Big Beat.* I was appearing on the television shows of Red Skelton, Bob Hope, Donald O'Connor and Steve Allen, but my agents were not able to finalize any of the film offers that were presented to me.

I began to spend all of my free time with my sweet baby, who was starting to walk. Out of a need to dispel my romantic illusions I decided to change and redecorate the Beverly Glen house. We chose to repaint the walls and the woodwork white, the window frames and doors in Chinese black lacquer. The sofas were re-covered in white leather, and when the bright orange carpet was installed my gloom disappeared for awhile.

Still restless, I took up my paintbrushes again, but even that didn't fulfill me. I began to look into Yoga and metaphysics, searching for answers. At the same time Mr. and Mrs. Stone became very social, renowned as great party givers. All we needed was an excuse to give a party.

In the living room we had our own piano bar, creating all the intimacy necessary to make entertainers want to perform, and our evenings were often filled with private concerts. Angela Lansbury, the composer Jay Livingston, Nat King Cole, and my old friend, Diana Lynn, a virtuoso pianist, were all frequent guests.

For the party celebrating Henry Willson's first trip to Paris we had among our guests Judy Garland, Mel Tormé, Glenn Ford, Donald O'Connor, Peter Lawford, Rock Hudson, Jane Withers, Blake Edwards, Jeanne Crain, Shelley Winters, and Montgomery Clift, who were all having fun translating the French sayings decorating the windows. The evening was balmy, and it was soon quite late. Luminaries surrounded the piano bar. Judy started singing "The Bells Are Ringing for Me and My Gal," and Donald O'Connor joined in. So did June Haver, Fred MacMurray, Rosalind Russell, Debbie Reynolds, June Allyson and Van Johnson.

I leaned against a wall looking at Hollywood's greatest stars, here in my living room. I was not dreaming! It was beyond my wildest childhood dreams.

"C'mon Corinne, join us," Dan Dailey said as he came back after getting his trombone from his car.

By four in the morning Judy Garland was singing "Have Yourself a Merry Little Christmas," and the mood of the party was changing. We all became misty-eyed.

At the end of our private concert, the maid and I got busy in the kitchen and soon our guests were welcoming the dawn with a breakfast of scrambled eggs and coffee.

"It's the best party we've ever been to," our happy friends thanked us as we stood by the door bidding them good-by. Jeff was beaming. We were finally accepted and appreciated by the Hollywood elite.

That was the good part of my marriage. Unfortunately, there was a negative side. Jeff had not capitalized on the deal with Universal. He had also managed to alienate innumerable producers and directors with his womanizing, chasing after their girlfriends who worked at odd jobs in the studios.

When Jeff's option at Universal was not picked up I did not let it deter me. Our agent arranged for both of us to tour in the play *Light Up the Sky*, which took us East. We had rehearsed for a few weeks when a film offer I couldn't refuse took me out of the tour. After making arrangements for my friend Denise Darcel to take my place playing opposite Jeff, I returned to Los Angeles to do *Plunderers of Painted Flats*, produced and directed by Albert Gannaway, with Skip Homeier as my co-star.

Gannaway, a tall man whose enthusiasm was contagious, paid me considerably more than my agent had led me to expect, and I became smitten with his obvious adoration for me. He had the capacity to make me feel that my welfare was the most important thing in his life.

During the filming we spent a great deal of time together. Gannaway respected my lack of interest in moving our friendship to a sexual plane, but he made himself a welcome part of our life, giving a great deal of attention to Robin, and then gaining Jeff's trust on his return.

I was busy making arrangements for my birthday party when Jeff announced that he had invited Johnny Stompanato and Lana Turner.

"Stompanato, isn't he one of the guys that was with Mickey Cohen, the gangster?"

"Yes," Jeff answered. "But that was years ago."

"What's he doing with Lana?"

"It looks like love," Jeff said whimsically. "He now has an antique shop in Westwood."

At the party Lana was radiant. Johnny Stompanato, a dark-haired, extremely handsome man, towered over the petite silver-blonde Lana. He was attentive, and Lana kept giggling happily at his intimate whispers.

Soon after, Lana left for London to do the film *Another Time, Another Place*. Johnny could not leave the antique shop in Westwood.

"She's furious with me. She begged me to close the store and come with her; but you don't fool around with my investors."

"Hey, Johnny," said Jeff, "she'll be back after the film is completed. You've got a good deal in Westwood, don't blow it."

"She's driving me crazy," Stompanato complained. "She calls me every night, crying, begging me to come. She doesn't like the place the film company rented for her; she tells me they're taking advantage of her because she doesn't have a man there to defend her rights."

"Do you love Lana?" I asked him.

"It's impossible not to. She's an all-encompassing woman. She calls when I get up, she calls when I'm ready to go to sleep, and she spoils me," he said grinning, showing off his gold jewelry.

"Can you put someone in charge of the shop for a week?" I suggested.

"I guess I could."

"Maybe you could go to London on a shopping trip for the store."

Johnny's smile reminded me of a cat that had just cornered a mouse.

He left the next weekend, and stayed longer than planned. When he returned he was gloomy and angry.

"She made me stay by promising the money to reimburse the investors, but when it was time to come up with the dough she refused, and told me to close the shop and let the investors sell the merchandise as their share. Well, no broad is going to play that game with me, so I roughed her up a little bit."

"You did what?" I was outraged.

"Listen, dames need to know who's boss."

"So what happened?" Jeff said, putting his hand on my shoulder to cool me down.

"That bitch complained to Scotland Yard. They came and escorted me to the airport."

Jeff and I were stunned.

"What are you going to do about the shop?" I said, breaking the silence.

"I'm going to close it up and salvage what I can get out of it."

It was only a few days later that Johnny announced, "Lana called. She told me she's sorry, that it was the film that made her nervous. She's calling four times a day. She says she can't live without me, but I can't get back to London, so she wants me to meet her and her daughter, Cheryl, and go on a vacation, the three of us."

After spending some time in Acapulco with Lana, Johnny returned to Los Angeles, called Jeff, and planned to stop by in the next few days.

We were watching television when the news broke.

"Lana Turner's boyfriend, Johnny Stompanato, was stabbed to death with a kitchen knife in Miss Turner's bedroom. . . ."

Cheryl, who was 13 years old at the time, was arrested and tried for the killing. It was ruled justifiable homicide. She had tried to protect her mother during a brutal beating by Johnny Stompanato.

There was one avenue open to me for making money, the offers I was getting to do a nightclub act. Overcoming my fear of singing, I borrowed from the bank to prepare an act and accepted my first booking.

We left for New Orleans. Dick Steward, the manager of the Swann Room in the Monteleone Hotel, walked with Jeff and me from the service elevator through the immense kitchen. We were followed by admiring whistles. We paused at the back door of the stage where I was going to launch my career as a singer. The Swann Room went dark. During the drum roll I moved to the center of the stage and leaned against a lamppost we had brought with us as a prop. Dick Steward made a flattering introduction. I heard the first notes of the music. My head was down, a pink spotlight coming up slowly. I started singing "Autumn Leaves" in French. The light man was supposed to enlarge the spot to take in my whole body. Wider, wider, I wanted to scream. Let them see my décolletage. The song was over. The lights came up. The applause was polite. The jokes that followed fell flat. I couldn't stop now. I started moving around on the stage, taking the audience with me, transporting them to the streets of Paris. Through sheer energy I had raised the audience to a high pitch of enthusiasm by the time I took my last bow. I left the stage and strode through the kitchen, wiping my face with a towel. Alone, I rode the freight elevator to the security of our suite. I had made a decision. I would completely rewrite my act.

I knew what to do. I would let the audience know where I

was born, how I got to America, and how I liked my leading men. I could see myself speaking of my first film, *Rope of Sand*, and, looking at the list of my songs, I picked the most appropriate tune. "And when Burt Lancaster took me in his arms, I felt like . . . 'Running wild, lost control, running wild, mighty bold.'" I sang the lyric as a tag to my recollection of Lancaster.

Now, for Jimmy Stewart in *Far Country*, I could sing, "They're not his lips, but they're such tempting lips, that it's all right with me."

Jeff was at the door.

"What's happening? We're waiting for you to change your clothes and join the club owner and the mayor. His honor is here to welcome you to New Orleans." Unzipping my dress to change, I announced to Jeff that I didn't want to stay with them more than a few minutes because I wanted to rewrite my act before tomorrow night's show.

By the time I opened in Washington, D.C., the reviews were promising.

> The Casino Royale has brought us some toothsome bon bons before, but this week the selection is truly splendid with a shapely Gallic siren named Corinne Calvet. For the most part, this stacked-uesque and alarmingly beautiful creature has confined her activities to moviedom. However, she recently took to the open road, and the swank saloon circuit. If you're wondering she sings.

I did sing. Armed with new confidence, I went on to the Empire Room at the Statler Hotel in Washington, then to El Morocco in Philadelphia, where the reviews were even more favorable.

> The town is completely full of Hollywood personalities these days, and far from the least of them is blonde Corinne Calvet, who is heading the show at the El Morocco. Miss Calvet is a well-constructed girl, brings bright, boundless energy and great enthusiasm to the stage. She obviously enjoys what she's doing a great deal, and transmits this enjoyment successfully to the audience. There is nothing more pleasant than watching a happy contented performer, and that is exactly what Miss Calvet is. She

sings in a big, not too accurate voice, and she infuses even the most banal numbers with a generous measure of her strong personality. Her movement and her phrasing are broadly theatrical, but she is a theatrical personality, so the note she strikes is just right for her.

It was also the right note on which Jeff saw fit to leave. He returned to Los Angeles to relieve his parents of the care of Robin.

The thought of being alone in a strange hotel room with no one to share the exhilaration and excitement I felt after a performance was terrifying. I didn't have the right personality for mingling and drinking with club owners and their customers, to their great disappointment. Even more than before I was afraid of meeting strangers, adding to the list of people who would remember me, and whom I would probably forget, adding to my embarrassment when they approached me. That anxiety was turning me into a recluse. The more invitations, the more flowers I received, the more phobic I became.

In Boston roses arrived with a note from Albert Gannaway, the producer of my last film. He would be taking in the late show, and wanted to know if we could have dinner afterward. His timing was perfect.

Seeing Albert walk toward me backstage, I felt secure again. His arms were around me, his head leaned lightly on top of mine. He was a charming giant, coming to the rescue of the lovely damsel imprisoned in her ivory tower.

The next day Albert advised me to hire two new musicians. My arrangements were rapidly modernized. From the lighting booth he directed the cues for my singing moods. Decisively he guided me wherever we went, candlelit dinners after my last show, sightseeing in places of interest during the day. I was vulnerable. He was my protector. I grew dependent upon him. He stayed with me for a few days until he knew I was comfortable with the new band.

When I got back to Los Angeles and looked at the bills that had piled up on the desk in Beverly Glen I was in shock. By the time they were paid we would be broke again. Later, I spoke to Jeff.

"Jeff, I don't want to go back on the road alone. You're not

working. I want you to become my road manager. I need someone. I will share what I make, so we'll both be able to share the
expenses."

"No way," he said quietly. "That would be bad for my image.
I have to think about my future. I'm no stage door Johnny."

I was tempted to say, "What future?" Instead I blushed.

"You could act like a man in love with his wife, knowing and
respecting her talents, protecting her and handling her affairs."

He was silent.

"You just want to play around when I'm out of town. That's
what you really want, to spend all the money I'm out there earn-
ing." I fled the room, banging the bedroom door.

Trembling, I dialed my booking agent.

"I'll take that club in New York, the Living Room. Book me
for three weeks, right away."

"Don't you want to wait for an opening at the Plaza?" he ventured.

"Can't wait. I need the money."

"You what?" He was laughing. "What did you do? Stop in Las
Vegas?"

"Hold whatever checks come in. I'll pick them up at your
office next week. After New York I'll take Montreal. Also, try to
find another club back East to fill in before I go to Miami. Then I
may as well do San Francisco."

"I thought you were dead set against doing three shows a
night?"

"I may as well have that experience too," I said sarcastically.

"Corinne, is everything all right?" I could hear the concern in
his voice. "Can I do anything?"

Sincere caring always made my emotions grip my throat.
Holding back the sorrow I felt for myself, my voice shaking, I
brought the conversation to a close.

"Don't worry. It's nothing that cannot be handled. Thank
you, and I'll be waiting for the confirmations."

I could see Jeff silhouetted outside the window, listening to
my phone conversation. Lighting a cigarette, I inhaled deeply,
tasting the salt of my tears.

I spoke loudly enough for Jeff to hear. "I'll take Robin and
the maid with me, that's what I'll do."

Jeff remained moody but he reluctantly decided to come with

us. Robin had resented my absences on tour, so it was a very happy boy who flew to New York. His amazement at the height of the buildings reminded me of my own years ago when I first arrived in the States.

At the Living Room in New York I was a huge success. The reviews were very flattering. Every night they added tables, and as the dance floor became smaller and smaller, my movements became more restrained. I was gaining confidence in my singing at the same time as I was losing hope for my marriage.

Jeff was absent from the club more often than not, and I was worn out worrying about where he was, and losing too much weight. It was Albert Gannaway who often joined me to meet friends I had not seen in years. Many nights Jeff didn't come home before dawn, and when he did his return was underscored by my violent accusations and recriminations.

I was breaking all records so the club owner offered to hold me over for another two weeks.

"I can't. We open Friday in Toronto."

My agent was smiling.

"Corinne, to be held over in New York means two thousand dollars a week more as soon as *Variety* prints it."

Variety, the show business bible. I could see my bank account bulging as he continued.

"I've already talked with Toronto. The publicity is good for them, so they'll give us the following two weeks. And I told them we'll send a replacement."

"Well, I guess I'm on. I mean you're on."

My career soared as my personal life crumbled.

"Albert," I confided to Gannaway. "Jeff is driving me crazy, out every night. I don't know what to do. I can't sleep. At least when he's in L.A. and I'm on the road I don't have to see it. What should I do? How can I pretend that I'm on top of the world, a beautiful woman, loved and desired, when I feel so insecure?" I was shaking uncontrollably. I felt Albert's hand on my shoulder.

"If you were to be cast in the role of a murderess you wouldn't be one." Albert's voice was solemn, his eyes were fixed on mine. "You're just playing a role out there . . . but this situation with Jeff, something must be done."

My eyes were playing tricks on me. Gannaway had become a

doctor. The round mirror I thought I saw on his forehead was making me blink.

"Robin would be better in Beverly Glen, and from there Jeff couldn't ruin your health. You can't take anymore; you're at the breaking point.

He was right. Robin was cranky from my stress. Robin and I were both crying when they left for Los Angeles. My son needed me and I was failing him. I felt like a hollow container.

At the club greasy cooking smells penetrated the thin walls of the cubicle in which I changed clothes. I hated the smell of grilled meat fat that permeated my dresses. Dousing myself with Shalimar, I would go out in the lights and be the toast of the town. Albert was back in L.A., but he called on closing night.

"I wanted to be back for your closing, Calvet," he said, addressing me in his usual fashion, "but I have some scoring problems here. I'll be up in Toronto by the middle of the week." Then in response to my silence, "You'll be all right. You're great. The act doesn't need me anymore. It's perfect."

"Albert, I think I need you."

In Toronto, the air was pure, the city was clean, the smiling faces felt European. For a moment I was happy. The room at the club was large and intimate at the same time. Jumping onstage to rehearse with the new band I felt secure.

In front, at a table, the two club owners sat with a public relations man. With each number I could see them looking more and more baffled, exchanging looks of consternation. Finally, the public relations man walked up to my pianist.

"Can we have a list of her numbers?"

After glancing at our program, he addressed himself to me.

"Excuse us," he said. He took the pianist by the arm, and the four of them conferred.

As I approached, three of them left, leaving my pianist behind. His face had turned white.

"Caroline Greene replaced you for the last two weeks. She did the same act, even some of the same songs; just singing the songs to different actors she was dreaming she could work with."

Caroline had watched my show many times in New York. She had copied my act and taken it to Toronto in my place while I was held over at the Living Room.

Betrayed. I had been betrayed once more. I felt the familiar pain pulling, distorting my right eye. My ears felt as if they were floating away from my head. My heart dropped like an elevator into my feet. My life was running out of me like a raw egg from a broken shell. I grabbed my purse and walked aimlessly until I found myself in front of my hotel. I remained silent. I was surrounded by a thick, protective wall made of cotton balls. People were talking. I barely heard their comments.

"Don't worry, you can sue Caroline. Could you just sing French numbers for tonight?" my pianist suggested.

I attempted to lift myself out of the armchair in which I was sitting, but fell back hopelessly.

"Should we call Jeff?" he asked.

"No," I managed to utter.

"Your agent said to fake the show for the press tonight, and to return to New York tomorrow."

"Mr. Gannaway is on the phone," another voice said. "He insists on speaking with you."

"Albert," I managed.

"They want you for 'What's My Line?' Meet me in New York tomorrow. Announce that some family illness is forcing you to leave tonight. And listen, Calvet. They would love for you to make them join in singing 'Alouette, Gentille Alouette.' I'll be right there," he said to someone where he was calling from. "I've got to go. Calvet, I love you. I'll fix everything when I see you tomorrow," I heard Albert say before the phone went dead.

"At least the act was good enough to steal," I said cynically.

After the pianist announced that our arrangements had been in our lost luggage, I sang a few French songs with only piano accompaniment that night, making everyone sing with me. They loved it. I did not return to take a second bow, but left for New York, anxious to be back in the comfort of Gannaway's guidance. Albert was not there when I arrived, but he called every few hours, delaying his departure time.

"I want to clear everything I need to do here so I can spend some time with you, my brave soldier," he said from Los Angeles. "Have fun on 'What's My Line?' Say hello to Bennett Cerf for me."

"I hear they called Caroline to finish the two weeks in Toronto," I said woefully.

"Don't worry. We'll stay ahead of her on our bookings, and

I'm sending a description of your act to all the clubs we want to play."

"Good," I said, somewhat encouraged.

"But I don't think you should sue. Her husband has connections, so it's delicate. You could lose a lot of bookings."

"Albert? What are you telling me?"

"I'll see you in Milwaukee the day before you open."

With Albert on my side, everything went smoothly. My Milwaukee opening was also a huge success. Sipping champagne from a frosted silver goblet, sitting on a high-backed, red velvet armchair, I saw that the red candles in the chandelier gave a glow to Albert's face. He looks handsome, I reflected with tenderness. My throat was dry.

"More champagne," I requested. "Albert, I love you. What would happen to me without you?" My hands were lost in his.

Back at the hotel, in my room, Albert undressed me. Feeling like a silent movie queen, I let him make love to me.

Headed back out to the coast, I had a stopover in Los Angeles before going to San Francisco for my next engagement. I asked Jeff to bring Robin over to the airport so I could see him for an hour or so before I left. He turned me down vigorously.

"I can't. I have an appointment. You'll only be in San Francisco for a few weeks."

"That's right," I said. "And I won't be taking any more bookings."

There was a moment of silence on the phone.

"Do you want me to come to your opening?" Jeff said.

"Would you?" I answered hopefully.

"OK, but I can only stay a day. Good things are happening here for me."

Bill Brown, an ex-newspaperman I had known as a friend during my Bromfield days, met me at the airport in San Francisco. His publicity office was handling the public relations for Bimbo's, the club where I was booked. I was glad to see him. Reminiscing about the old days, we went from talk shows to newspaper interviews drumming up business for my appearance. Something good is happening to Jeff in L.A., I kept thinking, my mind full of foolish hope.

I called Gannaway.

"Jeff is coming for the opening. I think you should come later," I ventured.

"Calvet," Gannaway said, "do you remember asking me to help Jeff?"

"Sure," I said with concern.

"I'm embarking on a project, and I've been speaking with Jeff about being my assistant."

"Albert, you would do that? You're too much. Jeff did say he had something cooking in L.A."

"He would have to move to Florida," Gannaway went on, getting no reaction from me. "We'll all have to move to Florida."

"Your wife too?"

"My wife and my son. . . ."

I interrupted him. "Albert, if Jeff is a success I can stop working and be a real wife and mother. I'll always be grateful to you, you know that."

"I know that when it comes to Jeff you have a bottomless amount of forgiveness. The most important thing is your happiness, Calvet."

"Albert, what can I say?"

"If it takes making your husband a successful man, then that's what it'll take."

"How soon do we have to move to Florida?"

"Not for a few months."

"Thank you, Albert. Bless you. You're my friend."

"And don't forget, your hopeful lover," Gannaway added wistfully.

Bill Brown had done a tremendous job. San Francisco was not going to miss Corinne Calvet at Bimbo's.

Jeff arrived, and left almost as quickly as he came. He listened to me, but his mind was miles away. His responses to my questions were monosyllables. He was condescending.

"You're breaking all previous attendance records," Bill Brown announced during my second week. "You've even broken the record of Lily St. Cyr, the stripper."

"What are you talking about?" I was stupefied. "Is this a strip joint?"

"No," Bill laughed. "It's just that Lily St. Cyr is an entertainer who takes off her clothes." Responding to my consternation, he added, "Look at it this way. If you can make more money than the top stripper without taking your clothes off, then Madame, you've really got it made."

"I don't appreciate your humor Bill," I said, laughing. "Get out of here. I've got to get dressed for the next show."

"There's a newspaperman, second table, stage left," Bill reminded me.

How could my agent have booked me in such a club, even if I had told him I wanted to work? Well, I thought, what's done is done. Somehow, I was feeling great. It's going to be a great show, I told myself.

During the show an overly enthusiastic heckler gave me a chance to show that I was in charge. But then, making a spectacular turn, I kicked my fur train with a brisk movement and heard the only seam that held my dress together tear. Like a creeping snail, the cool air was moving up my moist flesh. Still singing, holding my body still, I knew one move would tear the rip the full length of the dress, exposing my naked body. Inch by inch, I tried to reach for the microphone stand. The panels of the dress came apart. Without losing a beat, I slumped to the floor. Lying on the side on which the dress had torn, I finished the song. The frenzy of applause was deafening. The men at the back tables were standing up. Some of them were on chairs. I gestured to a man sitting at the closest table. Moving slightly off the floor, I let him see my condition. Comprehending my dilemma, he stood up and grandly pulled the tablecloth out from under the contents of his table, sending glasses flying in all directions. The club bouncer was on him in an instant, picking him up by the back of his coat. The man tried to explain. No one could hear. The turmoil was at a peak. I looked over toward Bill Brown, begging with my eyes for help. He was looking around, smiling in amazement. I knew what he was thinking. What great copy this would be. He couldn't have planned it better. I turned to the band and motioned for them to start the next number. The noise subsided, and instead of singing I announced that I required a large raincoat brought to me on the stage because my dress had split and I wanted to change.

The reaction was like the roar of an approaching storm, thunderous applause mixed with laughter and the heightening of endearing calls. Someone came to my rescue, dropping a coat over me on the floor. Holding the garment against me, I walked to the safety of my dressing room where I collapsed, laughing hysterically. I was alone. I didn't want to laugh. I wanted to cry. I looked in the mirror. My eyes had a red glow.

"I feel as if there is a demon in my body," I spoke aloud, making the sign of the cross. I heard myself utter with total authority, "I order you to leave, in the name of the Holy Ghost. Now." Kneeling down, my eyes closed, my head on the floor, my arms extended, I waited. Slowly I felt my arms being pulled out of my sockets by invisible powers. The pain was excruciating, yet there was an infinite pleasure. Holding my breath as if I was giving birth, I abandoned my will.

"Not my will, Father, but Yours." I let go and felt free. Bill Brown was knocking at the door. I admitted him to my dressing room.

"You were magnificent. What class. That's what I call presence. Wait until the press gets hold of it."

"Please take me back to the hotel," I spoke quietly.

I survived San Francisco and Bimbo's. We went to Florida, but Gannaway's deal failed so we returned.

Back home, life with Jeff took on a dreamy sameness. I remained committed to the proposition that a child, our child, needed a family, and I continued to hope that somehow things would change. Periodically, I made efforts to get my agent to find me work. The only thing I could muster was one New York television show. I went to New York, and added a final chapter to the Hall Wallis–Corinne Calvet saga.

One night I was out with Cy Howard, the well-known television and film writer, now married to the daughter of Jack Warner. Cy and I had gone to a Broadway opening. Afterward, I was feeling feverish, but on Cy's insistence I accepted his invitation to have dinner at a club. As we walked in, to my surprise I saw Hal Wallis sitting at a large table with a man I didn't recognize.

"Join us, Cy," Wallis spoke authoritatively. "You know Joe," he said, pointing to the man with him, who looked like a banker.

"Slide in," Cy said to me, as Wallis moved over to make room for both of us.

My throat was swollen. I ached all over. I was coming down with something. Overcoming difficulty in swallowing, I asked Cy to dance, and I could see that Wallis was watching every move we made on the dance floor. When we sat down, fresh drinks were served. Carefully, with the corner of my dinner napkin, I removed the cold sweat that was covering my forehead. In shock, I felt a hand on my knee, moving up my leg. I dropped the napkin on the leather seat, and pulled roughly on Wallis's arm.

"Excuse me," I said. "I must go and powder my nose."

While Cy was standing up to let me pass, Wallis muttered sweetly, "Hurry up, we're going to miss you."

I felt dizzy. Something was definitely wrong. Looking in the mirror above the wash basin, it was obvious. I was running a high fever. I stuck out my tongue. It was a strange color; so were my gums and throat. I have to get to bed right away, I decided. And then the thought entered my mind, "It's a chance for the perfect revenge."

Back at the table, I asked Wallis to dance.

"You know, Hal," I whispered, "you could have had me if you had put romance into your approach. If you had courted me instead of treating me like one of your cattle, I could not have resisted you. You see, tonight, it's snowing. That's romantic. And a ride in Central Park in a horse and carriage would be a perfect start."

"Let's go," he said, walking me back to the table. "Take care of it," he said to Joe.

We walked arm in arm toward the Plaza hotel, the large snowflakes falling softly, the streetlights creating the effect of an eerie Christmas card. We were silent. He put his arm around my waist, helping me cross a mound of snow. The soles of my shoes on the newly fallen white carpet crackled a soft, Papa . . . Papa . . . Papa. My fever raged inside, my joints ached. No sooner had the horse started along his well-trodden path than I began to sing softly.

"*Un fiacre, allez trotinant, clochinant, cahe cahin, hudias, hop la.*"

"*Voulez-vous coucher avec moi?*" said Wallis, his hand reaching under the blanket that covered our legs. "*Baise-moi.*"

I woke up from my Christmas card dream. For a moment I wanted to forget my plan for revenge and ask him to take me home, but it was too late. There was no holding him back. Between kisses I told Wallis that tomorrow I'd like to receive a bouquet of roses. I was kissing his ear, his eyes. I passionately made sure that he caught whatever I had which was, I found out later, strep throat!

In bed the next day, shivering with fever, I waited for the flowers. They never came.

After three days I ordered four dozen red roses sent to Hal Wallis's hotel. With them I included a note.

Next time I'll give you something worse. Best wishes for your recovery.

Corinne

I never heard from Wallis, but rumor had it that he was quite sick and confined to bed for several days. Why is it I still sometimes have a funny, strange smile on my face whenever I think of that horse and buggy ride?

I returned to Beverly Glen. One night when the maid left after dinner, I joined Jeff in the living room after kissing Robin goodnight. A fire was burning. He was rolling a brandy snifter over the flames.

"Darling," he said, handing me the glass and taking a deep sniff of his. "I have been doing a lot of thinking. It's no good. I don't want to be married. I don't want to be tied down to a wife and child. I've tried, really, I've tried. But I'm too rotten to be married."

"That doesn't mean I don't love you. It's just that I can't live here anymore. So . . ." he paused to swallow his brandy in a single, long swallow, "before there's any scene I'll be going."

"Jeff . . ." I started.

"Don't." He put his hand over my mouth. "Nothing can change. It's too late."

He was gone.

Robin and I were left alone in the house. I yearned for the comfort of his little arms around my neck, but I couldn't let him see my pain. I must never say anything negative to him about his father. He would have his own pain at the separation. I could not add my bitterness and anger.

Pacing up and down the living room, I talked to myself.

"A lady does not show her sorrow, any more than she washes her undergarments in public." I sounded like Isabelle.

"OK Isabelle," I heard myself say angrily. "So what happens to that pain, where does it go? How do you get rid of it?

"If you must cry, do it alone. Keep your pain to yourself; it will make you stronger, more regal.

"How do I keep Robin from feeling doubts and anger?

"Tell Robin the reasons why his father left, and leave the emotion out of it."

Closing my bedroom door behind me for privacy, I relinquished my body to the bed, overpowered by tremors. My pillow became the recipient of my sorrow. Like great waves from a sea of regret, my pain continued to escalate until it reached its apex. Out of control, I howled against my fate.

"No," I screamed. No to the pain, no to the collapse of my family. No to the responsibility of raising Robin by myself. No, no, no.

I could hear my heart palpitating outside my body, and yet the whole room was inside my heart, which was swelling, pounding erratically. I surrendered to what I felt was my inevitable death, and fell into oblivion.

When I woke up the next morning I ventured out of my room. The house was desolate. The maid had taken Robin to school. Outside, near the pool, the consoling rays of the morning sun warmed my cold flesh. Suddenly came the jarring sound of the doorbell.

"I'm a friend of Jeff and Herb," the tall, skinny man said. "My name is Charles. May I come in?"

"Jeff doesn't live here anymore." There, I had said it. I had made it official.

"That's why I'm here. I thought you might need a strong shoulder . . . come," he said, pushing me gently out of the way.

"How did you know?" I asked.

He didn't answer. "May I make some coffee?"

"I'm sure there is some ready."

At one time or another I had heard Charles's name mentioned by most of our friends, yet Jeff had not been willing to make him a part of our crowd.

"I don't trust him," Jeff had said. "He smokes too much grass." I wondered if maybe Jeff had said this to frighten me. Charles appeared calm and competent.

The immense loneliness I had felt in the house was no longer there. I lit the old-fashioned pot belly stove in the lanai, and stood close to it, getting warm. Charles came back with strong, aromatic coffee on a silver tray with croissants and English marmalade. He had an extraordinary forehead, I thought, accentuated by a prematurely receding hairline. He was about my own age. I sat next to him as he poured the coffee.

"Jeff does not realize how cruel he can be," Charles said, buttering a croissant. "I was a friend of Barbara Lawrence, his ex-wife, when they were married. He came home one day . . . marmalade?"

"No, I couldn't eat a thing."

"First error. You must keep your body going. Anyway," he continued, without insisting that I eat, "Jeff came home one day and for no apparent reason told Barbara he was leaving." His brown eyes, full of compassion, were watching my reaction. "I think she would have gone crazy if I had not happened to stop by. It gave her a sounding board."

"Here." He passed me a lighted, rolled cigarette.

"Grass? Do you think it will help?"

"It can't hurt, and it may help you have a little more perspective."

Inhaling deeply, I coughed, releasing the smoke.

"Very strong, isn't it?" I said.

"There's a little bit of hash rolled in it," he answered, taking the cigarette from me.

Looking at me and shaking his head knowingly, he continued.

"He's got you down that low. I bet he's eliminated all your friends."

"Now wait a minute." Surprisingly, I was out of my lethargy and on the defensive. "We have lots of friends."

"Sure," he said, his arm sweeping over the empty house. "Real close friends. How about girlfriends? With Jeff around no girlfriends, not safe, right? So how many people did you think of calling last night after he left?"

"I didn't call anybody because my private life is nobody's business."

"Well, you'd better prepare yourself, because any minute now the phone will ring, and the columnists are going to ask you how you feel." He stopped, and let the fact that I was a public figure sink in, and that I had a role to play. "So what are you going to say?"

There was no way I could speak to the press just then, defeated and vulnerable. He saw my silent appeal, and said that he could stay and answer the phone for me.

"That's what I'm here for, to help you through this transition." Charles broke out into a reassuring smile, displaying a set of impeccable teeth. The pain inside me began to subside.

"Why don't you go and take a bath and make yourself even more beautiful than you are now?" He had taken a book out of his coat pocket and was settling down on the sofa.

"What are you reading?" I asked, probing.

"Gurdjieff, *All and Everything*."

"You are?" I was happy to discover we had intellectual kinship. "I have tried to read that book, but I get lost among all those complicated names," I admitted.

The phone rang. Charles picked it up. With his finger on his mouth he gestured for me to be quiet.

"No, Miss Calvet is not available for comment. I'm the houseman. Yes, I'll leave a message." After hanging up he bowed, one hand on his stomach, the other on the small of his back. "Voilà," he said. "That's a very pitiful smile, but at least I did get you to smile. That was the representative of United Press. Until you come back all refreshed, maybe I'll read some of this." He pointed to the book.

The press was insistent. The phone rang incessantly. After the last call Charles was at the bathroom door.

"Hurry up. We're going to take a drive to the beach; we've got to get out of here. The press is going to be camped in your driveway. Harrison Carroll of the *Herald Express* just asked me how you were taking the breakup. The last time your marriage failed, he said you tried to commit suicide."

"What did you say?"

"I just told him I didn't know anything about it. That I hadn't been working in this position for very long." His deep guttural laughter jolted me. In no time we were driving to the ocean. The glistening crests of the waves were blinding. As I looked behind me, I mused that my steps on the wet sand were marks indicating that I did not really exist, for the water came and left, and the footsteps were no longer there. That made me feel relieved, re-vitalized. I ventured to the water's edge.

"The house, it's still in your name I hope?" Charles questioned.

I nodded.

"What time does Robin get out of school?"

"Two-thirty, Charles. I must not forget to go and pick him up." I longed to hold Robin close to me. "Jeff tells Robin that it's all right to tell little white lies," I added, "and I'm teaching him that the truth is the only way."

"Little white lies, and big black ones, it doesn't make much difference to Jeff if it's for his own advantage."

"Poor Robin. I hope he does not end up confused."

"Kids can see right through people. I've seen Robin with Jeff a few times. He's sharp. He'll be all right." Charles was reassuring.

"Why would he see you when he didn't want me to meet you?"

"Afraid I might blow the whistle on him, I suppose. Listen," he said, changing the subject, "what are the things you loved to do that you haven't done since you married Jeff?"

"Charles, when I'm with a man I love to do whatever my man enjoys. Alone, there is nothing I want or love to do. Except maybe," I said, trying to be funny, "drink a lot of Pernod."

That night, after Robin had gone to bed, I toasted Charles with the French aperitif he had ordered from the liquor store. As the night sped toward light, the smoking, mixed with the drinking, destroyed my reserve, and floods of untamed, resentful tears burst out. Charles, like a psychologist, was skillfully irritating, directing the release of my anger, doubts, and pain. After three days, exhausted, but free, I picked up the newspapers.

"Corinne Calvet's husband is a man about town again. Are the divorce rumors true?" I read.

Mention of Jeff dancing cheek to cheek with a gorgeous brunette helped me make up my mind.

"I must get out of town, Charles. I can't stand to read about his conquests."

A call to my agent in New York brought an offer to replace

an ailing actress in the play *Amphitryon 38,* in Myrtle Beach, South Carolina.

"Can you learn the play in one week?" my agent asked me.

Charles, listening on the phone extension, nodded his head affirmatively.

Later, I was filled with consternation when I read the play. It was written in verse.

"No way can I learn this play in a week."

Before midnight Charles returned with a recording of the play on three separate continuous tapes. Each night I went to sleep, my head lying next to a pillow speaker. The actress who made the recording had read the words without any interpretation. Charles played the other parts on the tape. The words entered my subconscious mind for seven or eight hours every night. During the day the act I had been hypnotized into learning at night was reviewed carefully. When it was time for me to leave for Myrtle Beach, I knew the role perfectly.

"Maman has to go, my darling," I told Robin, "but Charles will come by often, and he may even take you to the amusement park."

The familiar frown was on Robin's face as he looked to Charles for confirmation. Charles winked back, his way of stating his commitment. Putting his arms around my neck, Robin let me kiss him, but showed his resentment of my departure by refusing to kiss me in return.

"I'll be back very soon, I promise," I said, giving him a last hug.

The marijuana we had smoked on the drive to the airport took effect. I felt numb. In a daze I watched Charles handle all the details at the airport. His hand on my arm guided me. Our good-bys were rapid. Handing me a small gift-wrapped package, he spoke.

"Open it when you're alone. It should be enough for you to smoke until I see you next."

Looking up, I imagined that I could see through the plane's interior to the bare fuselage. I felt as if I were caught in the guts of a huge prehistoric bird. The plane took off. The big bird was flying so smoothly that if the seatbelt hadn't held me down I would have been floating on the ceiling.

"Oh, Jesus," I prayed. "I attempted to find you in John and

Jeff—that's why I was attracted to their beauty. I thought through them I could find that family of my youthful vision. Why did it turn out wrong each time?"

There was no answer, but the roar of the engines became music played by a grand symphony. I merged with the music, each note ambrosia to my body. I was at once the orchestra and the leader. When a musical phrase surprised me with its graceful artistry I could make the orchestra repeat the passage at will. I was hallucinating.

In no time we landed in Chicago. The plane that was going to take me to South Carolina was an old DC-3. As we boarded, my fear of flying grabbed me again. The paint was peeling off the wings. The windows were blackened by the engine exhaust. My paranoia mounted. I was apprehensive, but it was too late for me to get out. We were already taxiing on the runway. Crestfallen, I knew I was in for another horrendous experience.

The decrepit plane, its motors sputtering with effort, slid and bounced. I had been recognized by the stewardess, and to save face I attempted to hide my fear by pretending to read a magazine. I was grumbling under my breath.

"So many times I have wanted to die, what am I so scared about? This flight is ridiculous. I can't even see the print in *Newsweek*. I would prefer to die alone, not in the midst of all these frightened passengers. Who am I kidding? I want to die only when I choose the time. It's when the decision is out of my hands that death scares me. Why shouldn't we have the right to choose the time of our death? Jesus, you chose yours, didn't you?" There was no answer.

"Why is it," I reflected, "each time I permit myself to feel secure in a relationship, the bottom of my world falls out and I find myself . . . please God, make the plane stop."

I bent over to reach for the disposal bag, and from the effort a film of moisture covered my forehad.

"Think about something else," I ordered myself. "Why am I here?"

There was no answer.

"Well then, who am I?"

"You are a star, a Parisian-born countess. You are thirty-four years old, and you look much younger," I answered myself.

"Yes, and I'm a mother who has just lost the father of her

son. Jeff is not dead, but it's the same. He won't be there in the house with us. It might be easier if he were dead. How am I going to raise Robin alone? How does a woman bring up a boy alone?"

"You are neither the first nor the only one." I heaved into the bag. I felt like a frightened little girl.

"Maman," I whimpered, "please don't let the plane crash. I can't bear the idea of Robin growing up as I did without his mother's love. What did I do to be punished this way?" I felt as if my rib cage was pressing on my heart, squeezing the life out of me.

"What would have happened if I had stayed in France? Would I have married Jean-Pierre and become a Communist? I wonder if our baby would have been a boy or a girl? What about André's child? I would not have been happy married to André."

The memory of André's abandonment after my forced abortion brought up the bitterness with a wave of bile. Exhausted from the effort, I closed my eyes.

"How did I become a star anyway? Because I wanted it, thought it and dreamed about it, and consciously visualized myself already there. So if I had that experience why didn't I continue visualizing what I wanted? Like a faithful, successful husband who would also be a great father? Why did I constantly entertain the fear of losing both John and Jeff through their infidelity? Why did I spend so much time worrying about Wallis holding back my future? Why didn't I keep seeing myself more and more successful? Why did I forget how I created my own opportunity?"

The realization of my own life's responsibilities and the futility of blaming anyone for my failures made me feel like a minute grain of sand, but at the same time it helped me understand the immense power that was mine to accept.

"Why did I lose enthusiasm in my own capacity?"

"It was easier to fall into my anxieties instead of overcoming them."

"But what about destiny? Can I really change the events of my life? Could I have done so?"

"We have the choice of seeing the events of our life from a positive point of view, as an opportunity for constructive change, or from a negative point of view, as horrible injustices," my other self said.

"That's easier said than felt."

"It works every time."

"Oh yeah? Give me one good example."

"What about the time Ray Milland was surrounded by all those admiring females?"

"Yes, it gave me the opportunity to meet Mrs. Milland."

"What about the time you just missed the elevator and decided to walk up the stairs on your way to meet Marc Allégret?"

"That's when I met the producers of my first film, right in the middle of the stairway."

"What about when Helen got you the Quebec City film?"

"Right, it was then I decided that Wallis was not the only avenue for presenting my talent as an actress. That's what I loved about Helen, she was always a positive thinker. She was never negative about anything. If she had lived I would have won an Academy Award," I mused.

"'If' goes with regrets and remorse, then turns into guilt. 'Guilt' brings on the fear that it might happen again. Leave all the 'ifs' in the past; they don't belong in this moment—or in the future."

The plane was sideslipping as if caught in a powerful current.

"So where did I go wrong?"

"It was when I was vulnerable and in poor health during the occupation that Jean-Pierre fell in love with me. And it was my vulnerability in the hospital that got John interested; and as for Jeff, it was the vulnerability of my heartbreak with John. And even with Gannaway, it was my unprotected situation in the nightclub act that got him interested in taking control of me. So they all fell in love with me when I was down and out, insecure and vulnerable. And when I became strong again from their love, they went out to look for someone else vulnerable who needed them. But I needed them too, desperately."

"Only to reassure yourself of your own beauty."

"And when I found out I could no longer count on their love I became so paranoid that my jealous anxieties and fears made me very unattractive and unappealing to them. I can see how that could happen. What should I have done?"

"'Shoulds' go with regrets. Regrets accumulate into guilt, and guilt is unessential. 'Shoulds' are like the 'ifs', wasting energy on the past."

"Enough. I can't take anymore. I feel as if my mind is going to blow up."

The plane was no longer dipping. We must be flying right into the wind, I thought.

As I bent down to get my compact mirror out of my purse the plane seemed to drop a thousand feet. I felt as if I were being pulled out of my body, suspended. I was falling head first. I became the hanged man of the Tarot cards, no longer in control of my thoughts. My mind had given up. I was putty in the hand of the moment.

It didn't matter if we crashed, and if I died it would not really be I who perished. I was no longer in my body.

"I am so much more," I sighed, as the plane leveled off.

"This is the captain speaking. Well, ladies and gentlemen, we've made it. That was really some ride. I must tell you that I'm as happy to be out of this storm as all of you must be. We'll be landing in twenty minutes."

There was no one at the airport waiting for me, no photographers, no welcoming committee. The lady at the theater box office said that arrangements had been made for me to stay at the Golf Club Inn of Myrtle Beach. The taxi driver in this humid little seaside resort questioned whether this was really my destination.

"Sure you want to go there, Ma'am? It's closed."

"Do they have a phone?" No need to panic; be in the moment, I attempted to convince myself.

"Sure, Ma'am, the bar's still open. It's just the hotel part of the inn that's closed down. It's quite an historical monument, Andrew Jackson once had his headquarters there."

The entrance hall smelled like a mating battleground for the neighborhood tomcats. A ghostly, round-shouldered young man was standing at the end of the lobby.

"You're the only guest," he said, welcoming me. "We've opened the facilities for you. It's a great honor, Miss Calvet."

During his interminable lecture on the past glories of the inn, I heard only the sound of a ceiling fan, complaining from old age. I was fighting against the fear that this place was a horrible, depressing tomb.

He was still declaiming when he showed me my room. A terrifying sound rose in my throat. I wanted to tell him to be quiet, but I kept my lips closed, afraid of what it would sound like if I let go. What was I doing here? I pressed my face on the cool window glass, as if the slippery raindrops could wash my thoughts clean.

When I turned around the hotel manager was gone. The door was closed. This is like a Hitchcock movie, I thought, as I threw myself on the old-fashioned four-poster bed. I miscalculated and hit my head on the headboard, ending up cheek to cheek with a fat wooden cherub. I could feel his pudgy hand making an indentation on my face. It hurts, I thought, but I didn't move. I was not in my pain. I was detached from my body. By habit, I felt I should cry, but there was no one to hear, so why do it? No sorrow, not even self-pity. My body was hollow. It was empty. I was in a tunnel. On the walls was an endless rerun of my fears. When the dawn came I woke up elated in the light of a new day. I had gone through a catharsis. I was free, and ready for a new beginning.

Full of enthusiasm, I arrived for rehearsal. The director sailed over to where I was standing, introduced himself, and handed me a script.

"What's this?" I said in shock.

"The play you are doing." He was smiling.

"No it isn't. I'm doing *Amphitryon 38,* not *Personal Appearances,*" I said, reading the script title aloud.

"Didn't your agent notify you that we thought *Amphitryon* would be too difficult for you with your accent, and," he lowered his voice to a whisper, "I thought it would be too hard for them." He pointed to the cast, who had stopped rehearsing.

"I have just learned this play in one week," was all I could say.

"So," the director answered. "It'll be a snap for you to learn this one. It's a comedy. We have already blocked it with your stand-in, so if you're ready we'll do a runthrough for you."

I picked up my purse and walked to the exit, then stopped, changing my mind. I went to the theater office and called New York.

"I'm sorry, Corinne. I thought my secretary had called you, and she thought I had. If you walk out on the booking now, it's going to look bad with AFTRA; the theater may even sue you."

I enunciated my next words slowly and clearly.

"You are fired!" Then I hung up the phone.

Without a word I went in and sat in the audience. I was pleasantly surprised. The cast was good, the play was not going to win me a Tony, but I could live with it for two weeks. We rehearsed for five days. I was having fun. It had been easy for me to learn the new lines.

Shelley Winters was in a play that was closing that night, and we concluded our final rehearsal just as it was time to set the stage for her play. After her last performance, she invited everyone from the theater for a wiener roast on the beach.

I arrived a little before midnight, dressed in my faded, custom-made Italian jeans and my favorite loose terrycloth shirt. I found myself dressing without underpants or bra.

What am I up to? I pondered. What sort of rebellion is this? It felt good. I was being female for myself, and my own sensations, not for anyone else.

A huge fire illuminated the beach. The moon was concealed behind the clouds. Shelley Winters came over, shoved a beer in my hand, and gestured for me to sit down on a blanket next to her. She was thanking the cast and her off-color jokes had everyone in stitches. I kept my head down, looking at the fire, feeling ill-at-ease. Across from me I saw an emaciated, handsome young man, his shoulders slightly slouched. An intense energy was shooting in my direction out of his eyes, from under heavy eyebrows. I shivered. I got up to leave, but was stopped by my leading man, who quietly announced that he wanted to introduce me to someone who was dying to meet me. "And he drives a big Cadillac," he added.

"No, thank you," I said. "I don't want to meet anyone." But it was too late. The young man from across the fire was standing in my way.

"Corinne, may I introduce an admirer?"

The young man was looking down. With a grunt he lifted his green eyes. His upper lip was covered by a thin moustache, reminding me of a young Errol Flynn, but I did not like the look in his eyes.

"Nice to meet you," I said. "I have to go. Excuse me." I felt that there was danger concealed behind his shy appearance.

I wanted to get away fast, and walked rapidly down the darkened beach. As my shadow grew more elongated with each step, its presence comforted me. I stuck my fingers in the sand.

Right below the surface the beach had retained the heat of the day. I removed my sandals, and pushing my toes downward, I walked briskly, totally involved in the sensation of pleasure I derived from the warmth left over from the sun. Suddenly, I felt as if someone were watching me. Afraid, I turned around, but there was no one in sight. The beach party was only a small orange glow in the distance. I sat on the sand and felt a bulge in my jeans—it was Charles's present. The moon had come out from behind rain-clouds, the tide was coming in. The sea glittered. I thought, Everything is so beautiful, why does it make me feel so sad? I smoked the small, hand-rolled cigarette.

I waited for an answer, a sign. There was only the sea, like a lover, calling me, inviting me, beckoning me. Unable to resist, I disrobed. Raising my hands and face to the heavens, I felt the moonbeams blessing my nakedness. Moving cautiously to test the water, I smiled with delight. The ocean was surprisingly warm. Lifting my legs like a prancing show horse, I moved into the sea toward the small, rolling waves. As the water filtered past my thigh, I stood with my legs apart, waiting for the contact of my lover's caress. The waves were reaching closer and closer to my pubic hair. I was resisting the approach by standing on my toes and jumping to escape the inevitable. I felt the sea swell in its urge to overtake me until I was captured by a bulging wave. Dipping myself to the waist, I started the teasing game again. This time the object of conquest was my breasts. Baiting my lover, the sea, I took a piece of floating seaweed and wrapped it around my shoulders. The dripping kelp teased my nipples. I dipped my shoulders into the water, letting my breasts float on top of the waves. They became weightless, and were transformed into an ethereal vibrating glory. Laughing, I dunked all the way. Turned on my back, I floated. I was in union with nature. Playing siren, I was calling lost sailors to my inner temple. The dark clouds above released heavy raindrops into the salty sea.

Rushing out of the water, I dressed and ran back to the inn. The wind was blowing the rain sideways with such intensity that I struggled to shut the front door. As I closed the bedroom door, the window burst open. Dropping my clothes, I stood naked in the rain, delighting in the natural shower. The deep roar of thunder sounded like the laughter of God, rejoicing at my pleasure. Lightning bolts were his spirit, revitalizing mother earth. I was a goddess, dancing my reverence. I lay down on the floor, my body stretched open as the thunder reverberated closer and closer. The rain had slackened. I was a connection between the earth and the infinite. My heart was like an empty cathedral, an echo chamber for the now menacing drum rolls in the sky. The wind in the trees was whispering the name of the Holiest. A branch scratched the window shutters like brushes on a sleepy jazz drum. I was elevated to a mystic recognition of my universal being. Within me there was an overwhelming tingling.

The rain had started again. Sheets of the warm cloudburst repeatedly chastised my flesh. Abandoning all resistance, I allowed my coiled energies to be released. I followed their parabolic dance into a spiral of love.

"Take me, Lord, I'm yours."

Nearby, lightning struck; the reverberations of its energy entered me. Like a cracked church bell, I was fused, and rang with the power of the Divine, a participating witness in this cosmic orgasm. Flowing out and following the resonant sound, I faced my own radiance. Before I slipped into unconsciousness I heard a whisper.

"Has Corinne been a good girl?"

"Oh yes, Maman, I have." I smiled as I drifted into nothingness.

I was aroused by the warmth of the morning sun on my feet. I knelt at the foot of the bed.

"Dear God, how can I face this life now?"

"Ask and it shall be given."

"I want to be close to you, without the fear of poverty. Please," I said sleepily, "could I have the love of a young, handsome millionaire?" I crawled into my bed, and slept until it was time to perform in the play *Personal Appearances*.

I got my wish. The young man on the beach with the intense green eyes was a millionaire. During the next six years I lived in luxury, the kind in which I had dreamed a movie star should live.

Epilogue

As a child, I had wished for a life full of excitement; the life I have led has fulfilled my youthful dreams.

It has been twenty years since I was introduced to the green-eyed young man on the beach. He was wealthy beyond my wishes. With him I had an intoxicatingly luxurious life and together we adopted a three-day-old baby boy. I enjoyed being loved by a possessive man who never looked at another woman. He was extremely generous, but full of surprises. When our affair ended after six years, he sued me for the return of the one million dollars he said he had showered on me.

That's when Albert Gannoway reappeared in my life. I welcomed his broad shoulders and married him for the father image he provided for my sons, but our marriage was short-lived. We soon discovered that our values were miles apart. By then I had fallen in love with a younger man. Ours was a classic older woman–younger man romance and although its ending was nightmarish, the affair was exciting.

For a while after that I stayed away from love affairs altogether, concentrating instead on my psychology studies. Then —incurable romantic that I am—I fell in love again with an even younger man. The experience was both exhilarating and rewarding.

Friends tell me I have always been incredibly naïve. I prefer to be naïve rather than bitter, and today I am a happy, contented woman who no longer needs a man's presence to validate me. My older son Robin is a handsome, delightful young man involved in finance. My younger son Michael is a good-looking athlete with an interest in electronics. They are my closest friends.

I thoroughly enjoy my present work. As a successful hypnotherapist I help others to realize their goals and to find humor in their lives. Periodically I have the chance to act in films and on television, both of which are great fun.

One thing I can say is that my life has never been dull—and I doubt that it ever will be. Perhaps I have not always been "a good girl," but I would not have it any other way. As I put the finishing touches on this book I feel elated. At last I have found inner peace, and I look forward to the future.

Index